Career Planning for the 21st Century

2nd Edition

by

Donald H. Blocher
State University of New York at Albany

Mary Heppner
University of Missouri

Joe Johnston
University of Missouri

LOVE PUBLISHING COMPANY
Denver • London • Sydney

Published by Love Publishing Company
Denver, Colorado 80222

All rights reserved. No part of this publication may be reproduced, stored in a retrieval system, or transmitted, in any form or by any means, electronic, mechanical, recording or otherwise, without the prior written permission of the publisher.

Library of Congress Catalog Card Number 00-104334

Copyright © 2001 Love Publishing Company
Printed in the United States of America
ISBN 0-89108-271-9

Table of Contents

Chapter 1
Getting a Life: Empowerment Through Planning 1
- **Chapter Overview** 1
- **The Nature of Human Happiness** 2
- **Using Self-Awareness and Self-Identity to Convert Developmental Transitions into Opportunities for Growth and Fulfillment** 3
  - Listening to Our Inner Voices 3
  - The Nature of Developmental Transitions 3
  - Types of Developmental Crises 4
  - The Danger of Rejection Shock 5
- **Framing Life Planning Around the Concept of Career Development** 5
- **Career Actualization** 6
- **Becoming an Adult** 6
- **Summary** 7
- **References** 7

Chapter 2
The World of Work: New Paradigms Mean New Challenges 15
- **Chapter Overview** 15
- **Themes Characterizing the Changing Workplace** 17
  - Theme 1: The term "career" has come to mean an integrative and holistic view of life roles, not simply an occupation 17
  - Theme 2: Diamonds are replacing pyramids 17
  - Theme 3: Information and service jobs have replaced many manufacturing jobs 18
  - Theme 4: Teamwork is the essential worker skill 18
  - Theme 5: Developing transportable skills is essential in today's less secure workplace 19
  - Theme 6: Understanding the culture of an organization is a key to success in that organization 19
  - Theme 7: Learning to manage change is a key to health and resiliency in the ever changing world of work 20

Theme 8: In today's employment market, you are paid to think,
not to produce a product 21

Theme 9: In today's global economy, people need to work with
diverse cultures and people 22

Theme 10: There are increasing trends toward becoming one's own boss 22

Theme 11: With the increased diversity of workplace options
comes an increased importance to know yourself 22

Theme 12: Workers today have a greater need for finding meaning
and mission in their lives 23

Summary 24

Chapter 3
Exploring Possibilities, Probabilities and Choices 27

Chapter Overview 27

Listening to Your Daydreams 28

Interpreting the Exercise Results 28

Considering Your Interests 29

Interpreting the Exercise Results 29

Thinking about Your Personality: The Holland Schema for Career Exploration ...31

Interpreting the Exercise Results 31

Considering Your Skills and Abilities 33

Considering Your Values 33

Timing 34

Sources of Career Information 34

Summary 34

Chapter 4
Planning Across the Life Span 41

Chapter Overview 41

Changes, Challenges, and Transitions in Adulthood 42

Early Adult Transitions 42

Midlife Transitions 43

What Is Involved in Adult Life Planning? 47

Throwing Away the Old 47

Learning To Live without Our Old Identity 47

Trying On Our New Identity 48

Life Planning as Lifelong Planning 49

Summary 50

Chapter 5
The Gendered Context of Our Career Choices 55

Chapter Overview 55

Uncovering Your Authentic Self 57

The Influence of Socializing Forces 58

Gender Issues in Today's Workplace 58

Taking a Closer Look at Gender-Related Issues That May Have
  Influenced Your Development 59

Some Positive Aspects of Gender Socialization 61

Summary 61

References 62

Chapter 6

Understanding Cultural Diversity: Implications for the Workforce 65

Chapter Overview 65

Living in a Multicultural World 66

Diversity and the Workplace 67

Racial Identity Development:
  Understanding Our Own Development and That of Others 68

  Black Racial Identity Development 69

  Minority Racial Identity Development 70

  White Racial Identity Development 70

Your Worldview: A Lens or Frame of Reference for
  Making Sense Out of the World 72

The Psychological Costs of Racism 73

Summary 73

Chapter 7

What in My Life is Worth Striving For? 79

Chapter Overview 79

Satisfying Our Inner and Outer Needs 80

Psychological and Material Needs 80

How Do We Try To Fulfill Our Needs? 81

  Progressive Mastery: Climbing Psychological Mountains 81

  Deficit Needs and Growth Needs 82

Values in an Inner-Directed Life 83

What Do People Really Want Most in Life? 83

Happiness and Young Adults 84

What Does All of This Mean for Life Planning? 85

Summary 85

Chapter 8

Goal Setting 89

Chapter Overview 89

Planning and Enabling Goals 90

Focusing and Prioritizing 90

Setting Specific and Immediate Goals 91

The Process and Power of Goal Setting 91

  Learning from the Examples of Others 91

McGwire: A Successful Goal Setter 92

Finding Your Own Goal-Setting Style 92
Bringing Our Strengths to Bear on Behalf of Our Goals 93
    Why Is Awareness of Strengths Important? 93
    Why Do We Often Deny Our Strengths? 94
    How Can We Assess Our Strengths? 94
    How Do Our Self-Estimates Limit Us? 96
Summary 96

Chapter 9
Generating Commitment, Reality Testing Goals, and Mobilizing Resources 101
Chapter Overview 101
Generating Commitment? 102
    Achievement Motivation 102
    Locus of Control 102
    Effort Optimism 103
    Determining if a Goal Is Worth Our Commitment 103
Reality Testing Our Goal 104
Mobilizing and Managing Our Personal Resources 104
    Action Planning 105
    Managing Our Behaviors To Achieve Our Goals? 105
    Managing Time 107
    Why Can't We Save Time? 108
    Why Do We "Run Out" of Time? 108
Summary 108

Chapter 10
Taking Care of Yourself, So That You Can Take Care of Business 113
Chapter Overview 113
The Importance of Self-Care 114
    The Role of Self-Care in Effective Career Planning 115
    Physical Self-Care 116
    Mental or Emotional Self-Care 117
    Spiritual Self-Care 119
Social Support: Developing a Powerful Network 120
Maintaining Balance in Life 120
Summary 122

Chapter 11
Confronting Obstacles 125
Chapter Overview 125

Problem Solving 126
    What Is Involved in Problem Solving? 126
    Putting Problem Solving to Work in Our Lives 130
Coping with Stress 130
    What Is Stress? 130
    Some Prevailing Myths about Stress 131
    Major Dimensions of Stress 132
    Learning to Deal with the Factors that Cause Stress in Everyday Life 133
    Using Our Resources to Manage Stress 135
Summary 136

Chapter 12
Putting It All Together 141
    Chapter Overview 141
    Representing Yourself to Others 142
        Types of Résumés 143
        Résumé Guidelines and Sample Résumé 143
    Networking and Cover Letters 145
        The Importance of Networking 145
        The All-Important Cover Letter 145
    Finding the Information on the Internet 150
        On-Line Job Hunting 150
        Organizing Your Internet Job Search 152
        Internet Job Search Strategies 153
    Interviewing 154
        Interviewing Tips 154
    Summary 156

Epilogue 167

Appendix A
Missouri Occupational Card Sort 171

Appendix B
The Strength Audit 197

Appendix C
Reality Testing Goals and Plans 217

Index 229

List of Exercises

1.1	Where I Am, Where I've Been, Where I'm Going, and What I'm Carrying with Me	9
2.1	Skills to Build On and Build Up	25
3.1	Using Your Inner Growth Compass	35
3.2	Occupational Daydreams	36
3.3	The Occupational Card Sort Deck	37
3.4	The Career Interest Game	38
3.5	Estimating Your Abilities and Skills	39
3.6	Values Exercise	40
4.1	Planning for the Unexpected	51
4.2	Career Navigation Lights	52
4.3	The Career Actualization Lifeline	53
5.1	Exploring the Effects of Gender on Career Choice and Development	63
6.1	Drawing a Genogram: A Vehicle for Exploring Your Own Cultural Heritage	75
7.1	How Well Are You Meeting Your Basic Needs?	86
8.1	My General Life Goals	97
8.2	Examine Your Goal-Setting Style	98
8.3	Getting Priorities Straight	99
9.1	Action Planning	109
9.2	Self-Contract	111
10.1	Analyzing Your Support System	123
11.1	My Typical Problem Solving Behavior	137
11.2	Stress Situation Analysis	138
12.1	Test Your Résumé Knowledge	157

Preface

Dear Fellow Travelers,

You are about to embark on a grand adventure, a journey of self exploration and deep reflection. This journey will ask you to work hard at understanding who you are and what you want from your life. We will ask you to carefully examine what is most important to you; what will likely give your life meaning and purpose; where your passions lie and how to bring those into your everyday life.

This book is based on the premise that people expect too little from their lives—especially their work lives. Some of us have come to expect little because many people we look up to have expected and received little from theirs. Many people get into a job based on very little information. They view their work as a means to an end. They experience work as drudgery. They dread going into work and once there, they spend most of their time waiting to go home—where their "real life" is. A pretty depressing picture, but all too typical of many workers.

But there are some people who experience work very differently. They are people who have truly found their passion. Work provides deep meaning for them—an important part of their life mission. They thrive at work, some days reaching that truly magical state of flow when they are so into what they are doing that they totally loose track of time and space. They become caught up in the moment. These are people who say, "I feel truly fortunate to go to my work each day. Can you believe how lucky I am? They are actually paying me to have this much fun." For these individuals, work and play, home and office, co-workers and family all blend into a seamless whole. They really feel that they are doing their hearts' desire, expressing that part of themselves that is most uniquely them.

We want this for you!

Who me?

Yes you! We believe that you can find meaning and mission in your life. We believe you can build for a life where you are living your passions. We believe your dreams are achievable, and we want to help you achieve them.

It is with great anticipation that we write this book. It is the culmination of over 100 years of combined experience of three authors. In that time we have worked with thousands of people who were trying to carve out meaningful lives. Some have not been successful and have settled for jobs of numbing boredom. Some have found jobs that are okay, that provide a paycheck and some sense of accomplishment. Others have really followed their deep, and authentic longings and developed a life of phenomenal richness and meaning. We have learned a lot from our combined experience about how these truly successful people got to where they are, and we want to share that knowledge with you.

This is not your typical career planning book which takes you through rote assessments and tries to match you up with jobs. This book will push you to reach deep within yourself for the map to your own unique life plan. It requires work on your part to get from it what it has to offer. But ah, how very worth it—to know yourself in a whole new way, to understand what drives you to excel, to examine the work world for those places and situations in which you can thrive. This work will pay off in a much better quality of life!

In developing this book, we carefully searched back through our own work as career planners, teachers, counselors and have brought together the best material we have used to guide you on this journey. We have also thought back about the people we have worked with over the years. We want to share pieces of their life stories with you. These people who have struggled hard, thought deeply, worked to achieve lives of meaning and mission. They are all quite ordinary people who took on the extraordinary tasks of understanding themselves in deep and important ways. Throughout the book we will bring in examples from the lives of individuals with whom we have worked to provide models for you as you take these courageous and life changing steps.

This book is divided into four primary parts. The first part (chapters 1–3) introduces the whole concept of life planning and helps you to understand the power that comes from taking charge of your life. These chapters will help you get in touch with your deepest strivings and to understand what is really important to you in your life. The second part (chapters 4–6) will examine the dynamic and diverse work world. We will explore the changing work place, the role gender and particularly gender role socialization has in your career choice and the importance of appreciating the growing diversity of workers. Part three (chapters 7–8) gets down to the nuts and bolts of career planning. You will learn about setting goals for maximum productivity, assessing your interests, skills and work related values and understanding what makes for a meaningful work life. You will also learn about managing and mobilizing your resources for maximum gain. Finally in part four (chapters 9–11), we will help you become active in putting this all together for yourself. We will talk about ways of finding people to help you through the career planning process, ways of taking care of yourself in the process, ways of confronting and overcoming obstacles you may face along the way, and finally, we will provide help on the specific tasks of résumé writing, interviewing skills and active job hunt strategies. Each of the chapters contains information about these important topics, as well as an exercise to really help you focus and reflect. So, with that said, let's get started on this grand adventure!

CHAPTER 1
Getting a Life: Empowerment Through Planning

CHAPTER OVERVIEW

This chapter examines the nature of human happiness and stresses the significance of *control* and *involvement* as key ingredients in quality of life. *Self-awareness* and *self-identity* are noted as keys to converting developmental transitions into opportunities for growth and fulfillment.

The basic concepts of career actualization and life planning are discussed, and the roles of personality development and developmental drives in energizing and focusing life planning are described.

Jack, Stan, Harry, and Elaine play together in a small jazz band. They are booked almost every weekend in a little bistro a couple of blocks off the university campus.

Jack is the leader and clarinet player. He says he is in his late 60s but looks older. He has been playing professionally for more than 50 years, including brief stints with several of the famous "name bands" of a bygone era. To eke out a living while devoting his energy to his beloved jazz, Jack has worked for most of his life as a short-order cook.

Stan is 23. He plays bass and uses his earnings to finance his dream of graduate school and an eventual Ph.D. in mathematics.

Harry is around 40. A successful stockbroker, he plays trumpet with the group strictly for relaxation and a change of pace.

Elaine is 21. She sings and plays piano. A senior majoring in theater, she hopes to be "discovered" and to achieve stardom in the world of show business.

Each member pursues a different set of hopes and dreams, and each confronts a different set of obstacles and realities. Yet, each of these very different individuals seeks much the same kind of richness and satisfaction from life.

More than 2,000 years ago Aristotle observed that all human beings are seekers of happiness. Everything in life that we prize, we treasure because we believe that it will somehow help to make us happy.

THE NATURE OF HUMAN HAPPINESS

As philosophers have pointed out for centuries, we can't achieve happiness by simply running after it. Nor does happiness just happen. It is not a prize won in some kind of cosmic lottery; it is not part of the genetic endowment of a fortunate few. One lifelong student of "optimal experiences," as happiness is sometimes called, put it this way:

> Happiness is, in fact, a condition that must be prepared for, cultivated and defended privately by each person. People who learn to control inner experiences will be able to control the quality of their lives, which is as close as any of us can come to being happy. (Csikszentmihalyi, 1990, p. 2).

This book is about the quest for personal happiness that each person undertakes along a developmental journey. It is literally about "getting a life." We know that what we call happiness involves at least two basic elements. The first is a *sense of control* over important aspects of our lives. The second is a *sense of immersion* or *total involvement* in what we are doing.

Most of us, most of the time, feel relatively powerless. Many of the things that are important to us lie outside our control. We can't choose our parents or our time of birth, control our stature, or determine our IQ. Wars, recessions, and natural disasters happen. Sometimes it seems that George Orwell was right: Life goes on as it has always gone on; that is, badly.

Despite our inability to control all of these outside forces, however, we always have opportunities to exert *some* control over important aspects of our lives. We have all felt at one time or another the exhilaration of being in control of our own actions and, for the moment at least, of being masters of our own fate. This exhilaration is the result of the first basic element of human happiness, having a sense of control over important aspects of our lives.

The second key element in "peak experiences," as noted earlier, is a sense of immersion or total involvement in what we are doing. In these moments we lose track of time, and our awareness of outside factors and extraneous disturbances is narrowed. It is like we have ripped a page out of time and space. These moments usually occur when we have stretched our bodies or our minds to the limits to meet a personally accepted challenge, when we have set ourselves to accomplish something very difficult but personally worthwhile.

Thus, it is when we make something happen that we get a life. No one experiences these kinds of peak moments of power and accomplishment all of the time. Sometimes we experience these moments when we achieve a kind of closeness and psychological intimacy with a loved one. Sometimes we feel a sense of spirituality in a mystical or religious sense.

Significantly, both *control* and *involvement* begin within ourselves. They begin in our unique and personal way of interpreting and construing the events and experiences that define our lives. We may perceive an obstacle as a challenge to be mastered or as a catastrophe to be avoided. We may define problems in ways that allow us to feel in control of our resources and faculties or perceive ourselves as put upon and victimized by a cruel and uncaring world.

Our experiences in life are *not* shaped solely by external events. Rather, they are shaped by how we *interpret* and *construe* events, by how we *make meaning* out of the circumstances, opportunities, and challenges that confront us. This book is about the possibilities that people can create for themselves as they perceive, plan, and organize to achieve control over the directions and distances that they travel across the life span. It is about the opportunities that human beings can come to recognize and even to create as they participate in the *flow* of wholehearted involvement in all that is compelling and rewarding to them. It is about how to avoid making life a spectator sport. That is what we mean by *empowerment through planning*.

USING SELF-AWARENESS AND SELF-IDENTITY TO CONVERT DEVELOPMENTAL TRANSITIONS INTO OPPORTUNITIES FOR GROWTH AND FULFILLMENT

Listening to Our Inner Voices

We all have a choir of inner voices that speak to the meaning of all of the outside events that we encounter on a daily basis. Our memories, and so our minds, are like a bank of taped messages stored in our unconscious but retrieved and played when we encounter new and unfamiliar challenges.

Many of these "taped" messages were given to us as children by parents, teachers, and other people in authority who may have been more concerned with bending us to *their* vision of the world than with helping us to build our own. Sometimes these messages combine to define our *identity*. They contribute to our sense of who we are or, at least, to who we think we are condemned to be.

However, we do not need to live out our lives within a prison whose walls consist of an externally defined and other-directed world. We do not need to have our identity continually defined and affirmed by the voices of others who may be blind to who we are.

Instead, we can, in our adult lives, look at our own inner world, at our own experiences, needs, and talents, and define our own personal identity. This identity can be built around what is different and unique and special about ourselves and our lives. When we have the courage to look at ourselves in this way, we gain the freedom to choose and the opportunity to control the directions and distances we travel toward what we want to become.

The Nature of Developmental Transitions

One of the reasons that it is difficult to define our own personal identity is that we are constantly changing, as is the world around us. As we change and the situations around us change, we have to constantly update our tapes. That is, the inner voices we listen to have to be valid in terms of our life, our experiences, and our stage of development.

One of the most important ways to begin this process of defining our personal identity is to begin to understand our own development. In a real sense, understanding the course and processes of human development over the life span helps us to understand where we have been, where we

What do your inner voices say when you are confronted with a new and difficult challenge?

What is unique, different, and special about you?

How have people you know reacted to developmental crises?

are going, and so, finally, who we are at this moment in time.

When we look at our life cycle, we can identify many of the milestones or transitions that have produced major turning points in our lives. They can be defined as events that force us to change our basic assumptions about ourselves and our world and that trigger corresponding changes in the ways in which we think, feel, and act in our daily lives. They can, in turn, also force alterations in our relationships with others. Finally, they can change our concepts of who we are.

We handle some of these transitions with only minor adjustments in our lives. Some transitions, however, trigger what we call *developmental crises*. Most of us, most of the time, operate in fairly consistent patterns in relative harmony with our environments. We tend to deal with problems in familiar ways with minimal delay and reasonable success. A developmental crisis, however, disrupts our lives. It is usually experienced as stressful and even painful. We may think we are having an emotional breakdown, but such crises are actually turning points and opportunities for further growth. When we are struggling with a developmental crisis, we are not sick—we are simply *stuck*. Resolving developmental crises and moving forward again is the process of *actualization;* it is the process of fulfilling our highest potentials. Each time we resolve a developmental crisis and move forward again, we need to pause a moment to savor our achievement and, above all, to update our tapes of who we are.

Have you experienced a developmental transition? What was it like?

How has your sense of identity or who you are changed as a result of developmental crises?

Types of Developmental Crises

Developmental crises can be classified as predictable and unpredictable. Predictable crises arise out of the inevitable transitions we face as we move through the life cycle. A college student falls in love and begins to question whether to drop out of school and get married. An honors graduate wonders how marriage and medical school will fit together. A new college graduate approaches an endless series of job interviews. A series of rejection letters from law schools dampens the aspirations of a college senior. A mother watches her youngest child pack for college. A professor approaches retirement age with a growing sense of panic.

Not all crises are predictable, however. A college junior runs out of money and has to drop out. A housewife of 15 years is shattered by the sudden collapse of her marriage. A career soldier faces a return to civilian life when politicians revise national priorities. A middle-level executive ponders the classified advertisements after corporate downsizing swallowed his 20 years of hard work and accomplishment.

Sometimes the onset of crises is much less dramatic. Many men and women simply pause to take stock of their situations, but then they find that their interests and values have changed, making a major transition an essential part of fulfilling themselves. Others come to realize that plans made for them by others are empty. They feel that the burdens of others' expectations and others' aspirations are too heavy to carry forever. So they bring their choices of colleges, majors, friends, and even spouses into review.

Still other men and women find that success and accomplishments have thrust upon them new challenges. The climb up a career ladder to positions of leadership and responsibility may have brought with it demands for which they feel ill prepared. These new demands may require special training or further education. They may even require a major reassessment of values and a reexamination of one's personal identity.

Developmental crises thus are triggered in many ways. Many of these crises, both predictable and unpredictable, are outside our own control. The death of a spouse, a divorce, a disabling illness or injury, for example, may bring sudden and drastic changes in our lives. Business failures, technological unemployment, wars, and recessions may all produce consequences that disrupt the pattern of our lives.

The Danger of Rejection Shock

Many times when we face developmental crises, we must cope not only with the practical challenges and demands that confront us but also with the depth of our own feelings of loss, failure, or rejection. A term used to describe this kind of deep-seated, emotional reaction to unwanted and unanticipated life changes is *rejection shock*. It is an apt description of our reactions to a wide range of frustrating situations.

Unfortunately, rejection shock often brings with it a loss of self-esteem, breakdowns in achievement motivation, avoidance of risk-taking, and strains on interpersonal relationships. The great danger in rejection shock is that it tends to sap our energy, optimism, and planning abilities precisely when we need them the most to get unstuck from our crisis and to start moving and growing again. When we give in to rejection shock, we are in danger of sinking into the helplessness-hopelessness trap that mires us down in depression and self-pity.

One of the major themes of this book is that even though developmental crises are often threatening, they are also opportunities. They offer us chances for a fresh beginning, a new start, and a challenge to reach out and regain control over our own futures. Crises offer these opportunities whether they occur in our college years, in midlife, or as we approach retirement. They are a chance to stop drifting and start directing our own lives once more.

FRAMING LIFE PLANNING AROUND THE CONCEPT OF CAREER DEVELOPMENT

To this point, we have discussed transitions and challenges in a very general way. We will now frame our approach to life planning around the unifying concept of "career development." One of the notions that has damaged the lives of countless people is the idea that we can readily separate our vocational lives from the other roles and relationships that define our total lifestyles and individual identities.

For millions of people, vocational planning is something considered for an hour or two prior to graduation from high school or college in the stuffy confines of a guidance counselor's office or in an occupational library. Too often, any assistance provided is very limited and of the "test them and tell them" variety. If any conscious effort at real life planning is made at all, it is in the narrow context of an isolated decision to apply to a certain college, enter a specific major, or seek a particular job.

The concept of "career" is an attempt to broaden the focus of our thinking about vocational life and its related aspects across the life span. The central idea behind the word career is a movement and progression. It is a dynamic, rather than a static, notion. We actively pursue and engage in a career over many years and often through many specific jobs and positions. A career involves an organized pattern of activities that may include what we commonly think of as both work and leisure, personal development, and family commitments.

The concept of career is basically psychological. That is, the unifying and energizing factors behind a career pattern are the psychological factors of personal needs, aspirations, and motivations. We accept a particular job at a particular time for a variety of reasons. We look at wages, hours, working conditions, alternative opportunities, and a host of other factors. However, we pursue a career pattern over many years because that pattern is psychologically relevant to our own personal identity and lifestyle. As we use the term *career* or *life planning*, we are referring to the vehicle we use to build or move toward a total lifestyle that embraces all of the roles and relationships that provide structure and meaning to our lives. It is literally the process of "getting a life." Take some time now to complete Exercise 1.1, which will help you to identify influences and experiences that have shaped your development thus far. Then think about how you can use this information in your present lifestyle.

Have you seen friends or relatives fall into rejection shock? What was it like for them?

How have you seen career patterns begin to emerge in your life?

What interests or values will you need to fit in around paid work to have a satisfying lifestyle?

How are the patterns that are emerging in your life similar to or different from those in your parents' lives?

Career patterns are products of our basic personalities. They are as varied and complex as are our individual lifestyles. There are no specific career patterns that are, in themselves, "normal" or desirable for all individuals. The pattern that most of us tend to consider typical, which is represented by straight-line progress from general education to specialized preparation to choice of occupation to movement up a single vocational ladder with family responsibilities thrown in along the way, is probably much more atypical than typical in our ever-changing world.

We live in a world of constantly expanding opportunities, changing technologies, shifting social mores, and other profoundly influential forces. Millions of people today are in jobs that did not even exist when they left high school or that they would have viewed as inappropriate or out of reach a few short years ago. Many are in family and relationship patterns that would have seemed unusual and unlikely a generation ago. Today, we realize that the best careers provide fulfillment, achievement, and satisfaction in terms of personal, family, and professional life.

CAREER ACTUALIZATION

The important considerations in examining any specific lifestyle or career pattern involve how that pattern facilitates the development of the individual in terms of fulfillment of personal needs and aspirations, the actualization of unique talents and potentials, and the ability to contribute to the general social good. We call those individuals who convert crises into opportunities *career actualizers*. The key elements to becoming a career actualizer are planning, organization, and commitment on behalf of a set of personally cherished goals.

The terms *career* and *work* are not synonymous. For some career actualizers, successful career planning could involve making their job or regular paid work *less* central in their total lifestyle. Such people may choose to accept and persist in jobs that are intrinsically unsatisfying in order to support other interests, commitments, and aspirations.

For such people, career actualization may mean devoting much greater time, energy, and resources to significant social causes or religious activities. It may mean organizing their psychological life around an avocation, hobby, or special interest that may be more engrossing and involving than a job. Career actualization may mean focusing on developing musical or artistic talents regardless of their immediate financial return. It is when we are able to identify the activities, interests, and causes that really "grab us" that we can begin to experience both the sense of control and the total involvement that are the key elements of human happiness. When we find these elements in or outside our paid work, we are ready to begin the process of planning. The key to career actualization, then, is focusing on what is truly fulfilling, satisfying, and growth producing. It is defining and locating what is exciting and worthwhile in life and then "going for it."

BECOMING AN ADULT

As noted earlier, for every individual, regardless of the unique characteristics of that individual's career pattern, certain challenges are imposed by developmental transitions. Becoming an adult is clearly the most significant and comprehensive transformation in the whole realm of human experience. So profound is this transformation that some people contend that the full process of moving from adolescence to adulthood may take as long as 15 years. There is no single event that clearly signals the attainment of adulthood. In our society we have a variety of indicators of adult status. Driving age, drinking age, voting age, and legal age for marriage, for example, all signal the approach of adult status. These cultural clocks rarely keep time with one another, however. All of these indicators are arbitrary and artificial. A good part of becoming an adult is coming to think of ourselves as adults.

It is important to realize that we continue to grow and develop even after we reach adulthood. Our development is driven by inner processes that move us to strive to grow and by environmental factors that tend to nurture or negate our efforts. Development, then, is a continuous, lifelong process. It is not limited to our early years. Developmental change is pervasive, touching psychological, social, and physiological domains, and life span development is influenced by a host of factors. Psychologist David Magnusson noted that no single characteristic, such as intelligence, education, or family origin, is all important in any human life.

Some of the inner processes that move us to grow seem to be wired in to the makeup of human beings across life stages and even across cultures. Called *developmental drives*, they are capable of moving people toward fuller realization of their talents and potentials.

Three basic developmental drives have been identified. The first of these inner tendencies is the urge to understand and comprehend the world in a rational and consistent way. As human beings we are not like ants programmed to perform and persevere in rigid and mechanical ways. Our DNA urges us to step back, confer, figure out, analyze, and understand our world. We are uncomfortable with unsolved puzzles and unexplained contradictions. Psychologist Jean Piaget pointed out that it is out of our need to understand, explain, and predict that we develop our capacities for logical thought and rational action.

The second of these inner tendencies is the drive toward *competence*. As psychologists Masten and Coatsworth pointed out, competence is reflected in our need to achieve some degree of control and mastery over the environment. Mountains are to be climbed simply because they are there. The stars are to be reached for the same reason.

Finally, we have a basic need to attach and bond with other human beings within enduring and emotionally satisfying relationships. Psychologist Mary Ainsworth has pointed out that within such relationships we learn more about ourselves. Above all, we learn that as we grow intellectually and emotionally we have more and more to give and that in giving we gain the most satisfying rewards of all.

As we move along the thorny path of individual development, we find that what is inside us is not some Pandora's box of psychological bumps and bruises from a less than perfect childhood. What *is* inside us is a set of needs and aspirations to understand and make meaning out of our lives, to exert some degree of control over the directions and distances that we travel across the life span, and to reach out to establish and maintain enduring and rewarding relationships.

Actualization is the process of recognizing these developmental drives and allowing them to energize and empower our lives. It is this process that defines *empowerment through planning*.

SUMMARY

We have looked at some of the basic concepts and principles that are involved in career actualization and life planning. We have seen that even though our development across the life span in an ever-changing world inevitably brings obstacles and even crises, we have the opportunity to convert those into new beginnings and new directions.

When we can identify those things in life that are truly exciting, involving, and deeply worthwhile to us, we are ready to achieve empowerment through planning.

REFERENCES

Ainsworth, M., & Bowlby, J. (1991). An ethnological approach to personality development. *American Psychologist, 46,* 333–341.

Csikszentmihalyi, M. (1990). *Flow: The psychology of optimal experience.* New York: Harper and Row.

How do you think of yourself right now in terms of adulthood?

How are relationships or the search for relationships shaping your life?

How will these developmental drives be part of your life planning?

How has intellectual curiosity been a part of your life and education?

What challenges are you striving to master in your life?

Magnusson, D. (1993). Human ontogeny: A longitudinal perspective. In D. Magnusson & P. Casaer (Eds.), *Longitudinal research on individual development.* London: Cambridge University Press.

Masten, A. S., & Coatsworth, D. J. (1998). The development of competence in favorable and unfavorable environments: Lessons from research on successful children. *American Psychologist, 53,* 205–220.

Piaget, J. (1970). *Genetic epistemology.* New York: Norton.

CAREER PLANNING 9

Exercise 1.1
Where I Am, Where I've Been, Where I'm Going, and What I'm Carrying With Me

This exercise will help you think about and sum up many of the important factors in your life right now. Answer the questions as thoughtfully and honestly as you can. Your answers are intended for your eyes only. You do not have to share them with anyone unless you choose to do so.

Where I Am

1. My Present Plans

Describe your present thinking about your vocational future. What experiences have you had? How did you arrive at your present interests and plans? If you feel that you have had unusual problems in selecting and pursuing goals, describe them.

Haven't really had any experiences, nor the opportunity to do so. Haven't had any unusual problems either except choosing a school which didn't really end up being a hard decision realistically. I feel good about now having a theoretical major even if I haven't gotten it official yet.

2. What About Money?

What is your present financial situation? Include any special problems you may have in this area.

I don't really have a present financial situation. I have a couple thousand saved up, I'll get a job after golf — for the first time ever! — then hopefully that'll my financial situation. My parents really can't help me so I will be paying off my student loans on my own.

3. The Most Exciting and Worthwhile Things in My Life

   a. What do you do for recreation?

Golf. I like to work out but I have never really had a regime or anything cause I was in vb and golf year round but after golf I'll go to the REC regularly.

b. What are your personal hobbies and interests?

I love to read and knit. I love to spend time with ppl I really enjoy. I especially love to travel – or rather dream and fantasize about travelling.

c. How would you describe your close friends, what you do together, and your role in the relationship?

Laugh. We all love to laugh. I am sometimes a leader, I make ppl laugh. We're mostly pretty easygoing.

4. *School and/or College*

a. What have your school experiences been like? What personal interests and family influences have affected the type of education you have completed or are now pursuing? How do you think your education is influencing your development as a person?

High school was okay, junior year was rough cause I wasn't happy, didn't really feel like I belonged, wanted to get out and go to college. Senior year was much better, much ... college is going really well right now. ... is really good, want what's best – what I look for in a good education.

b. What were your extracurricular activities in high school and college, and did you enjoy them?

Did volleyball for a long time, loved the game, not the system. Will do intramural with Caitlyn at UNM. LOVED band, really big in high school, esp. marching band which I did for 4 years, very involved – amigos. Had fun at jobs usually – too hard on myself, love the game.

c. How would you describe your past and present relationships with teachers, coaches, and advisers?

I struggle with authority. However my guidance counselor was amazing and she really loves me and she helped me a lot. Golf coach was nice, frustratingly disorganized. Knew golf but wasn't always helpful. One evil teacher who we first couldn't get agree on anything and we told each other. Most teachers were really good and I really enjoyed and appreciated them.

Where I've Been

1. *Relationships with Parents, Brothers, and Sisters*

    a. How would you describe your family experiences and relationships while you were growing up and now? What were your mother, father, brothers, and sisters like as individuals? How did you get along with them? How have these relationships changed in recent years?

    Very good. Our family is very tight. Sometimes we are a little too much for each other. My mom was a great mother - encouraging, supportive, wanted to make sure we knew she was open for anything, fun, spontaneous, loving. Dad pushed me to be my best in everything. High expectations for himself and me - passed on.

    b. In what ways are you like your father? In what ways opposite? In what ways different?

    High expectations for ourselves, frustrated if we don't perform at the level we should. Struggle with patience. Smart, like to learn. React the same. Love reading. He loves to talk and visit with his relatives. I like to listen but I don't talk as much, and I don't like it when he's pushy and loud.

    c. In what ways are you like your mother? In what ways opposite? In what ways different?

    My mother and I are so similar. Everyone says we look exactly the same but we very disagree. We hang out and run errands and like to be spontaneous. I can talk about anything, we're like bff school girls

Where I'm Going

1. Relationships and Family

Give some thought to and describe your feelings about what you want your family and long-term relationships to be like in the future. What are your feelings about children? In what ways do you want your own family life to be like and unlike that of your parents?

I want one. A family and a long-term relationship. I love kids and would want to have as many as everyone will allow. I would hope I am a similar parent to my parents because they did a very good job. I want a husband right now.

2. Hopes and Aspirations

What are your highest goals and aspirations for the future in each of the following areas? In other words, describe what your life would be like if it had no practical obstacles or limitations.

   a. Career

I would graduate with a degree in International Relations, prob Span, and something else, take all the necessary levels and positions to becoming a diplomat, including living everywhere.

   b. Family

I would develop a relationship, be steady and solid and fun and loving and caring and get married really young. We would travel and move and enjoy our lives together, adventuring, living life until we are old together. Have kids, more a lot.

c. Total lifestyle

Full of life, spontaneous, adventurous, exploring, traveling, experiencing, visiting, wandering, moving a lot, live in different kinds of houses, with different kinds of people.

What I'm Carrying With Me: Summing It All Up

1. At this time in your life, where do you see yourself in regard to:

    a. Resources?

    Personal

    Parents, Cameron, golf girls, grandparents, Julie, Jennifer, Naomi

    Financial

    Some savings, getting a job

    Family ←

    Other

    b. Goals?

    Personal

    to be happy and fulfilled

Financial

to be unconcerned. work hard, continuously be paying something. Save, spend little, work much

Educational

graduate from Harris (with honors) in three years max. Graduate school? unsure

Vocational

diplomat, travel and live and work all over.

Family

Stay close to my parents and sisters, have a family of my own — fabulous husband then great kids

Other

?

2. What are the practical obstacles, problems, and constraints with which you must cope to reach your goals?

a. In yourself?

work too hard too much too fast, too much pressure on myself, too high of standards, good self-discipline, motivation and work ethic

b. In others?

don't treat me the way I deserve (unintentional → nurse?)

c. In the world?

people are crazy, I wish I could have more faith in humanity than I already do but they make it difficult.

CHAPTER 2

The World of Work: New Paradigms Mean New Challenges

CHAPTER OVERVIEW

This chapter discusses some aspects of the changing world of work. We present these as 12 themes, all of which should be considered when planning for the future. An important caveat, however, is that companies and organizations vary widely. While the majority of work settings have incorporated these changes, there are organizations where this is not the case. Some organizations operate today in very much the same patterns as in past generations and may be doing so quite successfully. The themes presented in this chapter are thus meant to provide lenses or filters through which you can view organizations to see the opportunities and challenges they may present.

The contrast between today's workplace and the workplace 20 years ago is vast. The changes that have taken place in the last generation cause us to question the very basic assumptions of what it is to be a worker and what it is to have a career. The personal characteristics that were so important in the last generation of workers—stability, experience, and allegiance to a hierarchical structure of leadership and decision making—now are thought of as quaint remnants of a past time. Change and diversity characterize today's labor market. Companies are reinforced for being "lean and mean." The evening news reports buyouts, mergers, takeovers, bankruptcies, layoffs, downsizing, and outsourcing. The workplace is anything but stable. Lifelong learning is the reality. "Portable" and "transferable" skills that one can take from job to job and the psychological flexibility to make continuous transitions are what is valued most in today's job market.

All of this can feel overwhelming and scary to people at all stages of career development. But with change also comes opportunity. The new world of work supports growth, development, flexibility, tolerance, and the celebration of diversity. Broader and perhaps healthier definitions of career and an increased search for mission and meaning are now part of our vocational lives.

Nonetheless, many times it feels as if the old rules don't apply and we are not sure what the new rules are. These feelings are clearly indicated in the following quotes from people with whom we've worked:

"I guess I thought I would do like my dad did: Find a company that I would fit in well with, work hard, continue to be promoted to higher positions within the company, and, I guess, retire from that company. . . . It seems like that is not the way it is working anymore."

"I tried to stress on my résumé everything I had accomplished in part-time jobs and other leadership roles I have held on campus. The person I spoke with said that while that was important, it was more important to demonstrate that I could work as part of a team. I hadn't really emphasized any of that. I thought they would be looking for my individual contribution."

"I did an informational interview with a company that my next-door neighbor works for. The interviewer said it was really important that I understand the 'culture' of various companies and which culture might be the best fit for me as a person. I am not sure what she meant by that, or how I should go about trying to find out what culture a specific company has."

"As a woman I was shocked by the lack of women in any of the parts of the company the interviewer showed me. I had thought that type of thing was illegal . . . but I guess it still is alive and well. The interviewer did say there were some women in the Marketing Division, but the rest of the company is still very male. I guess I could try to be a trailblazer, but I am not sure I want to."

American companies are changing, and the changes are rippling out into employment settings throughout the economy. The dominant model of the last generation was one that rewarded loyalty and seniority within a single organization. Today, loyalty and longevity are no longer central values for many companies. As you go out into the job market, it is important to be aware of some of these basic changes. The remainder of this chapter describes the new paradigms in the world of work. They will affect a range of issues as you think about various companies, such as what you will look for when you interview, how you will present your skills, what types of skills and personal attributes you will try to develop, and how you will fit yourself to the organizations for which you might want to work.

THEMES CHARACTERIZING THE CHANGING WORKPLACE

Theme 1: The term "career" has come to mean an integrative and holistic view of life roles, not simply an occupation.

When we used to think of the term *career development,* we would think about our occupation, what we did from 9 to 5. Increasingly, people are realizing the interwoven quality of their careers and redefining the term *career* to incorporate many life roles and contexts. One's occupation is no longer seen in isolation but rather is thought of as one of many parts that form the life story of the individual, or the narrative that the individual is living. This story has the individual involved in many life roles, such as worker, parent, partner, and volunteer, and particular life contexts, such as being a person of color, a woman, a Jew, a lesbian. All of these roles and contexts are important to understanding the meaning and purpose of career in one's life.

Each of you has unique values and needs that grow out of your own particular cultural and historical context. What will be meaningful to you as you develop your career will be highly personal. As you plan your career, it is important to think broadly and holistically about your life and its unique characteristics.

The following stimulus questions are helpful for reflecting on what life roles and contexts are the most important to you. Take some time now to answer them thoughtfully.

1. What life roles are most important for you to integrate as you try to plan the most meaningful career?
2. What life contexts are important to you as you think about your career (e.g., family, religious affiliation, ethnic group, etc.).
3. What historical and cultural elements of your history are important to consider as you plan for the next phases of your life?

Theme 2: Diamonds are replacing pyramids.

In the last generation, most organizations could be visually depicted as pyramids. An organization would have a large base of workers, a small number of managers at the middle levels, and a smaller number of executives at the top. The managers were the people who *thought* for the company, the so-called white-collar workers. These administrators saw it as their job to develop the plans and to supervise the bulk of the labor force in carrying out those plans as fast and efficiently as possible. The majority of workers were not valued for their intelligence, creativity, or ingenuity; they were valued for the speed and efficiency with which they could carry out orders.

Individuals typically entered the company at the bottom, depending on the type of industry and the qualifications of the worker, and then spent many years working their way up through a series of well-established career paths that had increasing responsibility, higher status job titles, and greater pay.

Today, most companies can be depicted as being diamond shaped. The majority of workers need to be highly skilled people capable of working responsibly on tasks. There is very little room for low-skill or no-skill workers. The bottom level of the organization is small; there are few jobs that require no skill. There is also less of a hierarchical progression to the jobs at the top. Most workers know that they might make horizontal moves or moves out of the company, but they know that becoming the CEO is not likely. Workers at all levels are seen as offering creative solutions to company problems. Workers are encouraged to be part of the company in very real ways: to join in decision making, to coach others, even to own part of the company.

Thus, the world of work as we have moved into the 21st century is one of rapid change and enormous possibilities. While it provides less stable job patterns, it also provides the opportunity for lifelong learning, a higher level of professionalism, and being valued for suggestions and input.

The following stimulus questions are helpful for reflecting on how you and your personality might fit in today's higher skilled workplace.

1. When you hear or read about changes taking place in the workplace, what is your first emotional reaction: Excitement? Fear? Worry?
2. What aspects of your personality seem best suited for the new workplace?
3. What aspects of your personality seem least suited for the new workplace?
4. What do you need to do to prepare yourself for the new workplace?

Theme 3: Information and service jobs have replaced many manufacturing jobs.

One hundred years ago most people were farmers. Only 30 years ago most people worked in manufacturing. Today, the majority of people work in information-related industries or in service industries. This shift from agrarian to manufacturing to service and technology has created a great many shifts in all aspects of the labor market, one of which is the need for education. While some unskilled jobs still exist in the service industry, many of the newer jobs now require a high level of skill. Even jobs in service-related industries often require knowledge of and ability to use technology to perform functions done manually in the past. Thus, gaining important skills through college or technical training is of great importance for today's worker.

The following stimulus questions are helpful for reflecting on how you and your personality might fit in today's technological workplace.

1. What skills do you have that may be an asset in the technological marketplace?
2. What skills could you learn that would strengthen your ability in the technological marketplace?

Theme 4: Teamwork is the essential worker skill.

In the last generation, individual accomplishment was highly valued. People were taught to carve out their own niche, accomplish their own goals, and be recognized and promoted accordingly. Résumés focused almost solely on what the individual had accomplished. Today, the workforce has become more and more an interdisciplinary team. Workers function as part of a larger group brought together to work on specific projects. While workers within companies are expected to have good ideas for new project developments, they are also expected to bring those ideas to a team, which will then work on all aspects of the project from beginning to end. As one worker for a major telecommunication company said:

"I work as part of a team. I come up with the best ideas I can, and I bring them to the team. Then, they are no longer my ideas. They quickly belong to the team. It is my job then to be a good team member and contribute my expertise to seeing if this is a feasible and profitable idea to develop."

This focus on working as part of a multidisciplinary team requires quite different skills than those needed when individuals reported to their bosses and worked autonomously on their own ideas. Interpersonal skills have become paramount in all kinds of organizations. One must be able to work with diverse people and to express oneself clearly and assertively. Workers must learn to disagree and resolve conflict in appropriate ways. Teams may be made up of people from all parts of a company, each with his or her specific expertise. In some companies, team members are drawn from all parts of the world. They may represent new developing markets or resources. Developing communication skills, interpersonal sensitivity, and relationship skills is a very important part of being successful in a job. Having such skills may also be the most important factor in landing a job. As one recruiter recently told us:

"For entry-level job applicants, my main question is how will they fit into our type of organization. I know that we will need to do training to get them familiar with our products and services, but those things are trainable. It is less easy to train people to work well with others, which is essential in our line of work. My questions for new applicants are less about what they have accomplished (the product) and more about how they have accomplished it (the process). I want to hear how they work with other people in bringing projects to fruition."

The following stimulus questions are helpful for reflecting on how you and your personality might fit in today's team-oriented workplace.

1. What interpersonal skills do you have that may be an asset in the more team-oriented marketplace?
2. What interpersonal skills could you learn that would strengthen your ability in the team-oriented marketplace?
3. What specific accomplishments can you point to that demonstrate skills you have in working with diverse people on teams and accomplishing mutual goals?

Theme 5: Developing transportable skills is essential in today's less secure workplace.

Many companies today do not expect that workers will stay with them for all of their working lives. In fact, many companies intentionally develop disincentives for doing so. They want and expect people to move on, because as people stay within the company they become more expensive to the company. They see the typical worker as coming in, developing skills, contributing in substantive ways to the company, and then moving on.

This expectation has a number of implications for workers. It is no longer okay to come into a job with a given level of skill and then "settle in" at that level. The worker who is not constantly learning new skills, keeping well informed about cutting-edge issues in his or her field, and constantly growing with the company will probably not prosper in today's workforce. Thus, today's workers are asking themselves such questions as, "What skills will I best be able to transport to my next job? What is my growth potential? What do I need to learn, and how can I learn it?"

It is important for you to ask yourself some of these same questions. The following stimulus questions are helpful for reflecting on how you and your personality might fit in today's less secure workplace.

1. What is my reaction to working in an organization that does not provide long-term security for me as a worker?
2. What skills do I want to develop that can continue to make me marketable in a range of organizations?

Theme 6: Understanding the culture of an organization is a key to success in that organization.

In trying to determine where you want to work, the most important thing to understand is the culture of the company. By culture, we mean the underlying philosophy that influences all aspects of the company, from dress codes to when coffee breaks are taken to where and how employees report to superiors and how they get promoted. Cultures can vary dramatically from company to company, and whole texts have been written on this topic. A leading best-selling magazine called *Fast Company* (which is also on the web at www.FastCompany.com) is a great source of information on organizational cultures.

We encourage you to do some reading and thinking about differing cultures and where you might fit best. Perhaps you are the type of person who fits best in what would be described as an entrepreneurial culture. Such a culture is typical of many new companies run by young managers. Policies and procedures may be unwritten, which means that there may be a great deal of ambiguity about who is responsible for what and what the "rules" of the company are for a whole host of issues, from how to get office supplies to who controls employee stock options. These companies rely strongly on employees' using their best judgment. There is little in the way of "chain of command," and it is likely that senior people will ask directly for employees' opinions rather than going through layers of other people. In addition, these organizations are often very casual, as reflected in dress codes and the fact that employees may often decide for themselves when and where to do their work. Further, there is an emphasis on tearing down the walls. Employees are much more likely to be housed in a modular office and to sit in a group with others including their boss. But expectations are high in these companies and success depends on producing at a very high level. These tend to be high-turnover companies, where workers move on to other jobs frequently and other less expensive workers are hired to take their place.

Other companies are much more traditional. Such companies have clear rules in place, and employees are expected to live within them. Policies and procedures are clearly stated, and workers spend little time having to make their own judgments about day-to-day functioning. There is much more of a hierarchy in place and a chain of command for responding to issues. Dress is more formal; the business suit is preferred for both men and women. When, where, and how employees work is clearly defined. In some of these traditional organizations there may be paternalistic attitudes toward workers. There may be the perception that the company knows best and that management will make career decisions for employees that are in their best interest. There may be more emphasis on seniority and job security within these organizations, as well as less ambiguity and more formal structure.

These somewhat stereotypical descriptions represent just two of many types of organizational cultures. Indeed, many companies have a blend of several cultures. As you research companies and organizations for which you may like to work, try to get a sense for the corporate culture and think about your own personality and where you might fit best.

The following stimulus questions are helpful for reflecting on how you and your personality might fit in different cultures in today's workplace.

1. What type of corporate culture best fits your personality?
2. What would be the hardest type of work environment for you to fit into?

Theme 7: Learning to manage change is a key to health and resiliency in the ever-changing world of work.

Change is the norm in today's workplace. As Will Rogers commented, "Even if you are on the right track, you will get run over if you just sit there." Businesses and organizations are in a constant state of flux and change. Many people believe that to be competitive today they must be very fluid. Some people like change and are able to go with the flow of such change without a problem. Other people, however, are resistant to change. Many people need stability and predictability in their work lives and the thought of constantly having to change is very difficult. Given that change is constant and pervasive in most workplaces today, it is important to think about your own personal reactions to change and how you can remain healthy and resilient in the midst of the turmoil that change often brings.

Listen to the voices of two individuals who work for the same organization and are about to go through the same change:

"I can't wait until we move. I think it will be great being located more in the center of the things, rather than where we are now, which is way out on the fringe. We are going to be joining a whole new group of colleagues. It is going to mean some cross training in what these people do, which really appeals to me. I am

especially interested in learning about the new technologies that will be part of this new work environment."

"I don't understand why we have to move. Our current facility has worked very well for a long time. Who is to say that we are going to get along well and be productive when we are thrown in to this new work group. No one has really studied this properly. I think we should shelve this idea for the time being, and perhaps take some time to study the ramifications that such a move would entail."

These two people sound as if they are talking about very different kinds of situations. In fact, they are talking about the exact same change, albeit through very different eyes. Our openness to change can be conceptualized as a basic personality trait. Where do you see yourself fitting on this continuum that runs from "very resistant to change" to "seeking out change—the more the better"? Where you are on this continuum may have been influenced by the kinds of changes that you experienced as you were growing up, by how comfortable your parents were with change, and how positive your experiences with change were.

Given the fluid nature of the workplace today, there is a need for workers to be able to manage change and to facilitate change as they work with colleagues and supervisees within their organizations. A CEO of a major corporation indicated that she viewed openness to new ideas as the single most important personal characteristic that she looks for in upper-level managers. She indicated that what separates those who rise within the organization from those who linger at the lower levels is the attitude that change is necessary in every organization for it to remain useful and productive in the global economy.

In studies that we have examined of highly successful people, some of the following behaviors were apparent. These successful individuals read widely. They read extensively both within their own discipline and in a wide variety of other areas. They peruse books, magazines, journal articles, and websites that focus on change, innovation, and trends for the future. They also surround themselves with colleagues and friends who enjoy thinking about the way the world is changing and how individuals must change in order to stay effective and productive.

Use the following stimulus questions to reflect on how you experience change.

1. When you hear the word change, what is your immediate reaction? Where do you think that reaction comes from in terms of your past experiences?
2. What can you do that may increase your own openness to change, and your ability to resonate to changes that will be relevant to your success in your chosen field?

Theme 8: In today's employment market, you are paid to think, not to produce a product.

As the shift occurred from a manufacturing economy to an information economy, thinking skills became much more valuable. High school and college teachers and guidance counselors are continually saying, "We are trying to help you develop your thinking skills," but students often do not realize the importance of achieving that goal. Critical thinking skills have become increasingly important in all kinds of jobs. Constructing products with tools is no longer descriptive of most jobs. Rather, you are typically hired to think—creatively, critically, and independently.

Many people go through high school, college, and sometimes even graduate school just pouring facts into their heads. They sit in classes filling their notebooks with exactly what the professor has said, memorizing it, and regurgitating it on exams. This is not the kind of thinking that will be expected of you in your future work life. You will be expected to synthesize information, develop new ideas, analyze problems, and come up with possible solutions. It is essential to develop these active critical thinking skills if you want to be successful in the work world.

The following stimulus questions are helpful for reflecting on how you and your personality might fit in a workplace that demands critical thinking.

1. When have you used critical thinking on a project or issue? How would you describe what you did to a potential employer?
2. If you have not yet developed critical thinking skills, what are ways that you can start developing these skills?

Theme 9: In today's global economy, people need to work with diverse cultures and people.

Today's marketplace is a global one. Many companies interact daily with markets all over the world. Workers are expected to understand this global economy and to be able to work with people from cultures vastly different from their own. The walls that used to represent the borders of the United States have been broken down by technology, and the Internet has allowed even small companies to compete in the global economy. With this increased diversity has come a need for workers to really understand and be able to deal sensitively with people from other cultures. At the same time, workers need to understand more about their own cultural heritage and the worldview from which they operate.

The following stimulus questions are helpful for reflecting on how you and your personality might fit in today's global workplace.

1. What skills have you developed that demonstrate your ability to work with diverse individuals?
2. What are specific examples of ways in which you have demonstrated cross-cultural awareness, knowledge, and skill?

Theme 10: There are increasing trends toward becoming one's own boss.

Today's workplace does not meet the needs of many workers. Some of the trends we have already discussed have made it difficult for some workers to be a part of someone else's workplace. Many of these workers have started their own businesses. Quite often, the businesses are home-based. With the advent of the Internet, fax machines, and cellular technology, workers are finding that they can set up a company and operate it themselves from their home with relative ease. While home-based businesses have become a more and more popular option, statistics show that these types of businesses continue to have a high rate of failure. Nevertheless, for certain people the home-based business is a lucrative option and one that allows them to have a great deal of flexibility and control.

The following stimulus questions are helpful for reflecting on how you and your personality might fit in today's increasingly self-employed workplace.

1. What aspects of becoming your own boss are appealing to you?
2. What aspects of becoming your own boss are unappealing to you?
3. What parts of your personality seem like a good match for self-employment?
4. What parts of your personality seem like a poor match for self-employment?

Theme 11: With the increased diversity of workplace options comes an increased importance to know yourself.

As has probably been evident in the discussion thus far, today's marketplace is truly diverse. Job options are more varied than at any other time in our history. There are numerous kinds of organizations, each with its own unique culture. Technology has opened up a truly global economy and has also opened up greater possibilities for developing one's own business. All of these options make it imperative that you know yourself, and the type of job situation you might best work within.

The following stimulus questions are helpful for reflecting on how you and your personality might fit in today's changing work settings.

1. Given everything you know about yourself, what type of workplace seems like the best fit for you?
2. How can you gain more information about yourself and different workplace cultures to help you make decisions about the type of workplace you would like best?

Theme 12: Workers today have a greater need for finding meaning and mission in their lives.

With today's workplace changing faster than ever, becoming more global and more virtual, workers are increasingly feeling more isolated. This isolation was expressed humorously in a recent cartoon that went like this:

> A man was praying to the heavens: "All this technology has made us feel so remote, so disconnected, so devoid of human contact, life seems so impersonal lately." Down from on high came the response: "If you want to report a sinner, press 1. If you've had trouble with a sinner, press 2. If your scripture is garbled, press 3. If you want absolution, press 4."

While we can all appreciate the humor in the new technological world, we must also recognize that for many workers this isolation has created an "existential emptiness." As workplaces become less stable, as workers readily take their portable skills to other companies, as job mobility is increasing, and as workers are increasingly working out of their homes via fax and modems, much of the meaning and solidarity that workers used to obtain from their jobs is no longer there. When we asked workers to comment on how meaningful they found their work to be, some interesting themes emerged. As you read the following comments made by John, Marian, and Susan, think about how similar or different your reactions might be to theirs:

"My dad seemed to get meaning in his job. He worked for the same company [since] right out of high school. Most of the people he worked with also spent their entire lives with the company. It seems like he got a lot from those life-long relationships. I don't have that same feeling. Most of my colleagues are turning over within 5 years—moving on, moving up. It feels a lot less intimate and a lot less personal. My dad used to think of his workplace as his second family. I can't ever imagine feeling that about the place I work."—John, 39

"I get a lot of meaning out of learning new things in my job, especially learning how new technologies can make my job easier and more efficient. Teaching others the skills I have learned makes me feel like I am doing something important—like my work matters."—Marian, 22

"I think I am like a lot of other workers who get meaning from things other than their jobs. I really view my job as a way to get money so that I can do the things I find meaningful—like exploring art and music. Sometimes it makes me feel sad that so much of my time goes to making money to live on. I feel like I have little time left for those things I really thrive on. I wish there was a way to integrate more things that I would find meaningful into my job, but so far I have been unable to figure out how to do that."—Susan, 29

While some workers, such as Marian, feel that they are able to derive meaning from their work lives, others like John and Susan are having a harder time feeling like their jobs are providing meaning or mission in their lives. Although it may be true that finding work meaningful may not be necessary in one's life, most would agree that it is desirable. Most of us spend in excess of 40 hours a week working. If we can find jobs that feed our spirit, jobs that we find meaningful, the chances are that we will experience greater all-around quality of life.

The first step in the process of trying to find meaningful work is identifying what we find personally meaningful. Susan found meaning through involvement in the arts. Marian found it in learning new skills and being able to share those skills with others. Once you have identified what will lead to personal meaning in your work life, all that remains is to find situations in which you will be able to perform those kinds of activities.

The following stimulus questions are helpful for reflecting on how you and your personality might fit in today's changing workplace, where many jobs do not provide meaning and solidarity.

1. How important do you think it will be to find work that you feel is personally meaningful?
2. What characteristics would make a job personally meaningful for you?

SUMMARY

While there are no doubt other themes that epitomize the changing workplace, we hope these 12 themes have given you an opportunity to think about yourself, the workplace, and what type of environment might best meet your needs. Finding a satisfying work environment has a lot to do with knowing yourself, knowing about different work cultures, and finding the best match for you. Take some time now to complete exercise 2.1. It will help you to inventory the skills that you have to build on.

Exercise 2.1

Skills to Build On and Build Up

This exercise is designed to help you summarize your strengths and areas of needed growth. We ask that you think deeply about the following three summary questions and respond in the spaces provided.

1. What are seven skills you currently have that you believe will be an asset to you in the changing workplace?

   languages
   friendly
   listener
   interested in people
   motivated
   eager   hard-working/determined

2. What are seven skills you need to develop further in order to strengthen your contribution to the changing workplace?

   knowledgable
   tolerance
   patience
   realistic
   stubborn
   open to change   authority

3. How can you develop the skills you listed in Question 2? Make your response as specific as possible.

   with time and learning and experience → being around more people and in situations where I am forced to deal with everyone

CHAPTER 3
Exploring Possibilities, Probabilities, and Choices

CHAPTER OVERVIEW

In this chapter, we discuss the complicated, fascinating, and ongoing process of exploring and considering career goals. We look at how dreams, interests, personality, abilities, values, and timing can influence the directions you should explore, and we provide a series of exercises that can help you determine the relative influence of each for you. We then engage you in informal assessments of each of these influences that may help explain choices you have made or shape those you are going to make. We conclude with suggestions and ideas for furthering your career exploration, and we indicate sources of additional information that might be helpful.

Career planning is a quest for self-fulfillment. It is one of the ways in which we come to terms with the basic issues of who we are, what we have to give, what we want to get, and how we will get along in this often bewildering world. This book is based on two truisms: People, like the world in which they live, are constantly changing, and empowerment comes to those who plan. Career planning must take those changes into account.

Before we can set goals—that is, before we can begin to define the directions and distances that we hope to travel in the course of our lives—we have to achieve some grasp of the multitude of possibilities that lie beyond ourselves in the outer world. We also need to sharpen our appreciation of the potentials, preferences, and aspirations that are locked within ourselves.

Most of us, since early adolescence, have listened to others tell us what we should achieve, what we should become, and how we should live our lives. Too often we have allowed this chorus of well-meant but usually unwanted advice to drown out the softer, more tentative inner whispers that have spoken of hopes, dreams, yearnings, and even fantasies that lie buried within ourselves.

Until we learn to listen to our inner selves, we are unable to even begin the process of career exploration. Exercise 3.1, which is called "Using Your Inner Growth Compass," helps you to look at both how much you attend to your inner self and how willing you are to act on what your inner self tells you. Complete this exercise before going on.

Even after we learn to listen to our inner self, we have to undertake the task of beginning to match up what it tells us with the myriad possibilities, probabilities, and choices that exist in the world of careers. Exploring that world and eventually beginning to focus upon a manageable number and range of possibilities involves considering your dreams, interests, values, and potentials. The discussion and exercises that follow will help you to begin that process.

LISTENING TO YOUR DAYDREAMS

One of the most widely used interest inventories, the Self-Directed Search (SDS), begins by asking you to list your daydreams. There are numerous other sections in the inventory in which you report your interests, abilities, skills, and the like, but the section that has been found to be most predictive of what people may eventually do with their lives is the daydream section. We are conditioned not to pay much attention to our daydreams, but the evidence supports the view that they can be powerful influences. They may also be a good starting point in career exploration for people who are looking for direction.

Exercise 3.2 illustrates the predictive nature of daydreams. It asks you to list five occupations you have daydreamed about or talked to others about that held some appeal for you in the past or do so now. For example, you might list that you have imagined yourself being an actor, a dancer, a musician, a politician, or a journalist. The exercise then asks you to rank the occupations starting with the one that presently holds the most appeal as a possible career role. Take a few minutes now to follow the directions and complete all six steps in this exercise.

Interpreting the Exercise Results

Now let's do some interpretation of your responses to this exercise. In the list of occupations should be clues to what you or others have thought you might be good at or enjoy doing. One or more of the occupations may represent what your parents, a teacher, or significant others have thought would be possible or probable for you. One or more may represent what you would like to do but are afraid to do. Perhaps one is something you can't do because you don't have the money, education, or drive to do it, but it still is what you would like to do. One occupation you have listed might represent a pure fantasy—you know it is not realistic but pursuing it would be sheer bliss, a perfect dream!

Making meaning out of your dreams will require some careful thinking on your part. We are taught not to take dreams too seriously or to spend too much time analyzing them. For the moment, however, assume that they contain important clues about what you might actually pursue as a career. It makes sense to look carefully at the list you have generated. Assume that each dream or choice contains at least one important clue or theme that you should consider in your search for what you most want to do with your life. Then ask yourself the following questions about each of the occupations you have listed:

- Is this still an important dream, or has the appeal worn off for one reason or another?
- Is this a dream that I've had for myself, or is it someone else's dream for me?
- Is this dream realistic or achievable?
- If this dream is realistic or achievable, could I be doing some things to move closer to it?
- What keeps me from it?

If you take each dream seriously and assume that it contains clues to what you are searching for, then you may want to share your list with others who know you well and care about you to get their reactions. You may ask them if they see other clues in these dreams that are relevant to you and your future.

Whether or not you share your list with others, you should apply your own judgment of reality to all of the dreams. You know many things about yourself far better than anyone else. You know, for example, that some of your dreams are just that: dreams that will always remain dreams. You may not see yourself with the desire, ability, or commitment to do what it would take to achieve a particular dream. Other dreams can't be dismissed that easily. They may represent real possibilities. If your dreams are an honest reflection of yourself, then they may provide as much insight into your possible future as the more objective inventories that we suggest you complete in the next section.

CONSIDERING YOUR INTERESTS

Closely related to daydreams are interests. What you dream about doing is usually related to your interests or preferences for certain activities. Because our interests develop over time and are generally supported by experiences we've had in particular areas, we often have more of a rationale for following our interests than for following our dreams. The data show, however, that measured interests (those determined by assessment instruments) typically support our dreams.

Interests are often easier to assess than dreams are, and many assessment instruments are available. Exercise 3.3, the Occupational Card Sort Deck, is one such instrument. Take some time now to complete the exercise. You'll need to photocopy the pages of cards from Appendix A, making double-sided copies, and then cut out the cards. Once you've done so, follow the directions given in the exercise. The process of sorting the cards has been consistently shown to help people gain clarity about their interests.

Interpreting the Exercise Results

We expect that you began to see "themes" or common reasons for placing the cards in particular piles as you completed this exercise. You might, for example, have placed certain cards in the "dislike" pile simply because you thought there would be too much stress involved in preparing for or working in the occupation. Stress would then be a "theme" that is important to you in deciding not to do something. Or you might have put the "chemist" card in the "dislike" pile because you don't like science or you didn't do well in it in high school. You would then have another theme: "science" or "don't do well with it."

Go through the cards in each pile again, making a list of themes that characterize what you dislike and another of themes that reflect what you like in the chart that is provided. Most people find generating themes to be quite simple. The following is a partial list of themes that we have seen emerge from others as they have completed this exercise. You may want to look this list over as a way of getting started on your own lists or adding to your lists.

COMMON THEMES

- Achievement
- Advancement
- Autonomy
- Benefits
- Challenge
- Effort Required
- Excitement
- Geographic location
- Job in demand
- Meaningful or meaningless work
- Monetary rewards
- Novelty
- Power
- Prestige
- Responsibility
- Results are obvious
- Safety
- Security
- Stress
- Structure
- Supervision
- Travel
- Variety
- Virtue
- Work environment
- Working outdoors
- Working with numbers
- Working with machines
- Working with animals

MY THEMES FROM THE OCCUPATIONAL CARD SORT

Dislikes
- disinterest
- not skilled

Likes
- travel
- people
- outdoors
- free
- interests

A Summary Statement About the Themes That Are Most Important to Me:

things I like and want to do

Exercise 3.3 usually presents some surprises. Some people may feel that they have too many or too few titles in the like or the dislike pile, and as a result they may feel that the exercise hasn't clarified their situation. It has, however. A person who has many cards in the dislike pile and few in the like pile might realize that he or she often makes decisions based on a process of elimination. This type of decision making is often expressed as "I know what I don't want to do, but I can't decide what I do want to do."

If you were candid and reflective in completing this exercise, the piles and lists you have created will give you a good start in identifying what interests you have and the occupations that might provide opportunities for pursuing them. For a more thorough assessment of your interests, we suggest that you take the Self-Directed Search, which is available at most college career centers across the country. It takes about 45 minutes to complete and does a more thorough job of helping you identify your interests, skills, and abilities. We will take you through a similar process and use the same vocabulary in our exercises. They are briefer, however.

THINKING ABOUT YOUR PERSONALITY: THE HOLLAND SCHEMA FOR CAREER EXPLORATION

At the start of a career exploration it is common to feel that there are far too many career possibilities even to begin to give them all serious consideration. One way to narrow and focus the exploration was provided by psychologist John Holland. After many years of research, Holland defined six different personality types and six corresponding basic sets of activities, or work environments. His research has shown that a majority of people who are identified as belonging in a given personality type tend to remain throughout their careers in a corresponding type of work environment.

Holland's schema is based on the idea that people tend to succeed in, find satisfaction with, and thus persist in vocational environments that are compatible with their basic interests, attitudes, and other personal characteristics, that is, with their personalities. Similarly, people tend to find greater satisfaction and acceptance when their coworkers share their interests and characteristics.

To some extent, the Holland schema is an oversimplification. To a degree, people help to create their environments, and their interests and attitudes often change with time. However, the Holland schema does provide a useful way to begin to focus the career exploration process and reduce it to a manageable size and scope.

Exercise 3.4, The Career Interests Game, uses the Holland schema to help you look at how you may want to begin your career exploration process. Take a few moments now to complete the exercise.

Interpreting the Exercise Results

The ease or difficulty you had in choosing the areas that best described you in the Career Interests Game should provide you with additional clues about your possible career directions. Some of you may have gravitated toward one of the six types, with all other types fading by comparison. Your career exploration process may be relatively straightforward. When you completed the Card Sort exercise, you probably found a fairly consistent theme within your choices. Others of you may have found that two or more corners in the Career Interests Game drew you strongly. Your career direction is not as clear. It is important for you to look at where on the hexagon the corners to which you were strongly drawn fall. Corners that are close to each other are similar and make for relatively easy transitions, while those that are on opposite sides of the hexagon make for harder transitions. Simply stated, if you gravitate toward types that are close together on the hexagon, it will be easier for you to find an area that is compatible with your characteristics. Look at the hexagon in Exercise 3.4 and find yourself and the types that best fit you. If the types are close together, you may find that making career decisions is relatively easy. If the types are not close together, you may find that making career decisions is more difficult. Some examples may be helpful here.

Individuals who identify themselves as Social (S) and Enterprising (E), for example, likely know that they *want* to work with people; they have only to decide *how* they want to do that. For some, a social service orientation may be appealing; others may be drawn to selling or to influencing people. If you look at types that lie across the hexagon from one another, such as Realistic (R) and Social (S) or Investigative (I) and Enterprising (E), you'll see that the types are quite different. The careers that allow people to combine these opposites are fewer. A job corresponding with Social, for example, would have you working with people, whereas one corresponding with Investigative would have you working with ideas and one corresponding with Realistic would have you working with objects. You may like all three, but you may have to pick one as most important. Some people find a way to enjoy their interests in diverse areas by developing hobbies that they can pursue outside of paid work.

If you found it difficult to discern which of two types really is most important to you or are having trouble figuring out how to combine or choose between them, you are not alone. Many people experience these difficulties. The following examples illustrate such dilemmas and provide some possible ways to get further clarification for yourself.

If the two types you chose are close to each other on the hexagon, it is likely that you will be able to find career possibilities that accommodate both types, as we illustrated earlier with the Social (S) and Enterprising (E) types. The choice of one over the other may only be a matter of deciding which to emphasize, as both involve working with people. Other suggestions are to volunteer time in a social-type job or an enterprising-type job or to interview people who see themselves as these types. Doing so may clarify for you which is more important to you or which type you most resemble.

If the two types you chose are opposites, however, like Social (S) and Realistic (R), you may have to give thought to other factors, such as your skills, abilities, and values. These may sway your decisions to explore one area as opposed to the other.

Another consideration that sometimes complicates the process of career exploration is a lack of experience in a particular area. Without relevant experience, you may be led to explore or consider given areas only to find that although your skills are relevant you do not have the passion or commitment to pursue the career seriously. Conventional types and Realistic types, for example, may move into jobs that don't require much formal education and may quickly develop the skills, abilities, and experience to do the work. But as they get older, they may find that they want greater opportunities for advancement or recognition. They still have the skills, and our inventories would suggest that they would do well in conventional and realistic jobs, but their inner voices may tell them something very different.

The most common factors that hinder people from finding clues to guide their exploration from exercises like those in this book are not knowing themselves well enough or not having been exposed to many of the vast array of career possibilities that are available in the world of work. Most of the exercises assume that you are comfortable with who you are and that you are reasonably well informed about a wide range of opportunities and situations available. Often, however, that is not the case, especially for younger people. It is hard to sort out possibilities without having had relevant experience. If you are in this situation, you may simply need to give yourself time to acquire the insight and experience needed to take the crucial steps to make good decisions. Career planning for you at this time may focus on exploration, tryouts of new activities, and reflection about your own strengths and preferences, rather than on attempting to make major decisions or choices.

CONSIDERING YOUR SKILLS AND ABILITIES

In high school, a great deal of emphasis is placed on identifying students' skills and abilities. Students regularly take tests and are compared to their peers. As they finish high school, they typically take achievement tests or college entrance examinations, and inferences are made about what skills and abilities they have acquired. Sometimes decisions about courses they will take or colleges they will apply to are made based on these scores. By the time they are ready to explore careers, they are often able to assess their own skills and abilities with accuracy.

As you begin your career exploration, your concern now is more with which skills and abilities you want to further develop or which you see as keys to a career. While you may do things to improve in some areas, a basic pattern likely is evident. There are some things that you find easy and others that you find difficult. In your career, you will want to engage in tasks you are good at and avoid tasks you find very difficult.

You may feel it is difficult to know what you really do best and that you need additional objective feedback. We suggest that you probably have a pretty realistic idea of what you do best if you are willing to look at yourself honestly. That is, if we were to ask you to rate yourself on a number of skills and abilities—ones particularly related to work and the careers you are considering—we contend that you would be able to rate your skills with considerable accuracy. To illustrate, look at the list of abilities and skills in Exercise 3.5 and mark your estimates of how you would rate yourself on each in comparison with others your age. Most likely, you will have no difficulty completing this task. When you are done, ask yourself which of those abilities and skills that you marked high you would want to develop still further. Think about whether you can develop the area into a career asset. Think about whether it fits with some of the career possibilities you have been considering.

The abilities and skills in Exercise 3.5 can be related to the six Holland personality types and occupational areas discussed earlier. The 12 abilities or skills in Exercise 3.5 are listed in the order of the types RIASEC. A more systematic assessment of these areas and personality types can be obtained by completing Holland's Self-Directed Search. If you found that the skills you rated high in Exercise 3.5 correspond with the types you were drawn to in Exercise 3.4, you are on to something! You will likely find satisfaction in a career involving those skills and types.

CONSIDERING YOUR VALUES

In addition to dreams, interests, skills, and abilities, values also play an important role in the career choices we make. We may value our country, our religious faith, or our loyalties so much that we would pursue one area regardless of other considerations. In such cases, a particular value may overshadow everything else. Passions are usually related to values and can provide strong motivation. Physicians, for example, often are motivated by wanting to heal or cure those with particular illnesses, and it is their interest in a particular disease affecting a particular group of people that helps define how they will spend their time. Other physicians may have a dream to help the disadvantaged or people in developing countries. For them, dreams, interests, and values are all tied together.

When you make a career decision, it is important to consider your values. A job that is a good fit for you will incorporate your dreams, interests, skills, abilities, and values. Keep in mind that although work-related values can change, some may be pretty basic and long lasting. In Exercise 3.6 you will find a list of common work-related values. The list is not comprehensive, but it is enough to get you started in thinking about values that are important to you. Try to prioritize these values in order of their importance to you. Then ask a friend to rank the same values for himself or herself. Discuss how similar or different your rankings are. There is no right ranking. Feel free to add other values to the list that come to mind.

TIMING

The adage that "timing is everything" applies to career planning as much as it does to many other aspects of life. You have likely learned, over the years, much of what you need to do to establish yourself in a career. When you heard or read the information, however, you may not have been ready to apply it. By working through the exercises in this book, you can ensure that you'll be ready to make sound career choices when the timing is right. Opportunity doesn't always present itself at convenient times, but by seriously considering the ideas and suggestions contained in this book, you can be ready to grasp opportunities when they present themselves.

SOURCES OF CAREER INFORMATION

Career information is literally everywhere. Every newspaper, magazine, and flyer that you pick up contains information about work and workers. TV programs, documentaries, and motion pictures all may contain relevant career information. One of the best sources of career information is other people. Serious conversations with people who have spent their lives in various career fields or who have left or entered various fields for various reasons can provide invaluable insights.

Chapter 12 contains lists of career resources available on the Internet. As you explore possibilities and seek out information, you will need to determine for yourself the kinds of information that are most relevant to you. Keeping a small notebook of relevant facts and personal impressions about occupations, work environments, and the people in them may help make your exploration process more systematic and efficient.

SUMMARY

Knowing what careers may be good possibilities for you is dependent on knowing yourself. Your dreams, interests, values, and abilities all provide clues to the directions that you need to explore. The exercises in this chapter were aimed at helping you to see yourself and your interests, skills, and so forth, more clearly. In addition to getting to know yourself, you also need to learn where the opportunities are as you begin to plan. The many sources of career information that are available today are helpful in this regard.

CAREER PLANNING   35

Exercise 3.1
Using Your Inner Growth Compass

How frequently have you:	Never	Sometimes	Frequently
1. Done something you felt like doing at the moment, without regard to the consequences?			\
2. Risked sharing your innermost thoughts and feelings with another person?			\
3. Done what you wanted to do instead of what you "should" do in other people's eyes?			\
4. Done what felt right to you against the advice of others?			\
5. Allowed yourself to experiment creatively with new approaches to old problems?			\
6. Expressed an unpopular opinion firmly and clearly in the face of majority opposition?			\
7. Told others of your deepest religious and philosophical convictions?		\	
8. Made an important decision and acted on it immediately without discussing it with anyone?	\		
9. Acknowledged by your actions that you can direct your own life?			\
10. Asserted your feelings clearly and vehemently when you were treated unfairly?			\
11. Made a new friend or really worked on deepening your relationship with an old friend?			\
12. Taken a course in an area totally new and different from your past education or experience?			\
13. Traveled to a place you had never been purely for a sense of excitement, curiosity, and enlightenment?			
14. Taken a fantasy trip—allowed your imagination to run freely for a half hour or more?			\
15. Done something no one (including yourself) expected you to do?			\
16. Stopped to "listen" to what was going on inside of you?		\	
17. Gone all out, risking a great deal to get what you wanted?		\	
18. Spontaneously expressed a feeling—joy, anger, fear, sadness, caring—without "thinking about it"?			\

What did you learn about how well and often you *attend* to your inner self?

I do what I want when I want — and I live

What did you learn about how willing you are to act on your inner impulses?

I don't care what they think *by this*

Exercise 3.2

Occupational Daydreams

1. List five occupations you have considered in thinking about your future. List both ones you have daydreamed about as well as those you have discussed with others.

   - (diplomat) — 2
   - H (linguist) — 3
   - H (translator) — 4
   - (ambassador) — 1
   - FI. ballerina — 5

2. Now prioritize each in terms of their appeal to you today. That is, place a "1" to the right of the occupation that has the most appeal, a "2" by the one with the next most appeal, a "3" by the one with the next most appeal, and so forth.

3. Circle the occupation(s) that others think you should do (parents, spouse, best friend, relative, teacher, etc.).

4. Put an "I" in front of any that seem impossible because of requirements—educational, financial, personal, etc.

5. Put an "F" in front of any that represent "fantasy" choices—fun but not realistic in your opinion.

6. Put an "H" in front of any that might qualify more as a hobby or avocation than as an occupation.

Later, you may want to look carefully for themes that are present in these choices. We suggest you keep this list where you can use it again.

Exercise 3.3

The Occupational Card Sort Deck

1. Photocopy and cut out the 90 occupational cards, as well as the LIKE, DISLIKE, and NEUTRAL / UNDECIDED cards from Appendix A. Note that the occupational cards are double-sided.

2. Go through the occupational cards and sort them into three piles: one pile for those occupations you feel you might like to do (LIKE pile), one for those you dislike or would not choose to do (DISLIKE pile), and a third pile for those you are unsure about or could go either way with (UNDECIDED / NEUTRAL pile). If possible, talk with a friend about your reasons for putting the cards in the particular piles as you go along. Talking about your reasons will help you make more meaning out of the exercise. Your friend might continually ask you why you put a card in a particular pile, which will help you express your reasons. These judgments carry meaning that can be helpful to you in understanding what is important to you in a career.

3. If you aren't sure what a particular occupation involves, look at the brief definition provided on the back of the card. Some other information is there as well, which you may find useful in additional career exploration.

4. Suspend judgment about the outcome of this exercise. For now, go back to the chapter text, where we provide additional direction.

Exercise 3.4

The Career Interests Game

R for "Realistic"
People who have athletic or mechanical ability, prefer to work with objects, machines, tools, plants, or animals, or to be outdoors.

I for "Investigative"
People who like to observe, learn, investigate, analyze, evaluate, or solve problems.

C for "Conventional"
People who like to work with data, have clerical or numerical ability, and like to carry things out in detail or follow through on others' instructions.

The Party

A for "Artistic"
People who have artistic, innovating, or intuitional abilities and like to work in unstructured situations using their imagination or creativity.

E for "Enterprising"
People who like to work with people—influencing, persuading, or performing, or leading or managing for organizational goals or for economic gain.

S for "Social"
People who like to work with people—to inform, enlighten, help, train, develop, or cure them—or are skilled with words.

1. Which corner of the room would you instinctively be drawn to, as being the group of people you would most enjoy being with for the longest time? (Leave aside any question of shyness, or whether you would have to talk to them.) Write the letter for that corner here: **I**

2. After 15 minutes, everyone in the corner you have chosen leaves for another party across town, except you. Of the groups that still remain, which corner or group would you be drawn to the most, as being the people you would most enjoy being with for the longest time? Write the letter for that corner here: **S**

3. After 15 minutes, this group too leaves for another party, except you. Of the corners and groups that remain now, which one would you most enjoy being with for the longest time? Write the letter for that corner here: **A**

Note. From *What Color Is Your Parachute?* (p. 290), by R. N. Bolles, 1999, Berkeley, CA: Ten Speed Press. Copyright 1999 by Ten Speed Press. Adapted with permission.

Exercise 3.5

Estimating Your Abilities and Skills

	High	Average	Low
Mechanical ability		✓	
Scientific ability		✓	
Artistic ability	✓		
Teaching ability	✓		
Sales ability		✓	
Clerical ability	✓		
Manual skill	✓		
Math skill	✓		
Musical ability	✓		
Understanding of others	✓		
Managerial skills		✓	
Office skills	✓		

Exercise 3.6

Values Exercise

Rank the following work-related values in order of importance to you.

8	Creativity
7	Helping others
9	High income
13	Influencing others
16	Leadership
3	Variety
4	Flexible schedule
15	Authority
17	Competition
11	Working alone
12	Working with others
14	Accountability/responsibility
10	Security
2	Leisure time
1	Travel
18	Social status
4	Meaningful work
5	Use of skills
6	Knowledge

CHAPTER 4
Planning Across the Life Span

CHAPTER OVERVIEW

In this chapter, we look more closely at the changes, challenges, and transitions that people encounter as they move through the life cycle. We then describe the basic tasks involved in adult life planning and discuss the need for lifelong planning for dealing with both the predictable and unpredictable problems and opportunities that will be confronted. An exercise called the Career Actualization Lifeline is provided to assist you in using a life span perspective to examine the major events in your life and to help you plan for the future.

What was or is this period like in your life?

How did you deal with some of those storms and stresses?

Have you experienced any of these kinds of losses or disappointments? When? How?

Do your career plans involve someone else? How will you, or have you, reconciled your needs with another's?

One way to define life planning is that it is *intelligent cooperation with the inevitable*. As we noted in Chapter 1 the only certainty that we can count on throughout life is the inevitability of change. In children and adolescents, visible and dramatic changes are often evident from month to month and year to year. We see the turmoil and tension that these changes can bring as they collide with an increasingly complex and demanding environment. We remember adolescence as a period of storm and stress, emotional peaks and valleys, and fluctuating values, attitudes, and relationships.

In adults, too, change can be dramatic and stressful. For some of you, the prospect of experiencing *adult* transitions, particularly those associated with midlife and beyond, may seem remote and almost unreal. For others, the prospect may seem threatening, something to avoid thinking about. For still others, however, the realities of adult transitions may be a part of everyday life. These realities, in fact, may be what has brought you to look at life planning in a systematic way.

Adult transitions and challenges are an inescapable aspect of life. Fortunately, by facing these realities *now*, by incorporating the inevitable into our present planning, we can be ready to convert crises into opportunities and challenges into triumphs.

Changes, Challenges, and Transitions in Adulthood

Early Adult Transitions

Perhaps the most critical and turbulent period of adulthood is the mid to late 20s. A whole series of transitions come in quick succession as life becomes rapidly more complex and the stakes attached to success or failure rise ever higher.

Two major areas of early adult transition are related to the establishment and maintenance of long-term relationships and the establishment of first steps in progress toward a career. In many ways, early adulthood is the time in which earlier growth in education, emotional stability, and relationship building are put to the test.

For perhaps the first time, the young adult finds that he or she is "playing for keeps." For the first time, success and happiness tend not to be a function of parental support or social status but to depend on personal skills, wisdom, and accomplishment. Failures in personal relationships or vocational efforts may leave permanent scars and lifelong disappointments.

For many young adults these years also bring the new roles of being a spouse or partner and a parent. The spouse or partner is now at one time lover, companion, housemate, coworker, and confidant—roles that previously could be avoided or separated into different "compartments." He or she is in a close, long-term relationship that requires cooperative efforts and shared decisions in homemaking, money management, leisure, and recreation. The cooperative management of two careers within the family unit may mean that *two* sets of aspirations and priorities must now be balanced. If the young adult is also a parent, the realities of parenthood also put heavy demands on emotional equilibrium and on the ability to provide mutual support within the different family relationships.

In addition, the young adult faces career demands that are generally quite different from those confronted in earlier part-time or entry-level work experiences. When the career choices made are highly ego-involving, and when success within a career is central to the individual's self-esteem and satisfaction, heavy pressures and stresses are certain.

Inevitably, career and family roles and responsibilities tend to collide. Managing and resolving conflicts and competition between family and career responsibilities become a daily routine.

The key skills involved in handling the transitions and crises in young adulthood are *time management*, *problem solving,* and *negotiation skills,* as well as the ability to give and receive *emotional support.* A healthy set of *stress management strategies* is also usually needed. Because of the complexity of the challenges encountered, planning and organizational skills are vital. We will discuss each of these areas in later chapters.

Midlife Transitions

When one manages to move successfully through the troubling changes from adolescence to adulthood and beyond and to achieve a reasonably stable and satisfying lifestyle, we might suppose that life transitions and their accompanying crises will fade forever into the background. Unfortunately, that is only rarely the case.

As most of us think about the life span, we tend to divide it into three rather distinct periods: youth, middle age, and old age. Not surprisingly, however, the specific age limits and thresholds that mark these periods vary widely depending on whom you ask. Teenagers and people in their early 20s typically see middle age beginning at about age 35 and entrance into old age occurring at about 50. Those already in their 50s perceive midlife as beginning at about 45 and continuing well into the 60s and even 70s.

Actually, it is not very useful even to try to define midlife purely in terms of chronological age. Two centuries ago the average life expectancy was under 40. Today, with each advance in medicine, safety, health, and nutrition, the average life expectancy creeps steadily upward. In a strictly statistical sense, midlife was once represented by the 20s, while today it can be seen to extend into the 50s and 60s and beyond.

It may be much more useful to look at midlife in terms of status or roles. Markers such as having grandchildren, the high school or college graduation of one's youngest offspring, promotions within an organization, or achieving a degree of financial security may all be seen as "markers" of midlife. None of these is, of course, fully adequate. One 45-year-old may have school-age children, while another may have grandchildren or watch over an "empty nest."

How Do People View Midlife? Although it is impossible to know exactly when one reaches the midpoint of one's life, people have a sense of when they are middle aged. Their feelings may be based upon the age and health of their parents and siblings, their own social position such as seniority, or their leadership responsibilities within a community, company, or organization. Their feelings may be a function of their sense of health, vitality, or well-being.

Whatever the precise limits one establishes, we know that there are certain *psychological* properties associated with experiencing middle age. Midlife, for example, appears to be a time to both look back and look ahead, a time to reflect on how life is going and what is left for us to do. Whereas young adults are most likely to focus on the future and the elderly tend to turn their attention to the past, in middle age present, past, and future perspectives blend together. We constantly have one foot planted in the present and the other poised to step into the future, while all the time the past tugs persistently at our coat sleeves with memories of triumphs and tragedies, victories won and opportunities lost. Our concepts of self change, and we have to update our inner-voice tapes accordingly.

Earlier we pointed out that in our complex society many cultural clocks tick away to chime out the passing of the markers and milestones encountered throughout the life span. As individuals, each of us listens to three kinds of clocks. We have *psychological* clocks within us that are governed by our own deeply personal hopes, aspirations, and expectations. Outside us are the "cultural clocks" that are regulated by external standards, customs, and expectations. And always present but often ignored are the "biological clocks" that govern the physiological rhythms that regulate and orchestrate the ebb and flow of life itself.

When did your parents reach middle age? When will you or have you?

Do midlife changes seem far away and unreal? How did your parents handle these changes? How have their problems affected you?

How are you changing with regard to these characteristics?

How are you feeling social pressures in your life now?

Have you or someone you know gone through a midlife crisis? What was it like?

How did you feel when you found the first gray hair or wrinkle or lost a game to someone younger?

Our psychological clocks tend to track our accomplishments based on our hopes, dreams, goals, and aspirations. Promotions, pay increases, financial security, social status, relationships, and so forth, are measured against our own internalized goals and expectations. Midlife is a time when we review what we have accomplished and ponder what remains to be done in terms of finite time and limited resources. It is time when we savor past successes and set firm priorities about the future.

Cultural clocks are also ever-present, reminding us of outside approval or disapproval. Even though the expectations on which cultural clocks are based are always changing, many people still feel a degree of social disapproval if their schedules for marriage, child rearing, financial security, career moves, education, or retirement deviate from what is considered "normal" or appropriate within a given set of social mores and values. In midlife, people may feel such disapproval more keenly, as the opportunities that are available tend to narrow.

Midlife is also a time when one's awareness of biological clocks is sharpened. In midlife, men and women increasingly engage in what is called "body-monitoring," as they become more aware of changes in their physical vigor. Graying, wrinkles, sagging muscles, thinning hair, and rising blood pressure all increase awareness of the passage of time and the inevitability of mortality.

When the many studies of midlife adults are reviewed, a number of overarching findings can be identified. Generally, people in midlife report increased self-confidence, more warmth and tendencies to be outgoing in relationships, a greater sense of commitment to goals and values, and a deeper sense of responsibility and dependability in both work and social relationships. These self-reported characteristics are supported by interviewers who have examined the life histories of the people being studied. In a very general way, people do get better as they get older.

Middle age tends to bring increases in *competence, self-assurance,* and *self-control.* Motivations and aspirations also increase. In midlife, achievement needs, the importance of close personal relationships, and the urge for self-actualization or development all increase.

While midlife is sometimes seen as a period of relative stability and even tranquillity, it is not without its stresses and challenges. Many years ago psychoanalyst Carl Jung wrote about the *midlife crisis,* a serious reevaluation of one's personal identity and accompanying goals and values. In midlife, Jung felt, people have achieved enough emotional security to reexamine their needs and aspirations and to reassert those needs and aspirations regardless of the presence of social approval or disapproval.

In today's popular literature, the midlife crisis is often portrayed as a sudden and drastic kicking over of all traces of the past accompanied by bizarre behavior or flagrant disregard for traditional norms and values. In actuality, however, the midlife transition is often a reflective and thoughtful reexamination of personal values and goals, and the consequent changes in behavior are rational and planned.

How Do People Experience Adult Transitions? Psychologists have been studying adult life and the challenges it presents for more than 50 years. The period of life beginning at about the age of 35 has been seen as a time of reappraisal and transformation of an individual's basic identity.

As we noted earlier, the years of adolescence and early adulthood are periods in which people are hurrying and hustling in pursuit of external and often material or status goals. Understandably, in the midst of this hard driving and hurried existence, they may ignore or even deny dissonant parts of themselves. When their personal interests, attitudes, or values seem to conflict, seem to get in the way of their immediate progress toward their goals, or threaten to make life too complicated, young adults may tend to push them out of awareness. As youth, we are often too busy with the task of mastering the mysteries and challenges of the outside world to attend fully to what is happening in our "inside world"—that is, the world within ourselves. We fail to update our views of self and our sense of what is really important in our lives.

As we approach the second half of our life span, this preoccupation with the external world begins to change. In the words of a popular song, we begin to "stop to smell the roses" along the way. We pause to listen to ourselves, and perhaps to become fully aware of ourselves for the first time in many years. We update our internal tapes. In the process of listening to and understanding our inner life, we achieve the freedom to become fuller, more complete, and more balanced human beings. However, the process of examining and integrating long ignored or even denied aspects of ourselves is often painful.

The pain associated with adult transitions is a growth pain, not a sick pain. The pain of such crises is often simply the price we pay for getting better and better as we live and grow. It is the price we pay for becoming more sensitive, more aware, and more inner-directed human beings.

As we become more aware of ourselves, we experience new opportunities as well as new anxieties. One of these opportunities is the opportunity to round out or complete our development by accepting and building on long ignored or denied parts of ourselves.

We noted that youth often ignore or deny parts of themselves that they may view as foreign or incompatible with their fledgling and fragile sense of identity. Men, for example, may deny feelings of compassion, sensitivity, and tenderness because those feelings are threatening or disturbing to a "macho" notion of masculinity. Women may deny inclinations to direct, organize, and manage people and situations, believing that such talents and interests are incompatible with the "sweet young thing" image around which they have organized their emerging identities.

But in ignoring or denying interests, talents, and sources of achievement and satisfaction, young adults may, in fact, ignore or discard very important potentials for growth. In midlife, we get a second chance to develop a new, richer, and more realistic sense of who we are and what we are truly capable of achieving. This second chance may be disturbing and unsettling, but it can also bring with it much of the same sense of excitement, discovery, and wonder that we first experienced in adolescence. Even more wonderful, accompanying this second chance is the wisdom, experience, and maturity we have acquired in adulthood.

Our reappraisal of self can also involve a reassessment of our goals, values, and aspirations. Often, the goals, ambitions, and undertakings with which we enter the adult world are those that were given to us by others. As we review these goals and values we may realize that our families, the group of friends with whom we happened to be close, or even the temporary fads and enthusiasms of the day combined to move our lives along a particular path. Although we may have known that our direction was being set by others, we may have been too caught up in pressures to resist.

As we get older, the questions we ask ourselves get louder and more insistent. One study found that most people in midlife were asking themselves the following kinds of questions:

1. What have I done with my life?
2. What do I really get from and give to my spouse, children, friends, work, community, and self?
3. What are my central values, and how are they reflected in my life?
4. What are my greatest talents, and how am I using or wasting them?
5. What have I done with my early "dream," and what do I want to do with it now?

These are hard, disturbing questions. It is little wonder that researchers have found that more than 80% of people in midlife are experiencing a tumultuous

How do you feel when you think about aging? In what ways does aging seem to offer promise? How is it frightening?

Will your plans be flexible enough for a midlife course correction?

Are there parts of yourself that you have ignored or denied? Will you be able to find and fulfill them later?

Will midlife bring you fulfillment or frustration and disappointment? How can planning now help?

What does it feel like to picture yourself in old age? How will you change? How will you stay the same?

struggle within themselves and between themselves and the outside world as they wrestle with these fundamental questions. We can conclude that most people experience a moderate to severe crisis as they become more aware of their own mortality and at the same time experience a strong desire to be more productive, creative, and significant people.

What Are the Dangers in Adult Transitions? Given that adult crises are likely to be experienced as disquieting or even painful, what are the real psychological dangers involved? Contrary to what we might guess, the tension, restlessness, or anxiety that we feel in the midst of crisis is not where the real danger lies. The fact that more than 80% of adults in midlife experience such anxiety is proof that it represents a natural, if somewhat disturbing, part of normal development.

Jung believed that the great danger of the adult crisis was in clinging fearfully or stubbornly to the goals or values of earlier years and in doing so refusing to acknowledge the changes and challenges of adult life. Another noted developmental theorist, Erik Erikson, used the term *stagnation* to describe the danger of failing to meet the challenge of adult transitions . He referred to the adult crisis as being a struggle between the forces within that move us toward greater creativity and greater contributions to others and to society and the darker forces within us that drag us into frustration, stagnation, and consequent despair. In a real sense, these students of adult development are saying that when we stop growing and giving, we begin dying. Stagnation is perhaps just another name for a lingering psychological death.

If, as adults, we are unwilling to accept the risks involved in reappraising our identity, or in acting upon the new information, our future is likely to hold little more than an ever-increasing feeling of frustration with family, work, and even leisure roles. If we deny and bottle up the urges to invest our energy and ideas in something new and important to ourselves and society, we are, in a sense, giving up hope in the future itself. When that occurs, the resulting stagnation can lead to a gradual withdrawal of contact with younger people, to a preoccupation with ourself and the processes of aging, and, finally, to a sort of empty and robot-like existence where we merely go through the motions of work, family, and social life while feeling increasingly useless, unneeded, and dependent. It is all too clear that this kind of stagnation is behind many of the problems of depression, alcoholism, divorce, and psychosomatic problems that too often beset people in their later years.

The Crossover Phenomenon Although it is certainly possible to exaggerate the differences between the adult transitions that men and women experience, it is clear that such differences do exist. Researchers who have compared the impact of midlife changes on men and women have found that men seem to become more concerned with building relationships, nurturing others, and receiving personal recognition and responses from others. Women tend to become more concerned with acting on the basis of personal aspirations. They begin to feel less guilty about asserting their personal needs and in acting aggressively and determinedly to reach their goals.

These differing directions of personality changes, which we call the "crossover phenomenon," tend to pose different kinds of relationship problems for men and women. Even though in one sense these changes may mean that men and women are growing more similar, the net effect may be to put strains on existing relationships.

For women, midlife changes have been perceived as reducing dependence on others and as moving away from a role centered around providing nurturance and support. Women often tend to experience increasingly high aspirations for personal achievements and accomplishments. They tend to seek greater independence and autonomy. They are often attempting to incorporate and integrate into their personalities a greater capacity to compete, achieve, and excel on their own.

Unfortunately, such changes may come precisely at a time when men may be attempting to develop greater capacities to express themselves, to experience physical and emotional intimacy, and to ask for help and support from others.

A poem by Ric Masten entitled "Coming and Going" eloquently describes the crossover phenomenon:

> I have noticed
> that men somewhere around forty
> tend to come in from the field with a sigh
> and removing their coat in the hall
> come into the kitchen.
> you were right
> Grace
> it ain't out there
> just like you've always said.
> and she
> with the children gone at last
> breathless
> putting her hat on her head
> the hell it ain't
> they pass in the doorway

This phenomenon goes a long way toward explaining some of the difficulties in marital relationships that are frequently experienced during midlife. It also explains other tensions adults may feel. As just one example, the changes in needs and aspirations that women experience in adulthood may run directly counter to the social expectations of a society with relatively rigid and traditional concepts of female sex roles.

What Is Involved in Adult Life Planning?

When we recognize the basic tasks that confront everyone in adulthood, we can begin to marshal resources and come to grips with these realities. Rather than taking refuge in fantasies and illusions, we can intelligently cooperate with the changes that are inevitable.

Throwing Away the Old

One basic task in midlife planning is throwing away the old to make room for the new. The "old" in this case consists of ideas, attitudes, values, and habits. Often stemming from childhood or from early experiences, these are not easy things to discard. Literally, it means having the courage to examine and reevaluate the ideas, attitudes, and values that we acquired in childhood, adolescence, or youth and trying them on again to see if they still fit. In a sense, we have to begin listening attentively to a new set of inner voices with the new set of messages born of adulthood.

Part of this process involves emotionally accepting some of life's hardest realities. Among them: We are all finite, fallible, and imperfect human beings. We cannot accomplish everything, nor can we overcome all obstacles. The world is not perfect or perhaps even perfectable, at least in our time. We and our loved ones are mortal; we are all going to die. Complete safety, total security, and permanent stability are all illusions. Most important, we need to have the courage to be imperfect and to live in an imperfect world.

Learning to Live Without Our Old Identity

As we learn to accept these realities and muster the courage to live with them, we may begin to feel, at first, a sense of loneliness and even of alienation. Sometimes, these feelings come from pulling away from our earlier dreams and goals. We may begin to be impatient with our old, unwanted, or unachievable goals, and we may begin to set new priorities and to be impatient with rituals or relationships that seem to waste our precious time and energy.

In a sense, we are passing through a corridor connecting our old self with our new self. In this passage, one of the things that we experience is a new time perspective. People making this transition are much more aware of the passage of time. They feel more of a need to utilize time carefully. Unlike the harried and reckless use of time by children or adolescents, many adults experience each day as important and eventful. The waste of a day is

Have you heard any doubting inner voices that question your earlier values and goals?
When?
What did those voices say?

How will aging affect your closest relationships? How have you seen it affect your parents or other midlife people?

Have you felt any of this or seen it in others?

How will your present plans give you this kind of control at midlife and beyond?

How have you experienced this renegotiation process or seen it in your friends or family? How did it feel to all concerned?

seen as an irreplaceable loss. When we do feel *in control* of ourselves and our resources, and when we are *immersed* in worthwhile activities, we feel a sense of *flow* in life that is opposite to the sense of the empty passage of precious time.

For some people the new time perspective may bring with it restlessness and discontent. However, many people who master the tasks of planning and managing time feel more fully in charge of their own lives than ever before.

Trying On Our New Identity

Building a new identity is not just a passive process. We literally have to build a new identity out of new or renegotiated roles and relationships, new or revised goals, aspirations, and values, and new and improved ways of coping with problems, decisions, and obstacles.

A central element in building a new identity is *risk taking*. Trying on the new elements of our identity is like conducting a set of experiments with our own lives. We can and should plan carefully, calculate risks, and try to predict outcomes. Yet, despite all of our efforts, the final outcomes will always have an element of surprise and uncertainty. In this sense, adult life is an adventure and an exploration of unknown territory. Part of the joy possible in adult life is the excitement that can come with this process. The following sections describe several of the tasks involved in building a new identity.

Renegotiating Roles and Relationships

One fundamental area of identity renewal involves renegotiating roles and relationships in our family, social, and vocational life. As we discover and act upon new information about ourselves, we inevitably alter the roles and relationships that defined our former identities. Those with whom we have close relationships are forced to cope with our new aspirations and attitudes.

Often these changes are disturbing and even frightening to everyone concerned. It is an upsetting and unnerving experience, for example, to suddenly realize that a spouse of 20 years has newly awakened interests, hopes, and aspirations that have never before been discussed or perhaps even dreamed of in the relationship.

Similarly, our children, friends, and coworkers will be confronted with emerging aspects of our new identity. Unless we are able to articulate and discuss openly what is happening in a major adult transition, important others in our lives may experience these changes as rejections of themselves and feel that we are discarding or discounting formerly cherished relationships and values.

The key element in renegotiating roles and relationships lies in the word "renegotiating." When we are able to describe to others what is going on inside ourselves, listen in a concerned and open way to their reactions, and problem solve together around the mutual difficulties imposed by transitions, we can emerge with a stronger and more viable network of relationships than ever before.

As roles and relationships change in adulthood, special or intimate relationships often take on greater importance. We often discard our old needs to be popular, admired, and loved by *everyone* and focus instead on the few really significant people and relationships in our lives. Unless we explain and negotiate our new expectations, however, they may put strains upon our relationships.

Renegotiating relationships in adulthood often also involves dropping facades and decreasing the amount of time and energy we are willing to devote to "impression management." As we attach increasing value to the worth of friends and loved ones, we often set higher expectations for interpersonal openness and honesty in our relationships. Sometimes we begin to downplay the importance of money and status in forming relationships and yearn to be accepted and responded to in terms of ourselves rather than our possessions or reputation.

Relationships With Parents One set of relationships that undergoes marked change in adulthood is our relationship with our parents. Often we become increasingly unwilling to put up with attitudes in our parents that seem condescending or authoritarian. We may become dissatisfied with our own, sometimes childish, reactions to our parents. When we react with childish dependence or rebellion to them we may feel guilt and inadequacy. The realization that we may have very limited time to work through the old hurts and differences with them makes our feelings more urgent, and the role reversal that often occurs with aged parents sometimes makes the relationships even more difficult.

Strangely, the death of a parent before we have worked through our relationship with that parent can make the problem even more troubling. Instead, the death of a parent can trigger a disturbing and turbulent kind of transition, especially if we have been unable to take charge of our own lives because of unresolved feelings of blame or guilt in regard to our parents and our childhood. Perhaps the most challenging and important task of adult life is to finally, firmly, and fully take responsibility for who we are and where we are going. We need, finally, to give up the rationalization that we are merely the product of our parents' mistakes or the victims of their inadequacies.

Many adults report that their close personal relationships are their most important sources of strength in coping with stress and anxiety in life crises. Even though adults are often seeking greater competence and mastery in work and social settings, almost all report that they want a renewal of intimacy with their spouses and closest friends. Similarly, as people move through adulthood they report a greater interest in religious and club activities and in family gatherings than ever before in their lives. Supporting the observation that close relationships help in times of stress, adults who report that they have been overwhelmed by stress and anxiety tend to rate themselves low in terms of their capacity for handling closeness and mutuality in interpersonal relationships.

Setting New Goals Perhaps the most important task of adult life involves reassessing our goals and aspirations. As we reexamine and sometimes modify or discard our old views of ourselves, we are forced to reorganize and rethink the basic values that give purpose, direction, and meaning to our lives. Often, as we noted earlier, this means thinking through complex values questions for ourselves because we are no longer willing to accept the pat answers or solutions that were given to us by others.

Sometimes our new goals and aspirations mean that we must drastically revise our concepts of self. They may lead us to reassess our strengths and develop more fully talents and possibilities that we had ignored or denied in the past.

LIFE PLANNING AS LIFELONG PLANNING

People often see life planning as a kind of one-time exercise that provides a ready-made road map that they will be able to follow, or at least pretend to follow, for the rest of their lives. Unfortunately, such plans, like road maps, may quickly become obsolete as we change and the world around us changes. Life planning is *lifelong planning*.

Successful life planning involves learning the skills, insights, values, and habits that enable us to build a satisfying and productive life within a constantly changing world. One of the keys to building such a life involves cultivating *flexibility* and *readiness*. We can never plan in a rigid or detailed way for *all* of the events and contingencies that may impact our lives. One of the truisms in life is that *something unusual and unexpected happens every day.*

It sounds like an oxymoron to say that we should *plan* for unplanned or unexpected events, yet that is precisely what we are required to do to build a satisfying life in a kaleidoscopically changing world. Take a few minutes now to complete Exercise 4.1, which will help you to see

How are you feeling the stress of changing parental relationships?

How have you felt this desire to be more open, and honest in your close relationships?

How well will your present long-term relationships give you support and satisfaction throughout your life?

your own flexibility and readiness for the changes that affect your life.

Two of the keys to having the flexibility and readiness to convert unforeseen circumstances into opportunities instead of disasters are *self-understanding* and *self-awareness*. We all have personal values, attitudes, and preferences that interact with the outside events that impact our lives. Recognizing these aspects of ourselves and applying them realistically to new and unexpected situations can help us to determine if the situations are indeed opportunities waiting to be seized or merely circumstances to be accepted, coped with, or ignored.

We can call these personal characteristics our career navigation lights. They help us to find our way through the fog of unforeseen events. Exercise 4.2 will help you to determine what your career navigation lights are. They are often deep-seated attitudes, preferences and values of which we are only dimly aware. They often determine both our choices and our degree of commitment to choices once made.

The questions in Exercise 4.2 are the kinds of questions that generate the information needed to begin lifelong planning and decision making. In subsequent chapters you will be asked to begin to set goals and develop plans that take these considerations into account.

Before moving on to Chapter 5 and a discussion of gender influences on career choices, we'd like you to complete one more exercise. Exercise 4.3 asks you to recall some of the most significant events and experiences in your life and then to arrange them in chronological order. This is a chance to examine how your life has unfolded so far and to think about how the past will affect your future. It is also a chance to think about how you can gain more control over your future.

Summary

This chapter looked at some of the changes and challenges that confront people as they move through the life cycle. The implications of these changes on values, goals, relationships, and self-concepts were discussed. Such changes are inevitable and make lifelong planning a necessity if we are to build satisfying and productive lives. Flexibility and readiness were noted as two key aspects for building a satisfying life in an ever-changing world.

Exercise 4.1

Planning for the Unexpected

1. Recall an unplanned event that fundamentally changed your life in a positive way. Describe how it has benefited you.

   Made me realize my potential, and what I am capable of

2. Describe that event in as much detail and with as much accuracy as you can. If necessary consult with someone who shared the experience with you.

   When I first shot 89 at Lebevel. It was the first time I shot under 90 at a school match, first time in college (from the whites) second college match, three or four days after shooting a 103

3. Recall as accurately as possible what *you brought* to the event or situation that *enabled* good things to happen. Don't buy into your first impression that it was just luck. In the space below, write about your *thoughts, feelings,* and *actions* and how they turned the situation into a positive opportunity and outcome.

   Kept my head in the game, stayed in a good mood, focused on doing well, realized I could actually do really well, wanted to for dad.

4. Now write down your responses to the situation, including how you felt and thought about it at the time.

   Excited, couldn't believe it happened, excited to prove I could do it again, truly now I pleased, not a fluke

5. What did you learn about your own flexibility and readiness?

   Always ready for a pleasant surprise

Exercise 4.2

Career Navigation Lights

The following is a set of questions about your "navigation lights." Thinking about these questions will help you to see the personal characteristics you have that you can use to turn change into opportunity. Think about each question carefully. Then write down your *honest* responses in the spaces provided.

1. How central to my life is my work? How does it relate to my family, social life, leisure, and recreational interests?

    I want my work to be be a central part of my life, something I enjoy doing, and that works with the rest of my life

2. How much security and stability do I need in my life? How much change and uncertainty can I handle?

    uncertainty - life, living, security - family, work (job) - not healthy, change - never too much

3. How much opportunity for creativity, originality, and self-expression do I need in my career?

    enough

4. How important are autonomy, independence, and self-direction to me?

    rather important

5. How much risk (personal and financial) am I willing to take to improve my career possibilities?

    I will take those risks if I can be sure they will pay off

6. How much support will I have for career changes or plans with friends and family?

    enough support - all that I ask for they sure be I won't ask for much

7. How willing and able am I to defer immediate rewards in exchange for greater long-term rewards and opportunities?

    I am long term oriented, willing to make more sacrifices

8. How willing and able am I to obtain the training, education, or experience I need to qualify for new opportunities?

    don't want too much, but willing to do what it takes

9. How willing am I to move my residence and region to seek out new opportunities?

    Yes that is what I want to do - have all the time to gain more opportunities

10. How willing am I to take on new responsibilities, longer hours, less leisure, or less vacation time to grasp an opportunity?

    mmm, less so unless it's something I really want

11. How confident am I that I have thought through these kinds of questions?

    semi, but I don't know what work will be

Exercise 4.3

The Career Actualization Lifeline

This exercise is designed to help you begin to examine your inner world. Try to respond to each part of the exercise as candidly and honestly as you can.

This exercise is for you. It need not be shown or explained to anyone else. This is your chance to reflect on yourself, on who you are, on where you came from, and on where you are going.

Forget for the moment who others *think* you are or how they *expect* you to be. Instead, think about how you feel about yourself, your life, and your relationships. As you complete the exercise (write your responses on separate sheets of paper), think about these three major themes:

- What do I have that I want to build upon, extend, and develop?
- What do I have that I want to change, get rid of, or move away from?
- What do I want to create anew, build from scratch, experiment with, or get started in my life?

Part 1: Looking at Hills and Valleys

1. *Peak (High) Experiences*

    What are some present-day or past peak experiences that have really mattered in your life, that have enabled you to feel complete or whole, or that have helped shape your self-concept and worldview?

    doing well in golf, being somebody, graduating high school, moving to college, making a place for myself, finding and meeting people

2. *Valley (Low) Experiences*

    What are some present or past valley (low) experiences that have deeply affected or influenced you?

    taking fourth at conf when I thought I could get first, hurting Dad's feelings, being dumped by Kevin then Cameron

3. *Things You Do Well*

    Discuss the personal or professional skills, techniques, and capabilities that you possess. *Don't be modest!*

    smart, languages, reading, leading ppl, listening, traveling

4. *Things You Do Poorly*

    Discuss what you do poorly but in your current circumstances must (or are "required" to) do anyway.

    talking, being organized

5. *Things You Would Like to Stop Doing*

    Specify behaviors or habits you would like to stop. Ask those who know you well, such as family members, friends, or professional associates, for help in answering this question if you need it.

    being an insiduy bme

6. *Things You Would Like to Start Doing*

   Discuss what you wish to do well. Include aspects of interpersonal competence to which you aspire, skills that you would like to learn, and kinds of learning experiences you would like to provide for yourself.

   go out, french, get a job

7. *Peak Experiences You Would Like to Have*

   Shoot for the moon here within the limits of your imagination and aspirations.

   going to Greece/living, being in love, being loved, first art conf

8. *Values Yet To Be Realized*

   Discuss values still to be realized, choosing from within as well as outside your immediate world.

   work before play

Part 2: Drawing Your Actualization Lifeline

1. Draw a line across a blank sheet of paper to represent your life span. Put a "B" on the left for birth and a "D" on the right for death. Then put an "X" where you see yourself at this moment in terms of your age, development, and present status. Mark off the distance from the present to death in 5-year intervals. What were you feeling as you did this task?

2. What do you *expect* to be doing 5 years from now? Ten years? Fifteen years? Etc.?

   payer (traveling), new experiences, family, love

3. What do you *hope* to be doing in these periods of your life?

4. What do you hope *not* to be doing at these times?

   slobbing, unemployed, single, alone

5. What values do you want to be realized—relationships, material things, influence, recognition, competencies—during each period?

   payer

6. What immediate and long-range plans do you have now that will help you to realize these values?

CHAPTER 5
The Gendered Context of Career Choices

CHAPTER OVERVIEW

This chapter helps you to explore the context of your life in terms of gender and how growing up as a boy or girl may have influenced and may still be influencing your career choices. Included in the chapter are the comments of adults we have worked with about their own socialization process and how gender has been an important factor in their lives and choices. We will discuss the problems that confront both men and women as a result of sex-role socialization processes. We will also discuss the positive aspects of gender-based roles.

As you read this chapter, we ask you to think about your own situation and how your sex-role socialization may be both a strength and a barrier to making career choices. We begin with the voices of Michael and Judy, two individuals we have worked with who are reflecting back on their own socialization:

"I know that we are supposed to be past all of that sex-role stereotyping, but I find myself feeling that I should be going into something more 'manly.' Although I've always been good with kids and am attracted to jobs like elementary education teacher or day care operator, I find myself feeling like those choices are not okay. And when I mention those choices to others, there are oftentimes snickers or offensive comments related to my masculinity.—Michael

"I wish I had more courage when I was younger to follow my own path. I was so busy trying to be a "good little girl" and please everyone that I really didn't allow myself to follow my own dream.—Judy

Although society has changed a great deal in the past three decades in prevailing attitudes about male and female roles, there are still dramatic differences in how boys and girls are socialized. Boys grow up in a culture in which occupation is the key to the future. Mastery and competition are highly rewarded. Much of men's self-esteem is based on their ability to master their environment, and the paramount part of that environment for many men is their job. Girls' lives revolve much more around relationships, which often causes them to rule out career fields that they perceive as not allowing enough time or flexibility for them to attend to connections and relationships with others. Understanding how the gender-relevant context in which we have been raised affects our current assumptions and aspirations is a critical part of career development.

Socialization begins early in life, and the attitudes we develop follow us throughout our lives. Studies show that children as young as 2 and 3 identify stereotypic roles for men and women. As children move from kindergarten to age 8, their ideas about what is appropriate for girls and boys become more and more rigid. By the time children are between 6 and 8, many have already narrowed their career options to within a small range. Once established, this narrow list is hard to expand.

Promising research, however, has shown that this narrow kind of thinking can widen through contact with role models. Children with nontraditional role models in their daily lives have been found to be much more likely than children without such role models to believe that both men and women can succeed and thrive in a wide range of occupations.

It seems very curious that, after decades of addressing issues of sex-role stereotyping, we are still seeing the influence of stereotypic attitudes on career patterns in the lives of people across America. Thirty years ago most people grew up in homes in which there were strict ideas about what was considered appropriate for boys and girls. Many parents in the 1960s were influenced by the women's movement and civil rights movements and tried to give their children messages that they could do anything, be anything. Unfortunately, the media, their peers, and their children's schools and churches often tempered these messages with conflicting notions about what children should aspire to.

Even those of us who grew up in homes and social groups that encouraged our aspirations have experienced societal or institutional barriers that, many times, have kept us from fully exploring our dreams. For example, because there still is not enough good quality, available, and affordable childcare, many employed mothers have selected career options that allow them to be at home with their children in order to ensure their healthy development. And because women's salaries, on average, are still only 74% of those of men, many employed fathers, knowing that they need to be the primary breadwinner in the family, have chosen careers based on salary rather than fully exploring their career options. Thus, even under the best circumstances, gender continues to influence the way we live our lives, the careers to which we aspire, and the dreams we ultimately pursue or discard. Information about the influence of gender on career choices can help to change this, but only when we use it for reflection on our own lives.

Uncovering Your Authentic Self

As we noted earlier, the career dreams and aspirations that we have as children may hold important information about what we might find satisfaction in as adults. Indeed, those dreams and interests that we had before we were exposed to society's messages about what is appropriate or inappropriate may be the most *authentic* career information we have. In workshops that we conduct with adults, we often ask the participants to think about their earliest memories and recollections. Sometimes we ask them to go home and look at old photographs or boxes of memorabilia to help transport themselves back in time to childhood. We ask them to think about what they were passionate about then and how that might inform their present choices. As shown by the following quotation, this type of reflection can be very powerful:

"I always felt like there was something missing in my life, that although I had a great partner and a job that a lot of people would die for, I still felt empty. I got out photo albums and memorabilia from my childhood and adolescence. Memories of those times flooded back in. I remembered how much I wanted to be a veterinarian. I loved animals and I loved taking care of injured birds and pets. I remember having my heart set on being a vet, until my dad told me in no uncertain terms that women could not be vets, that we lacked the strength to handle large animals. I really started thinking about changing to a career where I could regularly be around and care for animals. Making that change has made all the difference. I no longer feel there is something missing. I feel like I am being more of who I was meant to be."—Janet

By getting in touch with memories of her childhood, Janet was able to uncover a part of her authentic self that had been buried for decades. While she didn't go back to school to be a veterinarian, she was able to find a job that allowed her to live out some of the interests that she had long forgotten.

Michael similarly identified and expressed his authentic passions as he poignantly reflected on his own compromised career path:

"When I was growing up in the rural South, I found my greatest passion was art. I loved to draw, to do photography, to study the raw aesthetic beauty in the countryside around me. I really didn't know anyone who was an artist, and it was only when I went to college that I visited my first art gallery. But somehow color, shape, and form were, from a very early age, truly engaging constructs for me. My artistic interests were tolerated and in some instances reinforced, but the clear message was, 'You are a boy. You will need to support yourself and a family. Art is a nice hobby, but you need a real job.' And so I did as I was told and got a degree in chemical engineering. I have made a good living with it and it has allowed me to support my family, just as the societal script says I should do. In that sense, my life has been successful. But if you ask me if I have been happy occupationally, if I have felt a passion for the projects I have worked on, if I have felt meaning in my work, the answer is, 'No! I certainly haven't.' I long for retirement where I can have time to pursue my real passion. It feels very sad that we have to go through so many years of our lives doing what we are supposed to do rather than what we would love to do."—Michael

How much has sex-role socialization influenced your career possibilities?

Try doing this type of reflection yourself. Think back to some of your earliest childhood memories and think about what you were passionate about then. When you really got lost in the flow of what you were doing, when time disappeared, what were you engaged in?

Sometimes it helps to talk to a parent or a sibling or to look at pictures of yourself as a child. This type of reflection has been referred to as "peeling back the onion," going further and further into your core to see if you can uncover clues to your authentic self.

THE INFLUENCE OF SOCIALIZING FORCES

As children move through childhood and become adolescents, even more influences affect their career development and choices. Adolescents spend much of their time in the classroom and with peers in extracurricular activities, both of which have a strong socializing effect. Although it is clear that the amount of affirmation and valuing that girls and boys receive is a critical factor in their healthy development, research has shown that many adolescents view the classroom as a cold, impersonal environment where their views are not solicited, heard, or affirmed. Girls seem to be particularly susceptible to being ignored in the classroom. A name has even been coined for classrooms in which girls are not actively discouraged or encouraged but rather ignored—the *null environment*. This lack of affirmation and valuing can result in girls feeling unsure of themselves and their views. It can also result in girls having feelings of lowered confidence in academic abilities and, eventually, to limited career choices.

For adolescent boys, sports are often a major socializing force. During this time of great peer pressure, conforming to group norms becomes a critical issue, and many boys feel the need to demonstrate masculinity through being tough and winning at any kind of competition, from sports to sexual conquests. It is during this time that boys often start constricting their emotions and putting on a tough facade. Having any of the characteristics of supposed femininity, such as emotional expressiveness, puts one in danger of being labeled as weak, a sissy, or gay by the powerful peer group. Many boys do not feel free to express interests or pursue occupational options that may be considered feminine. Possibilities of becoming a nurse, a childcare worker, artist, or the like, are often dropped out of fear of what they might imply about masculinity.

Take a few minutes now to complete Exercise 5.1, which will assist you in reflecting on your own adolescence and how gender-related issues may have influenced your development. As adults we must explore how the messages we received in our childhood may have affected our lives.

GENDER ISSUES IN TODAY'S WORKPLACE

Although the workplace has changed a great deal in the past three decades and many career fields are now open to both men and women, discrimination and gender inequity still exist in the workplace. Back in 1977, sociologist R. M. Kanter reported that organizations tended to stereotype women into one of four gender-familiar roles: *mother, child, iron maiden,* or *sex symbol*. Unfortunately, research conducted a decade and a half later found that these categories still existed in the workplace. Little has changed since this more recent research.

These stereotypic roles may help an organization feel comfortable by placing women in categories that are familiar and predictable, but they also undermine women's sense of professional competence and serve to reinforce structural discrimination. The "mother" role is the stereotype that describes women as nurturing and places them in charge of caring for others. Unfortunately, these nurturing characteristics, which should be valued and held in high esteem, tend to segregate women into jobs with the lowest salaries. The "child" role stereotypes women as being less mature, more dependent, more in need of help and supervision, as well as requiring protection from others. The "iron maiden" is the stereotype that is often used to describe assertive, competent women who are deemed to have taken on more traditionally male characteristics. While these characteristics are seen as positive when exhibited by men within an organization, they often cause women to be rejected and thought of as not being "real women." Finally, the "sex object" role focuses on women as solely sexual beings and leads to their devaluation in the workplace. This stereotypic view of women also puts them in danger of sexual harassment, which is still rampant in today's work environments. These gender-stereotypic roles form the basis for much of the sexual segregation and discrimination women continue to face in the labor market.

Even when women do very well within organizations, all too often they run into what has been referred to as a "glass ceiling," where women can rise only so high and then are stopped by an invisible barrier to further upward mobility. This glass ceiling may be supported in organizations through informal networks that exclude women from the kinds of information and relationships they need to advance. Mentoring, although a popular concept, is still not available to many women.

For men in the workplace, the issues are certainly different, but they nonetheless can be both restricting and demoralizing. As psychologist Tom Skovholt (1990) poignantly expressed: "Painting a picture of men's lives often results in a work-dominated landscape." Men's sex-role socialization tends to give the clear message that work is everything. Men often feel that they need to be successful at work to be successful in life, and they strive for those material things that are the visible signs of success: owning a home, owning a car, taking yearly vacations, providing for a family. Men have many role models of the traditional path to success. Fathers, brothers, and neighbors all provide clues about what is expected. As Skovholt noted, "Whether the job is loved, hated, intrinsically satisfying, or boring is much less relevant than the expectation that a man will work. A long-term non-working male adult violates this strong male principle and is usually shunned or rejected." Thus, there is tremendous pressure on men to do the right thing and very little flexibility in terms of what that right thing is. The few men who try to break out of traditional patterns of seeking success have very few role models. As feminist and social critic Betty Friedan (1981) remarked, "The trouble is, once they disengage from the old patterns of American masculinity and success—John Wayne, Charles Lindbergh, John Kennedy—men today are just as lost for role models as women are."

For those men who follow traditional routes to success, the road is a difficult one. For many men, being successful means being "on top"—rising to the top of organizations, being the boss. Unfortunately, as we pointed out earlier, today's labor market has fewer and fewer places at the top. The organizational pattern represented in the labor market today is much flatter than it was in the past. Few people really rise to the top. Only 8% of the total male population work in white-collar, professional jobs. If men's identity and self-esteem are based on rising to the top, many men are certain to be disillusioned with their progress. This disillusionment can lead to stress-related illness and other forms of psychological distress.

Thus, the "gendered context" in which we live and work can have a profound effect on both men's and women's feelings about themselves and their career prospects. Both men and women have many issues to consider when choosing their career path.

Taking a Closer Look at Gender-Related Issues That May Have Influenced Your Development

In a previous section of this chapter, we discussed and asked you to reflect on how gender-related aspects of the environments you experienced in early childhood, adolescence, and adulthood may have influenced your career choices. Making the satisfying career choice requires that you take a closer look at these factors. Women need to look, in particular, at four specific outcomes of gender socialization: math avoidance, lower expectations for success, lower self-efficacy for nontraditional career fields, and role conflict. Men need to look at, among other things, issues of mortality and gender-related stress and coping.

Math avoidance is one of the most insidious remnants of girls' gender socialization and one that may have an increasing impact on women's career development in the future. Psychologist Nancy Betz, who has devoted much of her professional life to assisting girls and women to consider entering into nontraditional career fields, has called mathematics the "critical filter" for women and has presented evidence that the avoidance of math courses starts women on a path of increasingly narrow career possibilities. By avoiding upper-level math courses, women remove the option of a huge number of science- and technology-related career fields. The problem will only increase as our society becomes increasingly technologically advanced and mathematics takes on even greater importance. The percentage of well paying, higher status positions that require a math background is high today and will only rise in the future. What is particularly sad about women's avoidance of these fields is that it appears to be primarily a socially determined phenomenon. The phenomenon goes like this: Girls outperform boys in math in elementary school; they like math and do well at it. By high school, socialization has had its effect: The majority of girls have lost their competitive edge and do similarly to boys. Then, on the SAT (Scholastic Aptitude Test), boys tend to do slightly better in math, and they receive more college entrance offers and scholarship funds. The greatest predictor of girls' lower math performance on the SAT has been found to be the number of math courses they have taken. Researchers have found that when the number and type of math courses taken is controlled, differences in performance tend to disappear. Thus, math avoidance appears to be a socially determined phenomenon and one that can have devastating effects on women's career options.

Another common outcome of gender-relevant socialization for women is a lower expectation for career success. Studies across a variety of ages and situations have indicated that girls, and women in general, tend to report less self-confidence about their ability to succeed. This lower expectation can be seen in scores on examinations, or the number and type of occupations girls consider and in the results on traditional career interest inventories. Even when girls' objective performance is demonstrated to be higher than that of boys, the girls consistently rate their abilities lower.

Not only do girls and women tend to have lower expectations for success, but they also generally feel that they don't perform as well as men, particularly in career fields that are not traditional for women. As with girls' performance in school, when men's and women's actual performance is held constant, women typically see themselves as doing more poorly at traditionally male occupations and tasks than males. Some researchers contend that part of this lack of confidence is due to a lack of role models of women in non-traditional fields.

Another issue of gender socialization that has taken on increasing importance for women is role conflict. More and more women are working full-time outside the home, yet most continue to be responsible for most of the work within the home. Data indicate that when women are working outside the home, they continue to do 80–90% of the housework as well. This dual role results in a great deal of role conflict for working women and, subsequently, a great deal of work-related stress.

Outcomes for men of gender socialization can also be very harmful. Probably one of the most tangible and dramatic outcomes is mortality: Women live, on average, 7 years longer than men do. Although some of this difference in mortality may be accounted for by biological differences in men and women, researchers argue that as much as 75% of it can be explained by the gender-role behaviors of men.

Researchers have also examined the relationship of gender-role beliefs to stress and coping. Their findings suggest that rigid adherence to gender-role socialization may result in a restriction in the types of coping that men employ. For example, although men may benefit from more social and emotional support, many feel that they cannot, or should not, ask for it. This feeling may be due to their beliefs about masculinity and the importance of strength and emotional independence.

SOME POSITIVE ASPECTS OF GENDER SOCIALIZATION

Much of what we have presented thus far about the gendered context of our lives has been negative. For many people gender stereotypes have created restrictions of dreams and aspirations, and for some of these people, the stereotypes have led to painful and damaging career experiences. However, it is also important to recognize that there are some positive aspects of traditional gender roles. For males, for example, psychologist Ron Levant (1996) pointed out, the same adolescent socialization process that breeds toughness and emotional inexpressiveness also promotes male strengths. These strengths include the ability to persist in difficult situations and the ability to strategize, think logically, stay calm in the face of danger, and take risks to achieve important ends. In addition, as psychologist Ron Levant noted, although the traditional male role in the workplace can lead to negative and harmful outcomes for men, it can also foster such characteristics as a willingness to sacrifice personal needs in order to take care of others, an ability to withstand hardship in order to protect others, and an ability to express love through action—by doing things for others and providing love in tangible ways.

For women, too, there are some positive aspects of gender socialization. Whereas theories of personality development have viewed traditionally male values of autonomy and independence as essential parts of women's healthy and mature development, more recent research has begun to question these basic assumptions. Women's needs for establishing connections and relationships are being increasingly valued, and their ways of connecting are being described as responsiveness to the needs of others and empathic responding. These skills are becoming increasingly valued in organizations where teamwork, rather than individual effort, is becoming more the norm and where skills at working with diverse individuals in a global context has taken on paramount importance. Thus, in addition to focusing on the negative aspects of our socialization as men and women, we must also recognize the positive qualities that this gendered context provides.

SUMMARY

We have seen in this chapter that our socialization as men and women strongly influences our career choices and development. Some of these influences are positive, but most constitute personal and institutional barriers that make it difficult for many people to achieve their dreams. An important step in overcoming the damaging effects of the gendered environment is to become aware of its existence and to analyze how these issues have influenced our own lives. An exercise was provided to help you start this process of reflecting on your own gender-role socialization and how it still may be influencing your career choice and development.

REFERENCES

Friedan, B. (1981). *The second stage.* New York: Summit Books.

Kantor, R. M. (1977). *Men and women of the corporation.* New York: Basic Books.

Levant, R. F. (1996). Masculinity reconstructed. *The Independent Practitioner, 16,* 1.

Skovholt, T. M. (1990). Career themes in counseling and psychotherapy with men. In D. Moore & F. Leafgren (Eds.), *Men in conflict* (pp. 37–54). Alexandria, VA: American Association for Counseling and Development.

Exercise 5.1
Exploring the Effects of Gender on Career Choice and Development

This exercise will help you to think about important stages of your life and the impact of your socialization at each of these stages. Please take some time to think about these questions as they apply to your own life experience. Then write your answers in the spaces provided.

Childhood

1. What occupational aspirations did you have when you were very young?

2. How did those aspirations change over time?

3. Were those aspirations linked to gender?

4. What messages did you receive regarding gender-appropriate occupations early in your life?

5. Who were your heroes and heroines? What influence did these people have on your career development?

Adolescence

6. Think about your years of schooling. Was your voice heard in the classroom?

7. Did you develop confidence in your academic abilities?

8. Did you feel affirmed for who you were and what you had to say?

9. How did the way you were treated influence your career development?

10. How about your peers? What messages did they give you about what was appropriate for you as a young woman or young man?

Adult Work Life

The questions in this section are for those of you who have already entered the work force. If you have not yet reached this life stage, you might still think about these questions as they may apply to your future goals before going on to the remaining questions.

11. In the workplace, do you feel stereotyped into certain predetermined roles?

12. Have you experienced being shut out of some jobs by a glass ceiling?

13. How do you define success?

14. When you look back on your life at age 80, what do you think will stand out as your key markers of success?

Positive Aspects of Sex-Role Socialization

Oftentimes when we speak of sex-role socialization, we speak only of its negative or stifling aspects. However, there are also many positive aspects to this process. The following questions will help you reflect on these positive aspects.

15. What positive personal characteristics do you have that are traditionally associated with your gender?

16. What traditional characteristics have you developed that may be helpful to your career development?

17. How can you value and affirm these characteristics in your life?

CHAPTER 6

Understanding Cultural Diversity: Implications for the Workforce

CHAPTER OVERVIEW

This chapter explores the meaning of diversity in the labor force and how it will (or does) affect you. You will be asked to think about your own cultural roots and your cultural heritage. You will be asked to think about your racial identity development and how it can impact your interactions with others. You will be asked to think about what makes up the core of your worldview and how your worldview is similar to or different from that of other people with whom you associate. Finally, you will be asked to think about the psychological costs of living in a racist society and how you personally feel those costs. We take this personal approach because we feel strongly that becoming clear about your own heritage, racial identity, worldviews, and how racism affects your life is the first step toward understanding and appreciating diversity.

Living in a Multicultural World

Nearly 400 years ago the poet John Donne wrote that "no man is an island." Yet, for better or worse, each of us is to some extent just that. No human being ever fully and finally understands, appreciates, or comes to know another human being. Indeed, because we are all constantly changing, we often do not fully know or understand ourselves.

We are separated from one another by a host of differences that tend to create the gulfs that surround our islands. Age and generation, gender, religion, family background, wealth and education all set us apart. In our society, with its long history of racial and ethnic strife, the chasms that separate and divide us are deepened and widened by skin color, ethnicity, and national origin. Often the way we regard these differences robs us of much of the richness, wonder, and beauty that our lives could contain. Far too often we regard diversity with fear and suspicion rather than as a vast storehouse of varied treasures.

At an objective level, we know that each of the world's cultures is, indeed, a storehouse of wonderful sights and sounds, tastes, and pictures. After all, Americans spend millions of dollars a year to travel to exotic places, eat marvelous ethnic foods, buy the art, and adopt the fashions from faraway places. Yet, at the level of human relationships, we react as though "different" means dangerous and "foreign" means inferior. We allow actual and presumed differences to keep us from interesting and rewarding relationships and seal us off from unimaginable treasures.

We can call the aggregation of these many differences and the feelings that surround them "social psychological distance." It is the expanse that confines each of us to our own island.

One of the many paradoxes that confounds human nature is that even though we often help to create and maintain the social psychological distance that separates us from others, we cannot really live comfortably for long on our own isolated and lonely little islands. We are, after all, gregarious, interdependent, and fundamentally social creatures. That, of course, is the essence of what John Donne was articulating. So we are constantly letting down and pulling up drawbridges as we try to reach out or pull back from others.

Because we live in a constantly contracting world, however, the cost of distancing ourselves from others is increasing. Reaching out to others today is an essential part of psychological, social, and economic survival.

Studies of the reaching-out process have shown that the first tendency for most of us is to reach out on the basis of what is called *assumed similarity*. That is, we reach out to those who seem to be much like ourselves, or at least like the way we perceive ourselves. We pull back from those who appear to be different even in the most superficial ways.

Interestingly, how we perceive others usually reveals far more about ourselves than it does about the people we are attempting to understand or describe. Our ways of perceiving others are a function of our intellectual development. As we grow and mature in our ability to understand the world, we may also grow in our ability to grasp the richness and complexity in others.

At the very lowest levels of intellectual development, we perceive others almost purely on the basis of *stereotypes*. That is, we focus on only one or two characteristics of the other person, usually membership in a particular social or racial group or occupancy of a particular social role. When we focus only on these superficial aspects, we begin to attribute all sorts of *assumed* characteristics, motives, or beliefs to the person regardless of the individual's actual behavior, accomplishments, or intentions. This kind of sloppy and primitive thinking creates a myopia that allows us to begin to believe that all men, all women or all members of a given racial ethnic, or cultural group can be treated as interchangeable objects rather than as unique, complex, thinking and feeling human beings. Stereotyping serves only to hurt others, distance ourselves from them and alienate ourselves from the best that is within us, which is the capacity to empathize and to feel with and for one another. Sadly, many people never develop higher levels of perceiving others because of the insidious effects of prejudice and bigotry that have permeated our society for generations.

Racism, sexism, ageism, and all of the other forms of prejudice that affect us are social diseases. That is, they are transmitted socially and mark or scar virtually every person who lives in our society. As with diseases like tuberculosis in the past, today almost everyone in our society "tests positive" for racism. Even though we may consciously abhor bigotry and all of the evil, cruelty, and stupidity that it represents, few of us have been able to escape completely from the contagion that permeates our society as a result of hundreds of years of racial conflict, exploitation, and intolerance. The essence of prejudice in all of its manifestations is the belief that one group of people is morally superior to another and therefore deserves to be heard, respected, and ultimately given power over others.

Sometimes when we are least aware, residual germs of prejudice stir within us and drop us back into a world of stereotypes, primitive thinking, irrational fears, and ancient animosities. Then, despite all of our sophistication and good intentions, we retreat to our little island or cluster of islands, pull up the drawbridge, and surrender to fear, fantasy, and ignorance. We adopt a social style of *exclusion* rather than *inclusion*.

Prejudice is not the only factor that eats away at our veneer of enlightenment and sophistication. Another factor is the presence of power differentials, which are often based upon vested privilege rather than upon competence and social responsibility. In terms of how people perceive others, we know that the powerless attend far more carefully to the powerful, who tend to control their destinies, than they are attended to by the powerful. Those who are not in power seek to "psyche out" the boss, anticipate mood swings, avoid irritability, and generally preserve the peace, whereas the powerful tend to listen less, be more oblivious to the subtleties and nuances of communication, and on the whole be less sensitive and complex in their perceptions of the less powerful. When we have unconscious attitudes of superiority, entitlement, and privilege, we often fail to listen to and learn from others with different cultural heritages.

How do we escape from the traps and tensions that push us back into retreat, discrimination, and isolation? How can we come to celebrate human diversity and come to enjoy the fruits of living in a world that is truly multicultural? For many of us, learning to adapt and, indeed, to grow in a multicultural world is both the greatest challenge and the greatest opportunity of our working lives.

We cannot undo what is done or completely eradicate the legacy of a tragic past. We can, however, learn to cultivate self-awareness and intellectual and emotional honesty. We can learn to take the risk of genuinely listening to others who think and feel differently from us. We can learn to find joy and appreciation in the treasures we discover. That is the celebration of diversity.

A good way to begin the process of thinking about racial and cultural diversity is to look at our own heritage and see how it has helped to shape our thoughts, feelings, and actions. Exercise 6.1 asks you to draw a genogram, a diagram that traces your primary family relationships and so, to an extent, your own cultural heritage. Take some time now to complete Exercise 6.1 as thoughtfully and honestly as you can.

DIVERSITY AND THE WORKPLACE

Cultural and ethnic diversity are realities that affect every worker in our society. As the 21st century begins, about one third of the U.S. population are people of color. By mid-century, this proportion is expected to reach one half. In some cities in the United States, nearly one half of the elementary school children speak English as a second language or not at all.

The range of cultural diversity in the United States is increasing rapidly. Only a few years ago, the term diversity was widely used to describe differences between African-Americans, Hispanic-Americans (largely those from Mexico or Puerto Rico), and Euro-Americans. Occasionally Native Americans were included. Today, most of our large metropolitan centers house groups of people representing all of the world's major religions, literally dozens of languages and dialects, and scores of nationalities from every part of the world.

Many of these people are recent immigrants, often refugees fleeing wars, revolutions, hunger, and poverty. Recent Spanish-speaking immigrants in these circumstances include people from Central America, South America, and the Caribbean region. African-Americans include Somalian, Sudanese, Ethiopian, and Haitian immigrants; recent immigrants from Asia include Cambodians, Laotians, Taiwanese, Filipinos, and people from any of a dozen other ethnic or national origins. Recent European immigrants include Moslems from Bosnia and people from any of a dozen different ethnic regions of the former Soviet Union.

We have never before experienced diversity of this breadth and scope. We are literally part of a world community in which the movement of populations across the globe is a norm, not an exception. For all of us, social, cultural, and environmental forces continue to shape who we are and how we will work and live together.

In U.S. society today, success in the workplace defined by diversity is dependent upon a personal and social style marked by a willingness and ability to work with others that is based not upon assumed similarity in cultural backgrounds but rather upon reaching out to listen, learn and come to appreciate the richness and variety of human experience. Indeed, diversity creates new opportunities for growth and learning for all workers.

Some labor analysts have said that diversity is the number-one issue in today's workforce. For individuals to participate in our global economy, they need to have the interpersonal sensitivity and skills to relate to people whose backgrounds are considerably different from their own. As one analyst recently put it, "Having good grades and technical skills is important, but having the ability to work with a team of highly diverse individuals is the kind of thing that is much harder to train into someone."

RACIAL IDENTITY DEVELOPMENT: UNDERSTANDING OUR OWN DEVELOPMENT AND THAT OF OTHERS

The effects of our society's history of intolerance, oppression, and divisiveness have been so powerful and profound that they have shaped and often scarred the personality development of virtually all of us. In recent years these effects have been subsumed under the concept of "racial identity." America, as a nation, has been described as a nation and society obsessed with questions of race and presumed racial differences. It is important to note, however, that "race" is a social concept, not a scientific term or category.

We are about to discuss some models of racial identity development, or research proposing how people develop their racial identity and how it impacts their interactions with others. We do so because these models can help you better understand yourself and others. In this discussion we use the terms "white" and "black" in describing groups or cultures knowing that these terms are labels given to groups or cultures that exist largely in the minds of people who have been socialized in a society torn by discrimination and oppression. People of different geographic origin would be described more accurately as African-American, Euro-American, and so forth. We chose to use these terms because they are used in both research and in popular discussions.

Racial identity models tend to focus on two sets of personal characteristics and attitudes learned out of experiences in the social environment and internalized to become virtually a part of the individual's personality. One of these sets of beliefs deals with characteristic attitudes toward racial oppression, prejudice, and bigotry—that is, questions of social justice. The other deals with questions of comfort, trust, and involvement in close relationships with members of other racial groups. Knowledge of how people, including ourselves, differ in regard to these factors as a result of their social experiences can help us to understand both our own reactions and those of people we work with in a multicultural world.

Several different models of racial identity development have been proposed, but all have as their central function understanding oneself and others in a society in which racial strife, oppression, and prejudice have been an ever-present reality. These models all assume that the statuses people present are not static but rather change as a result of life experiences. The racial identity states you see yourself in today may not be the one you are in several years from now, especially if you are open to growth and change. The three models that have received the most attention over the past decade are presented in the following sections. They were developed by psychologists who conduct research and training in the area of diversity. Janet Helms and her colleagues developed both a black and a white racial identity model, and Donald Atkinson and his colleagues developed a model for minority group members more generally. You will see as you examine these three models that there is a degree of overlap among the identity states that each presents. We encourage you to read through each of the different models, as they may help you to further understand your friends and colleagues. Pay particular attention to the model that best represents your state of identity development.

Black Racial Identity Development

According to Helm's, racial identity development is an interactive maturation process in which individuals increasingly become aware of racial prejudice and of themselves as racial beings. Racial identity arises out of an interplay between an individual's affective, cognitive, and behavioral attitudes and responses to the environment. According to this model, black racial identity development processes can be described using the following five states: contact, dissonance, immersion/emersion, internalization, and integrative awareness. Individuals do not progress through these states in linear fashion. Rather, the states are states of consciousness and may differ across environments. We describe these states in the following paragraphs. Quotes are provided from people we have worked with to help illustrate the characteristics of each state. If you are black, think about which state represents you best at this time in your life. If you are not black, think about African-Americans you know, and try to identify where they might be in their racial identity development.

Contact The contact state is characterized by ignoring racial differences and, at the same time, revering white standards and devaluing black standards. Someone in this state of racial identity development might say, *"I have always grown up around whites and have never really thought about myself as a racial being. I don't identify with blacks—most of them seem so different from me. I have always felt much more comfortable around whites."*

Dissonance The dissonance state is characterized by ambivalence or confusion about one's racial identity, that is typically ignited by a positive uplifting experience or a negative experience with racial discrimination. The following quote is illustrative of people in this state: *"In Alabama I never thought much about my race. Then I moved to the Midwest. All of a sudden people were noticing my race,* *and I started feeling like maybe it is a bigger deal than I thought."*

Immersion/Emersion The immersion/emersion state is represented by high racial saliency and the idealization of black standards while denigrating white standards. Consider the following quote: *"I really have no desire at all to be around any white folks. They may act like they want to be your friend, but when push comes to shove and you really need the help, they are nowhere to be found. I plan to find a job where I can work for and with blacks and stay as far away from the white community as possible."*

Internalization The internalization state is depicted by positive racial commitment and an objective view of white society and standards. *"There are good and bad people in both the black and white race. You have to get to know people and just see what makes them tick. You can't just hold preconceived notions about it all."*

Integrative Awareness This state of black identity development is characterized by both valuing one's own racial group and empathizing with and understanding other oppressed groups. A person at this state of identity development told us, *"I used to think we were the only ones that had it bad. But the more I get to know others, the more I realize they are feeling a lot of what I am feeling. It is really important for people to work together for the good of all of us 'underdogs.'"*

It is important to note that these states are not mutually exclusive and that individuals will often have some attitudes consistent with all of them. The strength of these attitudes for an individual may differ across the states and across environments. Thus, individuals typically have stronger attitudes relative to one state than the others, and the strength of endorsement may vary depending on the environmental condition in which the individual is currently operating (e.g., a predominantly white job setting versus a predominantly black social environment).

Minority Racial Identity Development

The model of minority racial identity development developed by Donald Atkinson and his colleagues is helpful in describing the racial identity development process of racial minorities in general. The model is similar to the black racial identity development model just described and consists of the following five stages:

Conformity The conformity stage is characterized by devaluing one's own group and other minority groups while appreciating the dominant systems.

Dissonance The dissonance stage is denoted by conflict between appreciating and deprecating all minority groups.

Resistance and Immersion The resistance and immersion stage is illustrated by valuing one's own racial group and supporting of other minority groups while denigrating individuals and institutions from the dominant group or culture.

Introspection The introspection stage is depicted by (re)evaluating and questioning the objectivity of previously held assumptions about one's own and other racial or ethnic groups.

Integrative Awareness The integrative awareness stage is characterized by a realistic appreciation of all minority groups and a selective appreciation of dominant systems.

White Racial Identity Development

Oftentimes in the United States, white (or Euro-American) individuals do not recognize themselves as racial beings. Because whites have represented the dominant culture in this country and have not suffered the kind of oppression and racial discrimination that minority members have experienced, the process of racial identity development is different for them. Whereas a main developmental task for racial and ethnic minorities is to disavow *internalized* racism—that is, to discard negative images of themselves drawn from the dominant culture—a major task for white individuals is to develop an awareness of and willingness to abandon perceived privilege or entitlement.

White racial identity development processes can be described using the following six states, as defined by Janet Helms and her colleagues:

Contact The contact state is characterized by ignoring race and racial discrimination, including one's own active or passive involvement in racial issues. The following quote illustrates this state of development: *"I don't know what the big deal is about race. I never think about it. I know people think they are always being discriminated against, but I don't see it anymore."*

Disintegration The disintegration state is denoted by confusion, conflict, and ambivalence caused by questioning social concepts of race. Individuals in this state are torn between their group allegiance and the obvious existence of institutional racism. This quote clearly shows the confusion and ambivalence that characterize this state: *"I know that whites have had it better, but I think it is because we have worked harder for it. But then again I guess there have been laws set up that hurt minorities."*

Reintegration The reintegration state is characterized by an idealization of "whiteness" and a denigration of other racial groups. Consider the following quote: *"I am so glad I am white, I can't imagine how crummy I would feel to be black or Hispanic or even Indian. It just seems like whites are smarter and more likely to be successful."*

Pseudo-independence The pseudo-independence state is portrayed by an intellectual understanding of social race in conjunction with a subtle endorsement of white cultural values or practices as normative. The following quote is illustrative: *"Yes, I know there are differences because of people's sociocultural history, but it would be nice if everybody could just fit in to American culture."*

Immersion/Emersion For whites, the immersion/emersion state is illustrated by an honest appraisal of racism and the realities of socioracial privilege as well as the development of a positive redefinition of what it means to be white. Someone in this state told us, *"I know that as a white I have privilege: the privilege to go into a store and not be watched, the privilege to not be 100 times more likely to have my car pulled over at a police checkpoint. A million small things that happen every day in my life remind me of the privilege that I have for no other reason than being born with white skin."*

Autonomy The autonomy state is characterized by a secure, positive, nonracist white identity that is informed by an understanding of other racial groups. This quote illustrates this state in white racial identity: *"The more I learn about and celebrate the differences of different groups, the more I understand about myself and who I am as a white person."*

It is important to reiterate that these are states of consciousness, not developmental stages. One does not move through these states in a linear progression. Rather, they are states of consciousness that many people who are confronted with a growing racial awareness may experience. Understanding them may help you appreciate where a coworker is and enable you to work with that person in a more sensitive and understanding manner.

For example, a black co-worker who has strong attitudes that are consistent with the contact state may be largely oblivious to racial elements of the work world, whereas individuals with robust "immersion/emersion" attitudes may be distrustful of non-black coworkers. Your interactions with these two individuals might be considerably different.

Take a moment to think about interactions you have had with individuals at different racial identity states. Then think about how these interactions were affected by your and their racial identity states.

Your reaction to this discussion may be, "This seems hard and complicated, and I don't understand what the big deal is anyway. I will just treat everyone alike. That should be good enough." This feeling is understandable, and it is one that many people have felt. The problem is that this attitude, which has been described by some as "colorblindness," tends to negate the importance of your culture and serves to isolate you from an important part of your own identity.

YOUR WORLDVIEW: A LENS OR FRAME OF REFERENCE FOR MAKING SENSE OUT OF THE WORLD

Thinking about your and others' worldviews can help you to understand some of the ways in which people differ as a result of their cultural heritages. Your worldview constitutes the frame of reference through which you experience the world. It forms the basis for your beliefs, attitudes, and relationships, and it develops out of your cultural experiences.

Worldviews can have many components, but the following five core concepts are discussed by many writers. Think about them in terms of your own worldview. What frame of reference do you use in each of the following five areas?

1. *Human nature is inherently good, evil, or a combination of both.* Do you view humans to be by nature good? Evil? A combination? How does this affect your daily living? How might this affect you in your current or future job? How would working with someone with an opposite worldview affect you?
2. *Human activity involves one of three modalities: being, being and becoming, and doing.* Does your worldview orient your activity toward being in the world, being and becoming, or doing? How does this affect your daily living? How might this affect you in your current or future job? How would working with someone with an opposite worldview affect you?
3. *Social relations are interpreted as hierarchical (involving leaders and followers), group-oriented (characterized by consultation and collaboration), or individualistic (emphasizing personal autonomy and control of one's destiny).* What does your worldview emphasize in your social relationships? How does this affect your daily living? How might this affect you in your current or future job? How would working with someone with an opposite worldview affect you?
4. *The relationship between people and nature involves mastery of people over nature, subjugation of people to nature, or harmony with nature.* How does your worldview portray the relationship of people and nature? How does this affect your daily living? How might this affect you in your current or future job? How would working with someone with an opposite worldview affect you?
5. *The concept of time is viewed with a past, present, or future orientation.* Which view of time is incorporated into your worldview? How does this affect your daily living? How might this affect you in your current or future job? How would working with someone with an opposite worldview affect you?

With today's changing workplace and the need to work closely with diverse teams, understanding how worldviews differ is more important than ever. It is also important to understand the worldview valued by the organization. For example, in the past a vertical or hierarchical view of social relationships in which the distinction between leaders and followers was emphasized was highly valued in the workplace. Today, a more cooperative and egalitarian view emphasizing shared ideas and joint responsibilities has emerged as workers operate in teams, consult with others, and work toward common goals within an organization.

Understanding your own worldview and realizing that there are other ways of viewing basic issues in human experience can be important to your development as a person and as a worker.

THE PSYCHOLOGICAL COSTS OF RACISM

It is not enough to understand models of racial identity and different worldviews. We must also realize the psychological costs of racism to all of us and strive to end it. Often, neither white Americans nor racial/ethnic minority Americans realize the full extent of the costs of living in an oppressive and racially insensitive environment. Yet racism affects our lives in many ways. Recently, we were with a group of college students who were discussing this issue. Listen to their voices as they talk about the impact of racism on them. To what level do you relate to their feelings? How are your feelings similar or different to theirs?

"When I hear about examples of racist hate and violence, I feel scared for us as a people. I get this knot in my stomach. I tend to think of people as being basically good, and these acts of racial violence make me question that. I fear for our humanity. I fear for our children. I don't understand how such hate exists."

"I think racism causes me to have limited relationships with people of color. Even though I have friends of other races, those friendships seem limited, like they will only go so far and then there is a line that won't get crossed. I won't be trusted when things get really hard. They will count on one of their own race at that point. It feels really sad to me that those feelings are so ingrained that even when I am aware of them I can't change them. It makes me feel very sad and kind of hopeless at times."

"I always have these nagging feelings like—did I just get this job because I am white. I know I have had more opportunities and privilege than a lot of people because of my skin color. Right from the moment I was born and throughout my life I have had better schools, better equipment, better options, because of my skin color. It makes me really wonder how much of what I get is really due to me—my skills, my core—and how much is just due to living in a racist environment that values white skin most."

"My knowledge of other races is really based on stereotypes. I have had so little actual contact. I fear contact and also want it, all at the same time. I want to get to know other cultures. I want to learn about how other people think and what they value. And yet, I feel like I have fear hard-wired into me. A hundred little things conditioned my fear, like I remember my mom automatically locking all the doors on the car whenever there was a black person anywhere in sight. Little acts, but they all add up and make me feel afraid to reach out and get to know others."

Thinking about racism in these ways may be new for you. Often when we talk about diversity, or multiculturalism, the focus is not on examining the costs of racism to us all. Yet, when racism is present in an office, a school, an individual relationship, or society generally, there are costs. Take a moment to think about and jot down the costs of racism to you personally. Does racism make you feel fearful or sad or angry like the individuals whose voices you've just heard? By thinking about the costs to each of us of allowing a racist system to continue, we may become motivated to do things each day in our own ways to end racism and to help ourselves function more fully as human beings appreciating the humanness of others.

SUMMARY

This chapter explored the importance of race and culture in highly personal ways. We asked you to examine your own cultural roots by creating a family genogram and to think about your heritage from your family of origin. We examined the concept of racial identity development and asked you to consider where you are in your own awareness. We discussed the issue of worldviews and asked you to consider how your frame of reference might be different from that of people with whom you work. Finally, we asked you to examine the psychological costs of racism and to think about how living in an oppressive society or working in an oppressive environment has hurt us all. We hope this journey has provided you with some new ways of thinking. As you move into the work world and work with diverse groups of people, we hope that some of the frameworks presented here will help you to be a more sensitive and effective worker.

Exercise 6.1
Drawing a Genogram:
A Vehicle for Exploring Your Own Cultural Heritage

A good place to start in this exploration of racial and cultural diversity is to examine your own cultural roots and heritage by drawing a genogram. The genogram is a tool for examining your family of origin and a stimulus for thinking about what you carry with you from your roots and how you are part of your family legacy. This exercise takes you through the steps of drawing your family genogram.

Step 1:

Begin your picture of your family of origin with your mother and father. Draw a circle for your mother and a square for your father about two thirds of the way down a sheet of paper. Connect the symbols with a line as shown below and write your parents' names under the symbols. Add their birth dates over the symbols.

Parents' Names

If either of your parents has died, put an X within his or her symbol and add the date of death just below the birth date.

Next, add yourself and any brothers or sisters to the picture as shown below. Make sure to place everyone's name under his or her symbol and birth date above it. If, for example, your name is Charles and you have a sister named Marge and a brother named Robert, your diagram will look like this:

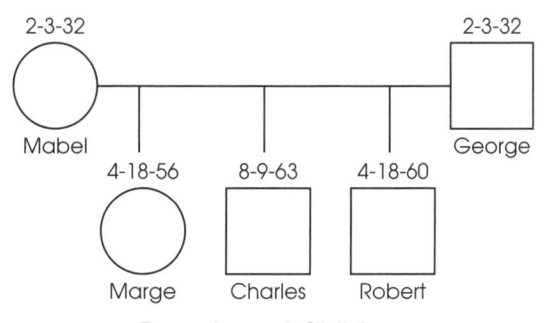

Parents and Children

The next task is to add your grandparents (seen below in the top line) and aunts and uncles from both sides of your family to the picture. Then add the occupations in which the members of your family of origin and extended family members are or were employed. Your career genogram will now look something like this:

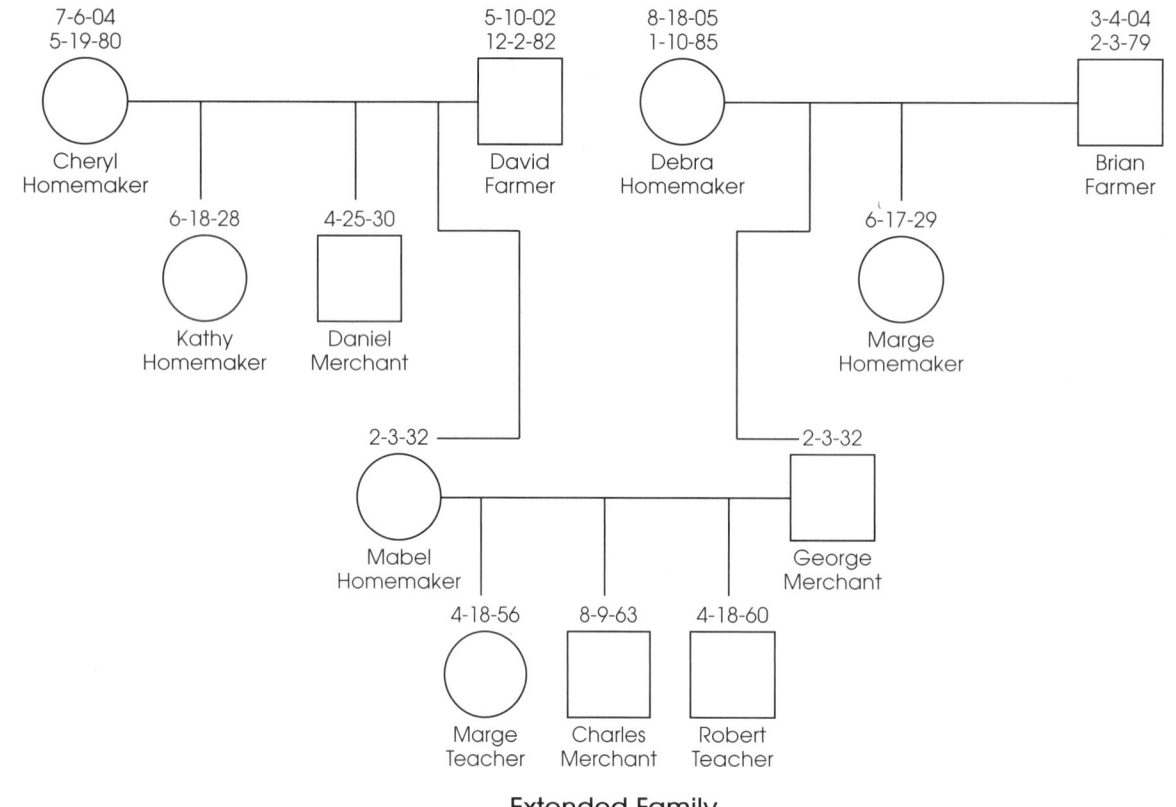

```
7-6-04              5-10-02         8-18-05              3-4-04
5-19-80             12-2-82         1-10-85              2-3-79
  ○───────────────────□               ○───────────────────□
Cheryl              David          Debra                Brian
Homemaker           Farmer         Homemaker            Farmer

      6-18-28    4-25-30                      6-17-29
        ○          □                            ○
      Kathy      Daniel                       Marge
    Homemaker   Merchant                    Homemaker

            2-3-32                 2-3-32
              ○───────────────────────□
            Mabel                   George
          Homemaker                Merchant

         4-18-56    8-9-63    4-18-60
           ○          □          □
         Marge      Charles    Robert
        Teacher    Merchant   Teacher
```

Extended Family

At this point, it is helpful to fine-tune your genogram so that it shows the family patterns that exist in your extended family. Perhaps there are single-parent families, blended families, or step-families as a result of divorce, death, illness, or remarriage. Perhaps a couple is living together but isn't married. The following are symbols used to represent many of the variations in family patterns.

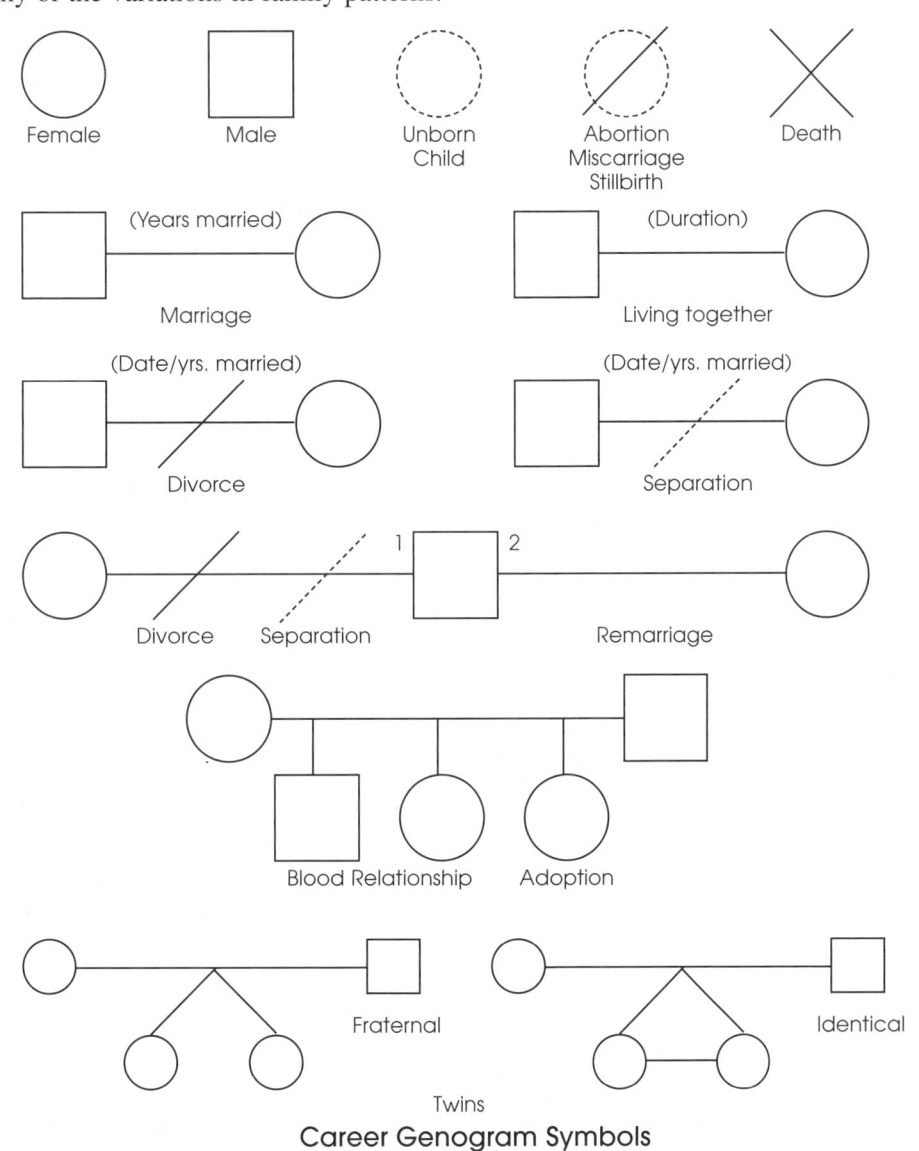

Career Genogram Symbols

Step 2:

Next, we want to you to look at your genogram and think about the family members shown and how their cultural heritage affects you. The following questions will help you start thinking about your culture and ethnicity.

1. What are your ethnic and racial roots? Add the ethnicities of your family members to your genogram. For example, if your grandmother and grandfather on your dad's side were Irish and your mom's parents were French Canadian, you would note those ethnicities near their symbols on the genogram.

_____
_____
_____

2. What parts of your heritage do you most identify with today? For example, some people identify with the food or music of their heritage, some celebrate holidays in a manner that reflects their heritage, and others identify with the political or cultural-historical aspects of their heritage.

Don't really do anything relating to my heritage. I like Czech, German & Norwegian food, some a little.

3. Have certain career behaviors or occupations been part of your ethnic or racial heritage? For example, some ethnic and racial groups tend to work to a much greater extent in certain occupations. Also, certain families value some occupations greatly, like teaching or medicine, and transmit this value to the following generations.

Nope, my cultural heritage is not a very strong aspect of my life or career

4. What personal characteristics that you see in yourself do you attribute to your racial or ethnic heritage? For example, some people attribute physical characteristics such as hair color, skin color, or body build to their heritage. Others attribute personality characteristics, such as their sense of humor or being particularly strong and stoic.

I have blue eyes, Czech bone structure, German nose all ethnic

5. Bias and prejudice can take many forms. If, for example, you were the only child of a certain religion in your community, other children may have made fun of you and even your teachers may have demonstrated insensitivity when your parents took you out of school so that you could celebrate important religious holidays. What biases, prejudices, and/or forms of racism have you experienced because of your racial or ethnic background?

None, I usually fall under the norm of holidays etc, never stick out for race

6. What biases, prejudices, and/or forms of racism have you seen your family members demonstrate toward other groups?

People make jokes about minorities don't mean to be racist, just commenting on how ppl are different

7. What biases, prejudices, and/or forms of racism do you find yourself carrying with you that you first learned in your family of origin?

Just some of that same stuff, ppl are different, just pointing out differences not racism just too truly

Chapter 7
Clarifying Values

Chapter Overview

This chapter helps you look at your values—specifically, those things in life that you feel are worth taking risks for, working for, striving for, and sacrificing for. Inner needs and outer satisfactions are discussed, as is the nature of human motivation. Finally, the factors that most people identify as important to quality of life are described.

Each of us has within ourself a picture of what we want to get from life and what we want to accomplish before we die. Each of us also has a set of fantasy goals: what we would do if we won the lottery, inherited millions, made a killing in the stock market, and the like. Although most of these fantasy goals are just that, daydreams and fantasies, and they may differ sharply from those things that we would work long and hard for or commit our lives to, they may, as we saw earlier in this book, offer important clues to our inner needs and aspirations. This chapter, however, focuses on the other type of goals—the things that we are willing to work hard for.

What are some of your fantasy goals? How have they changed lately?

How has your awareness of and attention to these kinds of needs changed in recent years?

Do you know people who seem to have wasted a lifetime of hard work? Why did it happen?

Knowing what we want and are willing to strive for seems deceptively simple. Everyone wants good things, health, money, popularity, leisure, and so forth. But we are not usually so clear about what we are willing to work for. For most of us, the process of really going after the good things usually involves choices, prices, and priorities. It involves knowing what in our lives is actually worth striving for, taking risks for, sacrificing for, and committing to over a period of years or even a lifetime.

Often, we are acutely aware of the choices that our elders have made. Sometimes we are appalled by how empty the values are upon which they mortgaged their lives. Sometimes we see the disillusionment that comes from a life spent pursuing status or power or money only to find that it brings little satisfaction and less real happiness. Sometimes it seems that none of the commonly accepted symbols of success are really worth a wholehearted, lifelong investment of time, energy, and self-esteem.

For many people, disillusionment arises from not really knowing what they truly want, what they are willing to mobilize all their energy for and commit themselves to in a wholehearted way. For such people, life is often experienced as empty, boring, and insipid. As we noted earlier, "getting a life" means being aware of and willing to act on behalf of our personal needs, motives, and goals. It is only when we listen to our inner voices and act on them that we begin to experience life fully.

SATISFYING OUR INNER AND OUTER NEEDS

As we noted in Chapter 1, three sets of inner needs, or developmental drives, seem to energize and shape the course of human development. These are the need to find meaning and understanding in our life experiences; the need to exert some degree of control and competence, over our environment and the need for enduring and emotionally satisfying relationships. To some degree, life is a quest in which we seek to attend to and satisfy these inner needs by what we engage in and strive for in the outer world.

As we engage in the outer world, however, we experience another set of psychological and material needs, or outer needs, that give practical substance to our strivings and searches. These are needs that lead to the motives and goals that we act on in our everyday lives. Some of these needs are listed below. As you read the list, think about the relevance of each of the needs in your life. We take some of these needs for granted until their satisfaction is threatened. We push others aside under the pressures of our daily routines. If we are unfortunate to be caught up in a natural disaster or some other catastrophe, however, we quickly realize their importance to us.

PSYCHOLOGICAL AND MATERIAL NEEDS

1. *Survival and Security*
   These are the most basic requirements for food, clothing, and shelter. They also include the need to feel secure in what you now have—your person, property, and essential personal relationships.
2. *Order and Certainty*
   This is the need for some degree of structure and predictability in your life.
3. *Growth and Development*
   This is the need to feel that you are progressing in becoming the person that you want to be. It is the need to feel movement and accomplishment in your most important undertakings.
4. *Hopes and Aspirations*
   This is the need to have genuine optimism and hope in your own future and in the world. It involves the hope that obstacles can be overcome and gains can be made.
5. *Freedom and Choice*
   This is the need to feel a measure of control over your own life. It involves feeling a sense of freedom to make choices and to implement them.

6. *Identity and Integrity*
   This is the desire to experience a sense of being a unique person with your own goals, values, and loyalties. It involves the desire to stand for something and to live for something.
7. *Worthwhileness*
   This is the desire to know that you are needed and valued by others. It involves knowing that your life makes a positive difference in the scheme of things.
8. *A Satisfying Value System*
   This is the need to have some set of values, causes, or commitments in your life that are worth devoting yourself to and that are important enough to transcend your own personal and petty problems. It involves a sense of participating in something bigger and more important than yourself.
9. *Confidence in Society*
   This is the desire to feel that your society will allow the attainment of significant goals, will afford reasonable opportunities, and will permit sacrifices and labors to be fairly rewarded.

All of these needs except for survival and security have a major psychological component. When they are unmet, we may feel discontented, anxious, or even depressed. It is easy to see why so many people are less than happy most of the time. Take a few moments to think about which needs in the list are most important to you now and what you can do to help yourself fulfill those needs.

How Do We Try to Fulfill Our Needs?

It is through our motivations that we attempt to fulfill our needs. Our motivations grow out of our basic needs. They are the energizers in our lives. They give the focus, purpose, and meaning that allow us to channel our energy. It is clear that all of us have, at any given time, a very complicated and often competing set of motives. Thus, we often experience confusion and ambivalence and find it difficult to make and follow through on consistent and enduring commitments.

Some of our needs are simple and easily satisfied. Among them are what are called tension-reducing needs. Food, water, and bodily comfort are ready examples. Other needs, however, require increasing levels of stimulation in order to be satisfied.

These needs have been called *stimulus hunger*. We can see that the need for stimulation in the environment is fully as real and essential as is the need for food and water. It is clear that human beings need appropriate levels of stimulation and opportunities to explore, interact with, and act upon the environment. These are essential "nutrients" that must be available if human beings are to develop the ability both to grow and to resist stress. These needs for stimulation can be called *growth needs*. The inner drive for competence that we noted in Chapter 1 is part of the source for these growth needs.

Growth needs cause people to seek out stimulation, to reach out, to explore, manipulate, and interact with the environment. Unlike other drives "stimulus hunger" has no fixed satiation point. That is, higher and higher levels of stimulation create demand for still more stimulation, so that in effect we seek to match the immediate level of stimulation with the chronic level that we have experienced through the past.

When we watch "extreme sports" on TV, we see people who are hooked on thrill seeking. In a sense, all of us are hooked on stimulus hunger. What we are really hooked on is growing.

People seen in this way, then, are beings who not only seek to reduce tensions and avoid pain but also need increasingly higher levels of stimulation and challenge in the environment and are strongly motivated to seek them out.

Progressive Mastery: Climbing Psychological Mountains

How do all of these concepts translate into a better understanding of motivation in

How are your favorite activities tied to growth needs?

everyday practical situations? What we can conclude is that many people acquire very powerful and enduring attachments to activities that provide steadily increasing levels of challenge. They are driven by the need for *progressive mastery*. All sorts of activities can provide the outlet for this kind of motivation. All that is needed is the opportunity for ever-increasing levels of mastery. Most lifelong commitments to specific activities have this character. Bowling or bridge, piano or Ping-Pong, golf or gardening, occupations from architecture to zoology that command lifelong, high-priority commitments tend to have in common the opportunity for progressive mastery.

As motivations for progressive mastery are developed, they tend to become unifying structures that shape our lifestyle in important ways. When no motivations for progressive mastery are developed, we may have difficulty in building stable or satisfying lifestyles and may flounder and fail in the pursuit of a host of temporary fads or enthusiasms. As noted earlier, studies of human satisfaction have found that personal happiness heavily depends on whether we find a sense of "flow" or progress in meeting the challenges in our lives. Pursuing a life of progressive mastery seems to provide both the sense of control and the sense of immersion that are vital for happiness.

Deficit Needs and Growth Needs

Psychologist Abraham Maslow thought of motivation as the drive to satisfy ascending levels of need. The basic, or lower level, needs which can be called deficit needs are those that insure sheer physical survival. According to Maslow, these needs are always dominant in determining an individual's behavior until they are satisfied. A cold, hungry, or frightened person has little energy available for anything other than securing his or her own survival. Deficit needs thus include the needs for food, water, and shelter. Until these basic needs are satisfied, we have little motivation for higher level, or growth, needs. As lower level needs are satisfied, however, we are increasingly motivated to pursue activities that are growth-oriented and that lead ultimately to self-actualization. Most of these growth needs (including the needs for recognition, acceptance, approval, love, and so forth) are met within the framework of good and healthy interpersonal relationships.

The psychological life of a human being is quite different when behavior is dominated by deficit motivation rather than growth motivation. The deficit-motivated person is dependent upon others for basic need satisfaction. Such people see others as need satisfiers, objects, or sources of supply for those basic physical and psychological needs that are strongest at the moment. They see other people not as whole human beings or as complicated and unique individuals but rather perceive them almost wholly from the standpoint of their usefulness or threat. Deficit-motivated people tend to treat others as a hungry and impatient person may treat a busy waiter. They tend to perceive others as objects to be used, exploited, ignored, or thrown away.

Growth-motivated people experience life quite differently. Once basic human needs are met and people move toward a *growth-motivated* pattern of interaction with others, they tend to appreciate others for who they are as well as for what they can offer. Mature social or sexual relationships are possible only when people reach this level.

In one sense, then, quality interpersonal relationships within a group, family, or community may be seen as the framework within which human psychological needs may be met. As lower level needs for physiological well-being, security, and safety are met, individuals begin to be motivated by social needs to belong, be accepted, and be loved. As these needs are satisfied, they give way to needs to be respected, to be valued, and to have recognition and status. It is out of these latter needs that personal and social responsibility and achievement grow. Finally, as the level of need satisfaction rises, self-fulfillment needs become more powerful. These

---

Are you on a progressive mastery escalator now? Would you like to be?

What do you do best now? How will that change in the next 5 years? Will you reach higher levels of mastery?

Are your present close relationships deficit or growth motivated? In what ways?

How are your present relationships meeting these needs?

are needs to realize one's full capacity to contribute to and appreciate others and society. Such needs are truly growth needs through which the developing individual moves toward fullest effectiveness and self-actualization. Much of the art of helping oneself or others to grow involves meeting these needs through positive achievement and prosocial behavior. Many centuries ago, Plato stated that the most challenging task of life is learning how to find pleasure in worthwhile accomplishments. His words are still true today.

VALUES IN AN INNER-DIRECTED LIFE

As we move toward satisfying higher level needs and become more inner directed, we form new values, preferences, and appreciations. Some of these include:

1. Preferring a responsible, self-regulated, and self-restrained participation in life, where we appreciate and conserve what we have attained rather than chase after remote or fantasy-oriented possibilities and illusions.
2. Finding satisfaction in taking vigorous action in overcoming obstacles and solving problems.
3. Finding joy and delight in our inner life and placing a higher value on aesthetic appreciation, sensitivity to others, and increased self-awareness.
4. Valuing more highly the simple pleasure of life, including an increased valuing of relaxation, occasional solitude, and opportunities to reflect and meditate on the mysteries of the natural world and the meaning of human existence.

Along with these changes come changes in aspirations for growth and development and in the ways in which we want to function in day-to-day life. These changes include:

1. Moving away from superficial facades and preoccupation with "impression-management" and striving to be as open and honest with others as possible.
2. Trying to act on our own judgments about moral and ethical questions rather than waiting for others to define what is right or wrong, moral or immoral.
3. Trying to set expectations about ourselves for ourselves rather than trying to please others or obtain praise and validation from others.

Overall, these changes in values tend to move us in the direction of seeking greater autonomy and greater freedom to act creatively and independently as well as toward an increased sense of personal responsibility for choices and actions.

WHAT DO PEOPLE REALLY WANT MOST IN LIFE?

"Happiness" is almost as difficult to define as it is to attain. It has been defined as the sum total of lasting pleasures, as contentment, as satisfaction and as the absence of pain or anxiety. As most people think of it, happiness is a transitory state of mind. Nobody is happy all of the time. Perhaps the surest way to be chronically unhappy is to expect to be happy all of the time.

A less ephemeral concept of happiness equates it to quality of life, a concept that has been systematically studied for more than 30 years. In the course of this research, thousands of people have responded to questionnaires or have been interviewed at length about their views of happiness and the values that they think contribute most to quality of life. The research has found that the sense of control and involvement that we described in Chapter 1 as essential ingredients in "peak experiences" are a part of quality of life, but only a part.

Perhaps the most interesting finding of the three decades of research on quality of life is that there is considerable consensus across age, socioeconomic groups, and ethnic groups about the most important ingredients in quality of life and that this consensus has remained quite stable over the course of the research.

What are the directions in which you are presently moving?

What would be your top three and bottom three quality of life factors? Why?

Surprisingly, such variables as age, gender, income, religion, occupation, as well as other demographic variables, have been found to be relatively minor determinants of well-being. Clearly, self-reported happiness is a psychological variable and not an automatic consequence of age, wealth, or social status. The research also indicates that the experience of stress in one's life is *not* a major impediment to quality of life.

Interestingly, although many people, when asked what will make them happier, respond "more money," there is almost no correlation between self-reported happiness and income from middle income levels on up. In fact, although personal, real income has more than doubled over the past 30 years, self-reported happiness has actually declined.

So, what are the factors that people in all walks of life have reported as being most crucial to quality of life? They are provided in the following list. Note that the rank-ordering of the importance of these varies from person to person.

1. Material comfort and financial security
2. Health and personal safety
3. Relationships with relatives
4. Having and raising children
5. Relationship with spouse (lover, etc.)
6. Relationships with close friends
7. Helping and encouraging others
8. Participating in government and public affairs
9. Learning
10. Understanding self
11. Interesting, rewarding, worthwhile work
12. Expressing oneself creatively
13. Socializing with others in recreation
14. Reading about, listening to, or watching concerts, sports, etc.
15. Participating in active recreation, sports, or hobbies

These 15 features of a happy or fulfilled life are agreed upon at a surprisingly high level of consensus. Although, as noted earlier, the ways in which these features are prioritized vary widely from individual to individual, people tend to place material comfort, financial security, and good health near the top of their lists as most crucial to well-being.

Beyond those values, people have rated work, close family and social relationships, and opportunities for personal growth as very important. These values correlate well with the basic human needs of *meaning, relationships,* and *competence* described earlier. It is when circumstances force people to choose among these values or risk losing one or more to obtain another that conflict, frustration, and indecision result.

The broad picture that emerges from these studies is that quality of life is fairly stable across time and is not usually radically or permanently affected by single isolated events. Further, the research shows that people who report high levels of happiness tend to be involved in close, positive interpersonal relationships, be actively engaged in and committed to work, be actively striving toward the attainment of goals, and perceive themselves as making progress in reaching such goals.

HAPPINESS AND YOUNG ADULTS

Most of the research on happiness has been done with adults aged 25 or older. The studies that have been conducted with post-high school young adults aged 18 to 22 have shown that the greatest levels of happiness are reported by those living independently (away from their family of origin), actively engaged in an occupation or preparing to enter an occupation, and newly married or engaged to be married.

Summarizing the information gleaned from the 30 years of research on quality of life, we could describe the happy person as one who (a) lives in a caring and supportive network of interpersonal relationships, (b) is engaged in or preparing to engage in work that is personally worthwhile and satisfying, and (c) is pursuing

Why would these factors predict happiness in young adulthood?

and making progress toward a set of consciously chosen goals that are reasonably congruent with personal values and psychological and environmental resources. In short, the happy human being is fully engaged in the mainstream of human activity and experience. As psychologist Carl Rogers put it, "The good life is a *process* not a state of being. It is a direction not a destination."

What Does All of This Mean for Life Planning?

The first step in making a long-term life plan is to endeavor to define our *personal life goals*. A life goal is more than a specific level of income or wealth or a certain social status or job title. It is a state of consciousness. Success in attaining life goals is almost impossible to define in a totally objective or external way.

We know that happiness is related to such psychological variables as optimism, self-confidence, a sense of mastery or control, emotional self-control, and self-esteem. We also know that happiness is related to situations in which we experience social support, intimate relationships, and adequate material resources. A life goal in this sense may be to have the respect of friends and colleagues, to feel loved by spouse and family, and to have contributed to building a better world.

Our problem in life planning is determining how to move toward external, material subgoals such as increased pay, promotion, job security, recognition, status, and power (that is, the conventional "success indicators") while at the same time holding on to and enhancing the psychological variables and personal supports that are crucial to happiness.

Exercise 7.1 asks you to look at how well you are meeting your basic needs and how you may want to rearrange your priorities to attain a greater level of happiness. Take some time now to complete this exercise.

Summary

In this chapter, we looked at a variety of human needs and motivations that can give purpose and meaning to life. We examined the concept of progressive mastery as a unifying set of motivations that lead to increasing competence, accomplishment, and satisfaction. Finally, we looked at the ways in which people typically define personal happiness or quality of life and that those factor into the concept of life planning.

How will life planning move you toward happiness?

Exercise 7.1

How Well Are You Meeting Your Basic Needs?

On the scale that follows each need listed below, estimate your present level of satisfaction. Use "6" to indicate the highest level of satisfaction and "1" to indicate the lowest.

1. *Survival and Security*
    1   2   3   4   5   **(6)**
2. *Order and Certainty*
    1   2   3   4   **(5)**   6
3. *Growth and Development*
    1   2   3   4   5   **(6)**
4. *Hopes and Aspirations*
    1   2   3   4   5   **(6)**
5. *Freedom and Choice*
    1   2   3   4   5   **(6)**
6. *Identity and Integrity*
    1   2   3   4   5   **(6)**
7. *Worthwhileness*
    1   2   3   4   5   **(6)**
8. *Satisfying Value System*
    1   2   3   4   5   **(6)**
9. *Confidence in Society*
    1   2   3   **(4)**   5   **(6)**
    theirs   *mine*

Which of these needs are being best satisfied in your life? Least satisfied?

Identity & Integrity ; value system

Where do you most want to make changes?

certainty

Where were you 5 years ago in terms of satisfying these needs?

Where do you want to be 5 years from now?

the same — can't ever be too certain

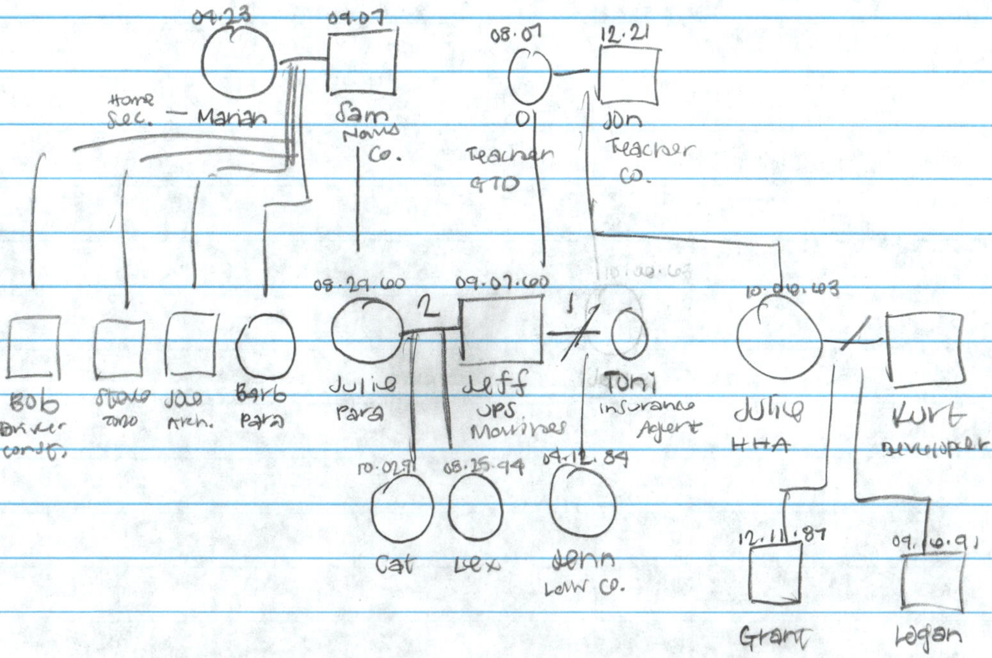
04.23
09.07
08.07
12.21
Home Sec. — Marian
Sam
Co.
Teacher
Jon
Teacher
Co.
08.29.60
09.07.60
2
1
Bob
Joe
Arch.
Barb
Para
Julie
Para
Jeff
UPS
Toni
Insurance
Agent
Julie
HHA
Kurt
Developer
08.25.94
04.12.84
Cat
Lex
Jenn
Co.
12.11.87
Grant
Logan

Now that you have rated each need in terms of satisfaction, rank order the needs in terms of your priorities for committing time, energy, and resources to each. (Use "1" to indicate the need to which you'd commit the most time, energy, and resources. Then continue your ranking through the number 9.) Rank the needs in terms of your present priorities and your priorities 5 years ago.

Now	Five Years Ago	Need
5	4	Survival and security
3	7	Order and certainty
7	1	Growth and development
1	2	Hopes and aspirations
4	5	Freedom and choice
2	3	Identity and integrity
6	6	Worthwhileness
8	8	Satisfying value system
9	9	Confidence in society

By organizing your priorities around the most important and current needs in your life you will be able to focus your time and energy more effectively.

Chapter 8
Goal Setting

Chapter Overview

This chapter discusses both the process and power of setting goals as a way of providing direction and focus to your life. Important criteria for goal setting are provided, and suggestions are given for refining your own goal setting style. Also discussed are the influence of self-concept on goal setting and the importance of recognizing and accurately assessing your personal strengths. Exercises are provided to help you identify your own style, assess your personal strengths, and set specific goals that will enable you to focus your energies and set priorities.

Setting long-term, or lifelong goals is a little like looking out across a vast expanse of trackless wilderness at a far-away range of lofty, snow-capped mountains. The mountains give us a destination and the general direction in which we want to travel, but they don't help a lot in getting us over the next hill or across the next river in our paths.

While such general life goals are vital, as they give us direction in our journey, they are necessarily abstract and sometimes even vague. Yet like the snow-capped peaks they become clearer and more sharply defined as we move closer to them. As we start out our goals may be simply that we want to make a difference in the world, that we want to leave a set of footprints that others might follow. They may involve earning the respect of others, building something that endures after us, helping to make the world more just and equitable, creating something of beauty, or helping to preserve what is already beautiful. They may involve raising a healthy family or developing our talents and abilities.

Our goals arise out of our values, those things, ideas, and expressions that we consider to be good and true and beautiful and that we want to be a part of or to have become a part of us. As we noted in chapter 7, we translate our values into goals as we begin the process of life planning.

As we go along on our journey, most of our attention and energy, most of the time is devoted simply to climbing the next hill or crossing the next valley. Often, we spend a lot of time exploring, seeking out the paths and trails and crossings that are possible for us in terms of our strengths and endurance and in terms of the loads we carry. Every once in a while, especially as we get older, we pause to catch our breath and look up to see if, indeed, the mountains are getting any closer or if the peaks are sharper and more clearly defined.

Life goals, then, can be thought of as representing the directions and distances between where we are now and where we want to be in the future. We reach them by developing life plans, or action plans of short-term goals that help us get to the next marker or milestone and move us a little closer to our ultimate goals or destination. Take a few moments now to complete Exercise 8.1 which asks you to think about your own general life goals. We will discuss more specific and immediate goals and plans in Chapter 9.

PLANNING AND ENABLING GOALS

Even though most people have a set of general and abstract life goals, only a small percentage of these goals are ever transformed into specific steps (or short-term goals) and more immediate planning and enabling goals. Many times when we are unable to set specific directions or zero in on a clearly-defined objective we tend to do nothing. Planning and enabling goals help us to begin the task of considering and mapping out new possibilities. They are part of the process of career exploration that we described in Chapter 3.

Many times, planning and enabling goals do not require us to make final choices or irrevocable decisions. They may involve the systematic exploration of new areas and options. They may involve tryouts in new situations, building upon existing strengths, and/or developing new strengths. They may involve building a stronger feeling of self-confidence and self-efficacy in a given area before even beginning a systematic exploration of its possibilities.

FOCUSING AND PRIORITIZING

Whatever your goal-setting style, ultimately you will need to both focus on and prioritize your goals. In *First Things First*, Steven Covey suggests visualizing our goals as elements—as small, fist-sized rocks or as gravel or even grains of sand—all of which we want to fit into a water pitcher. Clearly, if we think of our goals as fist-sized rocks, there are only a few that we will be able to put in the pitcher. If we envision our goals as smaller pieces of gravel or grains of sand, many, many goals will fit in the pitcher. But we also need to think about the order in which we will put the elements into the pitcher. If we fill the pitcher first with the gravel or sand, there will be no room for even one fist-sized rock. The metaphor illustrates that the larger pieces of rock, or our higher priority goals, need to be considered first.

SETTING SPECIFIC AND IMMEDIATE GOALS

When setting your specific and immediate goals, remember to bear in mind the following criteria below:

- Is it important to you?
- Is it reasonable?
- Is it achievable?
- Is it within your control?
- Can you visualize yourself achieving it?
- Are you willing to invest the time and effort necessary to achieve it?
- Are you ready to begin *now?*

Take some time now to complete Exercise 8.3, which will help you prioritize some of your own immediate and/or long-term goals.

THE PROCESS AND POWER OF GOAL SETTING

When we read the biographies of famous, highly successful people we usually find a recurrent theme. Most of these people set clear and immediate goals for themselves. As we read their life stories, we often get the impression that goal setting was a simple process for them. Indeed when people have clear goals early in life, their biographies seem to read like fiction. The process for them seems all so easy. Opportunities appear to present themselves at every turn, and these people seem to be clear about how to make choices and seize the opportunities. We can read about their lives and hope to learn something from them. For most of us, the process will not be that easy. For most of us, setting goals will not be a quick, easy, or simple process that leads us unerringly to success. It is, however, an essential part of any life plan.

Learning from the Examples of Others

Sometimes, looking at how others seem to attain lofty goals without ever experiencing failure or disappointment can be discouraging. The way others set goals does not have to define our own style, however. Goal setting arises out of our own needs, values, and experiences. Our goals and the way we pursue them are a part of our own uniqueness.

We can, however, learn some things from thinking about how others have been successful. The following themes emerge from their life stories. First, goals are, themselves, powerful sources of motivation. And second, when people set goals, modify them, struggle and seek help with them and make them public, those goals become unifying and energizing forces. These themes can be clearly seen in the story of Mark McGwire, which is told in the next section. It is important to note that people who set goals may (and often do) struggle. People who have no goals simply flounder.

The pursuit of goals in the manner that makes for a best selling biography may seem to read more like a fantasy than reality. That however does not take away from the importance of setting goals. For the famous and the rest of us, goal setting should be a guiding factor in our lives.

Goals are powerful sources of focus and direction, and we can learn how to go about setting goals by looking at how others who have been successful have done so. We also can learn to understand ourselves better as we begin to see the influence that goal setting has on our behavior. In the process though we need to be honest with ourselves. Goal setting can be more fiction than reality. It is like making New Year's resolutions and thus can become more a ritual than a way of life. If we are to attain our goals, they must be based on reality.

When confronted with your regular daily responsibilities, how do you react? Do you feel overwhelmed, or does your awareness of your goals urge you on to perform at a higher level?

McGwire: A Successful Goal Setter

In the late 1990s, much of the world followed Mark McGwire's pursuit of hitting the most home runs in a single baseball season. It was a long-term goal for McGwire. He had aspired to and nearly achieved the record several seasons in a row. From opening day in Saint Louis in 1998, it was evident that he was still in pursuit of the home run record. He was open about it. The fans knew his goal, and before the season was over millions followed his pursuit. He became the Babe Ruth of the 1990s.

In interviews as McGwire got close to the record, listeners and viewers could feel the power of the goal he had set for himself. He had come to believe it was realistic and possible for him. His clear focus and dedication were clearly apparent. As the drama unfolded, he talked of the importance of team goals as well as individual ones, and occasionally as he got close to the record, he tried to downplay the importance of the goal. It was his style to do so. But it was clear that the record or goal was a powerful force in his life.

Those who followed the story remember that it was often stranger than fiction. McGwire see-sawed back and forth with his rival, Sammy Sosa, in the last month of the season, always staying one up on him until the very last. McGwire hit his 60th home run on his father's 60th birthday, he surpassed Roger Maris's record of 62 home runs with the Maris family in the stands, and then he connected for two home runs in his final game in front of the home crowd, achieving his goal and providing a storybook September finish. Like the story of Babe Ruth, the saga of Mark McGwire is motivating and instructive. Though it is almost more like fiction than truth, it illustrates the power that goal setting can have in transforming an individual life.

Finding Your Own Goal-Setting Style

As we observe world-class athletes or others who have achieved high levels of accomplishment, it is clear that they have set specific and immediate goals and have established firm timelines within which to reach each goal. They see each goal as achievable for themselves and often have even visualized attaining the goal with all of the rewards that its accomplishment carries.

What emerge as common threads in the process of goal setting for these high achievers are the *power of the goal, the intensity of the individual's focus,* and the *belief in the possibility of achieving it.* We may not be able to find the kind of public acclaim for our successes that these cultural heroes receive, but we can incorporate these criteria for setting goals into our own goal-setting style and bring the power of goal setting into our own lives.

One fact that is usually left out of examples of the way others set goals for themselves is that life is seldom the simple pursuit of a single goal. Few people put their lives on hold while they pursue a single goal. When people try to do so, they usually suffer the long-term consequences of such a narrow focus. Most of us must continue to live our lives and juggle a complicated set of responsibilities while trying to place a high priority on one or two really important goals. This is the nature of reality, and it is what makes it so important to find a goal-setting style that fits with our own life situation.

Going to school, earning a living, attending to daily duties, family responsibilities, or obligations, keeping up friendships, maintaining your health, and continuing that ever elusive pursuit of happiness can complicate the single-minded pursuit of any goal. And often the pursuit of one goal makes it difficult to attend to others. Some people are better than others at juggling such tasks, others are overwhelmed by the process, become discouraged, and even abandon their goals. We don't suggest that there is only one way to bring the power of goal setting into your life. We intend this chapter to serve as a stimulus for you to come up with or better understand your way and then refine and use that way within a lifestyle that is uniquely your own.

When we often find ourselves overwhelmed by what we want to accomplish, we need to be able to focus on those goals that are most important and accept the fact we can't do everything at once. By prioritizing goals and working toward those goals that are most important to us, we are more apt to experience the process as empowering. Whatever your goal-setting style, it should be one that helps you to mobilize your energy and resources. The essence of goal setting is taking time to focus and prioritize. Setting goals enables us to devote our energy to those things that are *important, possible* and controllable.

Our experience suggests that far too few people consciously and consistently engage in a process of setting goals for themselves despite the overwhelming evidence that doing so often makes a difference in the lives of those who do. Before reading further, take some time to complete Exercise 8.2. Be honest with yourself as you consider how goal setting fits into your life and lifestyle.

Your answers to the questions in Exercise 8.2 will give you an idea of how, and how much, you may need to adapt your goal-setting style for it to become a method of personal empowerment. As we noted earlier, we are more interested in having you refine and adapt your own style than in trying to get you to find a new one. What works for your lifestyle may differ from what works for others. We hope that we have given you ideas about how to improve or refine the process you currently use to give direction and focus to your efforts.

BRINGING OUR STRENGTHS TO BEAR ON BEHALF OF OUR GOALS

While the directions in which we travel are determined by our values and goals, the distances that we move and the objectives that we reach along the way are determined by our strengths, our determination, and our ability to plan and to utilize our inner resources. However, we can use our strengths, or inner resources, only when we are aware of them, recognize them, and incorporate them into our identities. The greatest limitation to our attaining our objectives and moving toward our ultimate goals lies in our own concepts of self.

Too often, we ignore our strengths or even deny them. If a person is asked to list as many of his or her strengths as possible in 3 minutes and then to make a similar list of his or her weaknesses or failings in the same amount of time, the latter list will almost always be three to five times longer than the former. We usually tend to deny or deprecate our simple but very real and often invaluable strengths. "Yes, I cook well, but that's not important," we say. "Sure, I guess I do know a lot about art, but that's just a hobby," we protest.

At first glance, such denials may seem almost admirable. After all, we have all been taught that bragging is wrong and that modesty is a virtue. In reality, of course, the honest awareness of our strengths and abilities leads to the kind of quiet confidence that is the very opposite of the braggart's insecurity and bluff.

Why Is Awareness of Strengths Important?

A realistic assessment of our strengths is essential to the development of a positive identity, which, in turn, is essential for moving toward our goals. People cannot work or love, to use Freud's classic criteria, if they distrust themselves or are consumed with constant fears and doubts about their own competence. To build positive and credible foundations of self-respect and self-confidence, we must have genuine reasons for believing in our own abilities and determination. No satisfactory substitutes exist for such spontaneous and genuine feelings of self-esteem.

In a real sense, the foundations for such feelings of self-esteem, the reasons why we feel good about ourselves, so to speak, lie in our *simple strengths*. These are the practical day-to-day things that we do well. The relationship between simple strengths and self-esteem is reciprocal.

What are three simple strengths you have that you often ignore or deny?

How have perceived failures or rejections affected you?

Just as an accurate perception of our strengths aids in the development of a positive identity, so too does the existence of a positive self-concept assist in the development of additional strengths.

When we believe in our own competence, adequacy, and worth, we are free to venture into new areas, take new risks and challenges, and move farther and faster in attaining our goals. We expect to succeed rather than to fail, and the final result often reflects our high initial expectations.

Our sense of self-confidence is the psychological insurance that allows us to take risks and to hang on as we face obstacles and disappointments. Through our personal security, we are willing to take on new challenges and in the process discover still more strengths or strength potentials within ourselves.

Why Do We Often Deny Our Strengths?

One of the basic paradoxes in human behavior is our tendency to ignore or deny our strengths and strength potentials. Part of the reason for this denial is that every strength or strength potential we recognize represents both a responsibility and a risk. When we acknowledge the presence of a strength or strength potential, we are faced with conserving, utilizing, and developing that strength responsibly. When we acknowledge that strength openly, we are faced with others' expectations about how we should deal with those responsibilities.

Further, when we recognize our strengths and use them responsibly, we are faced with risks. Only the strong can fail. If, instead, we take refuge in a presumption of our own inadequacy, incompetence, and weakness, we can successfully avoid the risk of short-term failures. The long-term price that we pay is, of course, the certain eventual loss of self-esteem and the abandonment of our most cherished hopes and aspirations. Our presumption of inadequacy soon turns into a self-fulfilling prophecy that moves us along the path to lethargy, self-pity, and defeat.

Another reason we tend to ignore or deny our strengths is, simply, that we are often unaware of them. We may have outdated perceptions of ourselves drawn from childhood or adolescent experiences. In a sense, we have failed to update the album of personal snapshots that tells us who we are and where we have been. A bad experience in school with an inadequate teacher, a nagging or perfectionistic parent, a perceived failure in an athletic contest, a rejection from an adolescent "crush"—all of these can trigger perceptions of self that outlive any relevance to present reality.

There is yet another reason for our denial of our strengths. Many times, we are unaware of our strength potentials simply because we have not been exposed to situations in which we can appropriately demonstrate and assess particular strengths. And even when we are exposed to strength situations, we sometimes fail to attend to and note our own positive performance. An ideal opportunity for learning to recognize, assess, and reflect on our strengths is presented to us as we set goals and make life plans. The new awareness we develop will serve us well as we strive to reach our goals and aspirations.

How Can We Assess Our Strengths?

We have already examined three aspects of discovering and assessing personal strengths. First, we can learn to accept the risks and responsibilities involved in acknowledging our strengths and strength potentials. Second, we can update our self-perceptions by reality testing them in the light of our present capabilities and by systematically questioning the relevance of our childhood and adolescent experiences to our present self-concepts. Third, we can actively seek out strength situations and learn to become more sensitive to our own accomplishments. Probably the most important element in assessing personal strengths is determining the appropriate dimension on which to place our assessment. Basically, most assessments of personal strengths are made on either the vertical or the horizontal dimension.

Assessing Strengths on the Vertical Dimension The most common method that people use to assess their strengths and abilities is social comparison, or what we call assessment on the *vertical* dimension. When we use this dimension, we judge our strengths primarily in terms of how they compare to others. That is we view ourselves in relation to the performance of others.

When we judge or evaluate ourselves on the vertical dimension, our judgments or evaluations depend very largely on the particular sample, or social group, with whom we make the comparison. When we are making predictions about our relative performance in a highly competitive situation with a known group of competitors, this kind of assessment may yield accurate predictions. Very often, however, particularly in childhood and adolescence, a rigid and inappropriate use of the vertical dimension in self-assessments produces distorted and maladaptive self-concepts. Many times we use groups who are older, more mature, or more experienced, or groups who possess other advantages, as the sole reference groups for our self-estimates. Then we may overgeneralize from these very limited comparison opportunities and close out directions for exploration or tryout because of our unrealistic, unfavorable self-estimates.

Living our lives on the vertical dimension, so to speak, may also cause us to define ourselves both negatively and narrowly. When we see a strength solely in terms of the ability to win over or otherwise be superior to those who happen to be around us, we miss many opportunities and ignore many potentials. In a sense, living our lives on the vertical dimension is like climbing an endless ladder. We can only advance over the backs of the other climbers, and we are in constant danger of losing our grip on our present rung as others try to displace us. Further, when we base our primary self-evaluations on the vertical dimension, our self-assessments are in constant flux. Every new group with whom we associate invites a new set of comparisons and hence a new set of self-evaluations. Much of our energy and time goes into ascertaining our particular place in the pecking order. Every new relationship has to be evaluated in terms of its impact on our self-concepts.

As we become more mature and more involved in attaining our goals, the burden of living on the vertical dimension becomes particularly heavy. We grow to increasingly resent the wasted time and energy, games, maneuvers, and self-deceptions that go with "ladder climbing" as a way of life.

Assessing Strengths on the Horizontal Dimension Fortunately, there is an alternative way to assess personal strengths. The central notion that defines this method, which we call assessment on the *horizontal* dimension, is the concept of *personal best*. By personal best we mean movement toward the fulfillment of personal potential. When we assess our performances on the basis of the amount of potential that *we* have actualized, the performances of others become much less relevant.

Interestingly, even in highly competitive situations such as world-class athletic events, performers have generally learned to shift their long-term assessments of progress from the "win-lose" vertical dimension to the "personal best" horizontal dimension. Living our lives on the horizontal dimension gives us a kind of control over our own growth and development that is not contingent on how well others perform. Experiencing this kind of control over our thoughts and feelings about ourselves becomes an intrinsically rewarding event that maintains a very high degree of commitment and enthusiasm for valued activities. It is part of the sense of control that is an essential ingredient in peak experiences.

This kind of commitment is very evident in sports such as golf or bowling and in activities such as running, where keeping a record of individual progress is built into the scoring system. It is a part of the

How have you been caught up in ladder climbing?

How has a sense of personal best helped you to maintain interests and commitments and to progress in developing skills?

progressive mastery life-style mentioned earlier. It is interesting to note the degree to which enthusiasm in this kind of activity increases in adulthood after interest in many of the "win-lose" activities of childhood and adolescence has begun to wane.

Another aspect of the horizontal dimension is that it focuses on the practical consequences of an activity or performance rather than on social comparisons. Personal strengths and accomplishments are means through which we achieve our objectives and move closer to our goals. On the horizontal dimension, we focus on performance in terms of both personal potential and progress toward practical goals. We are interested in demonstrating effectiveness rather than superiority.

This focus on goal attainment and personal effectiveness allows us to utilize our limited time and energy more carefully, efficiently, and productively. One of the ways in which setting goals and developing plans can be liberating is in helping us to move from the vertical to the horizontal dimension of self-evaluation.

How Can We Learn to Assess Ourselves on the Horizontal Dimension? Many people are stuck on the vertical dimension because they lack awareness of and trust in themselves. As we grow more mature we begin to accumulate the experience, sense of awareness and self-knowledge, and self-direction to concentrate on meeting our *own* needs. We begin to assess ourselves in terms of how well we meet those needs rather than on how well we have met *others' expectations*. When we succeed in moving from the vertical to the horizontal dimension, when we are finally able to assess our own strengths in terms of our own potentials and purposes, we have taken the first step in a vitally important adult transition. We have come to terms with our own uniqueness

How Do Our Self-Estimates Limit Us?

We noted earlier that our perceptions of self can be a kind of prison that confines us and shuts us off from what we might become. Our greatest limitation lies in our view of what we think we can realistically accomplish. Those who have studied this sense of self-efficacy conclude that it is the central factor in determining how we react to new learning situations or opportunities. In career planning our sense of self-efficacy is just as important a factor as are our interests and preferences. We can sum up the enormous influence of self-efficacy on our behavior by pointing out that we seldom attempt what we believe is impossible to achieve.

Appendix B contains a useful exercise called "The Strength Audit." You will gain a clearer idea of the extent of your own personal resources, strengths, and capacities. If you attend carefully to this exercise, reflecting honestly on your own strengths, you will be able to begin to overturn the limitations imposed by ignoring or denying them. Please complete this exercise when you have some time to yourself and freedom from distraction.

SUMMARY

In this chapter we discussed the process of translating general life goals into planning and enabling goals, and we stressed the importance of setting priorities to better mobilize our energy and personal resources. We then examined the significance of being aware of our strengths and the importance of evaluating our efforts in terms of "personal best." We noted that even when we are unable to make final choices and decisions we can set goals in terms of exploring possibilities and readying ourselves to seize opportunities.

Exercise 8.1
My General Life Goals

In the spaces below, write down three of your present general life goals. Be sure that each is (a) really important to you, (b) reasonable in terms of accomplishment, and (c) within your possible control. After you write down the goals, think about the following questions:

1. When did I first become aware that this goal was important to me?
2. What important values are represented in attaining this goal?
3. What are some experiences in my life that have helped to form this goal?
4. Who are the people who have helped to shape this goal in my life?

Jot down your answers to these questions in the space provided.

Goal: Have a full, happy, successful, eventful life, don't live any twice

1. Origins: junior year high school when life sucked
2. Values: working hard to be successful, stay motivated
3. Experiences: not being happy and wanting to be
4. People: Mom, Dad, Cam, Dara, Neth

Goal: Get good grades in college (high school), be prepared for my career and for life

1. Origins: summer before school started
2. Values: staying dedicated, studying, work hard, sacrifice extra
3. Experiences: not getting good grades
4. People: DAD

Goal: Have a successful, happy, fulfilled, romantic, spontaneous, loving, caring, quirky MARRIAGE

1. Origins: throughout high school
2. Values: dedication, loyalty, honesty, love, respect, spontaneity, romance
3. Experiences: movies, mom and dad, others, dad and Tori, myself
4. People: Mom, Dad, Kevin, Cam, Dara, G&G, G&G

Exercise 8.2

Examine Your Goal-Setting Style

1. Do you set goals for yourself?

    no

2. Do you do it as part of a weekly routine?

    yes

3. Do you believe it is important?

    yes

4. Do you write your goals down? Post them? Carry them with you?

    yes

5. Do you set few or many goals for yourself? How does it work for you?

    many

6. Do you have categories for your goals, such as personal or professional, long or short term, important or not so important?

    no

7. Is goal setting a regular activity for you or only reserved for special situations?

    reg

8. Do you examine your goals on a regular basis?

    yes

9. Do you prioritize them?

    no

10. Do you share them with others?

    no

11. Are you usually successful in meeting your goals?

    yes

12. Do you rethink or adjust those goals with which you are not successful?

    yes

13. Do you make a practice of celebrating the achievement of your goals?

    yes — crossing them off, thats it

Exercise 8.3
Getting Priorities Straight

In the chart below, list two sets of goals for yourself: one set of personal goals and one set of educational or professional goals. These may include planning and enabling goals as well as those based on firm choices. Be reflective, and take some time with this. Note that many people find getting started to be the hardest part of this exercise. When you are finished, apply the following criteria to each goal:

- Is it important to you?
- Is it reasonable?
- Is it achievable?
- Is it within your control?
- Can you visualize yourself achieving it?
- Are you willing to invest the time and effort necessary to achieve it?
- Are you ready to begin *now*?

Then give each goal weight of 1 to 3 indicating the importance you attach to it ("1" is little, "2" is some and "3" is much importance). Be sure that you rate the current importance of each of these goals.

Personal Goals

1. MARRIAGE
2. CAREER
3. GOOD GRADES
4. STUDY ABROAD
5. ~~~~ KIDS

BE HAPPY
KEEP IN CONTACT
WAKE UP ON TIME
GET TONED / LOSE WEIGHT

Educational or Professional Goals

1. GOOD GRADES
2. GRADUATE EARLY
3. BE LOOKED UP TO
4. BE KNOWN
5. KNOW OTHERS

Here are a few more questions to think about.

1. Did you complete the exercise? Was it easy or difficult?
2. Did you find yourself with few or many goals?
3. Could you establish priorities for the goals?
4. Did it help you to recognize your own style in this process?

CHAPTER 9
Generating Commitment, Reality Testing Goals, and Mobilizing Resources

CHAPTER OVERVIEW

This chapter deals with *commitment,* the process that turns planning into reality. We look at the importance of achievement motivation, a sense of personal control, and effort optimism as basic attitudes that help us to hang in and remain committed to reaching our goals in spite of obstacles. The discussion then turns to action planning, the process of creating a step-by-step strategy for attaining our goals.

Generating Commitment?

The most powerful and pervasive reason for failure is that people do not translate their goals into *commitments* around which they orient their lives and concentrate their energies and talents. Most of us think we have goals, but often we find, upon honest examination, that what we thought was a goal is in reality simply a wish, desire, or hope.

The difference between hopes and goals is that goals are readily converted into commitments and then into practical plans. They become the basis for our choices, priorities, and decisions. Hopes, in contrast, remain vaguely pleasant fantasies that provide the stuff for daydreams and other needed escapes from reality. There is nothing at all wrong with hopes and dreams, except when we confuse them with genuine goals and deceive ourselves into believing that we are somehow being true to ourselves through our fantasies rather than through our commitments and actions.

Goals that are translated into commitments provide a sense of consistency and direction for our lives. They orient us so that we can act more directly to satisfy our needs and achieve the material and psychological rewards that we value most. Goal setting and the commitments we make to achieve our goals, generate the energy that helps us to mobilize our resources and to *act*.

It has been found repeatedly that making firm and public commitments to goals facilitates performance. That is, we are more likely to follow through if we not only set clear, explicit, and reasonable goals but also publicly affirm our intention to achieve them. Indeed, it seems to be this process of public affirmation that translates hopes and dreams into actual commitments and hence into concrete achievements. The way to do our personal best is to publicly commit ourselves to a goal that is challenging but attainable.

How are these tendencies part of your personality?

Achievement Motivation

Three basic attitudes that help us to remain committed to our goals are achievement motivation, a sense of personal control, and effort optimism. These attitudes are discussed in the following sections. In Chapter 1 we discussed the inner drive toward competence, or the need to have some degree of control or mastery over the environment. A closely related concept is *achievement motivation*, which is the tendency to be attracted to, and to persist in, situations that offer considerable challenge or opportunity to earn highly valued rewards through personal effort. In a sense, we can think of achievement motivation as the desire to succeed through personal effort. High achievement motivation seems to be one of the few general psychological characteristics shared by most successful people.

Studies of this kind of motivation have defined the following three basic characteristics of people with high achievement needs:

1. They like situations in which they take personal responsibility for finding solutions to problems.
2. They tend to set moderately difficult goals and to take carefully calculated risks.
3. They tend to get satisfaction from positive accomplishment rather than from simply avoiding failure.

The combination of these three tendencies helps people to channel their efforts into productive activities that lead to successful outcomes.

Locus of Control

An important way in which people differ in their thinking about goal setting and commitment relates to what is called "locus of control," or the ways in which people believe their lives and fortunes are determined or influenced. Some people primarily attribute the rewards, successes, and failures that they experience to their *own* behaviors and efforts. These individuals are said to have an "internal" locus of control. They feel they are in control of their own destiny and their own fortunes, and, they believe that the outcomes of their ventures will be determined largely by their efforts and choices. This belief is closely related to conditions necessary for peak experiences, as discussed in Chapter 1.

Other people experience life very differently. These individuals believe that their fortunes, rewards, and misfortunes are controlled from outside by others, or by blind fate and circumstance. They are described as having an "external" locus of control.

Neither view is, of course, right or wrong in an absolute sense. All of us recognize that the outcomes of some undertakings are determined by forces outside our control, and the outcomes of other undertakings are dependent entirely upon our own behavior. The general tendency, however, to attribute the outcomes of important life events to either internal or external causes has profound implications for how, or indeed whether, we actually make commitments and take action. If we feel predominantly that the crucial events and rewards in our lives are controlled by forces outside ourselves, we tend to behave passively, like "pawns" in a larger game over which we can exert little or no real influence. We make genuine commitments only in areas in which we believe that we have some control over the outcomes.

Having an extremely external locus of control can have two devastating sets of consequences. First, it can make us vulnerable to pervasive and overwhelming feelings of powerlessness in stressful situations. We may become prone to the "helplessness hopelessness syndrome" that is the breeding ground for depression. Second, and perhaps more important, it tends to produce a set of "self-fulfilling prophecies" about our lives. When we believe that we are unable to control our lives, we fail to set goals, make plans, or participate in those decisions that may, in fact, represent the only possible way to establish some sense of order, control, and responsibility for our own lives. The concept of internal-external locus of control helps us to understand how we react to both opportunities and obstacles.

Effort Optimism

If we were all completely internal in our view of the world, when things went wrong we would be apt to be overwhelmed by guilt and self blame. This is no doubt one of the reasons that so many people are largely external in their attributions.

A more tempered and reasoned approach is what we call the *effort optimism hypothesis.* Basically, effort optimism is the belief that our personal efforts, if properly directed and energetically applied, can lead to some degree of positive control over our own lives and over the world in which we live. Anthropologists have said that effort optimism represents a belief system that has been a distinctive part of the American culture. It is the belief that hard work that is intelligently performed pays off for both the individual and the society most of the time in most situations. Effort optimism is not a Pollyanna approach to life but rather is an approach fueled by a reasoned faith and confidence.

People whose life experiences have seldom confirmed the hypothesis of effort optimism, either because of inadequate coping skills or because their world has, in fact, been capricious and dangerous beyond their capacity to cope, may tend to assess even moderate obstacles or problems as overwhelming. Such people may, therefore, fail to make commitments, to plan, or to reach out to grab opportunities. The effort optimism belief is an important part of commitment to planning and action.

Determining if a Goal is Worth Our Commitment

A goal is an endpoint, a desired state of affairs, even a state of being that arises out of our values. Commitments, however, come from a reasoned belief in our own capacities, a careful assessment of our opportunities, and reality testing of both.

How have self-fulfilling failures affected people you know?

How is effort optimism a part of your worldview?

How do you typically look at the causes of success and failure in your life?

Most of us have plenty of people around us to tell us what our goals and commitments should be. Few of us, however, take the time to think through the many considerations that are involved in setting our own goals and generating our own commitments. The result is that we seldom generate commitments. We are much more likely to generate a commitment around our own goals than around goals that are given to us, or forced on us, by others.

How do we know that a goal really is worth committing to? One way is to ask the following kinds of questions:

1. Did I choose this goal for myself rather than primarily to please others?
2. Am I ready to make a specific public commitment to this goal?
3. Am I willing to commit myself to a specific timetable to measure my progress toward this goal?
4. Are the first steps in my progress toward this goal fully within my own control, or am I waiting for someone else to give me permission or encouragement?
5. Have I really thought through the consequences of setting this goal? Do I know the price, and am I willing to pay it?
6. Does this goal arise out of values that I have carefully considered and have been willing to act upon in the past?
7. Can I visualize this goal clearly and see myself at the endpoint that it represents?
8. Have I thought out the short-term objectives or milestones along the way to this ultimate goal? Do they seem real and feasible?
9. Does commitment to this goal assume a high priority in my life right now? Am I willing to sacrifice other activities or to downgrade other priorities in my life?
10. Am I excited and eager to begin to work on this goal *now*?

When you can answer a firm yes to these kinds of questions you are probably ready to make a real commitment.

REALITY TESTING OUR GOALS

What are the reality considerations in making commitments? Everybody wants good things. If goal setting were nothing more than a grown-up version of writing a letter to Santa Claus, we would all be able to make out our lists with great ease. For goals to generate commitments, become part of our lives, and matter in shaping our futures, they must be reality based. This does not mean that our goals cannot be challenging or that they cannot stretch all of our potential resources. But unless our goals are tied to our own personal characteristics, abilities, and opportunities, they are likely to remain as dreams rather than become solid commitments. Appendix C contains an exercise that will help you to reality test, and if necessary revise, your goals in terms of your experiences and personal characteristics.

MOBILIZING AND MANAGING OUR PERSONAL RESOURCES

The most critical and difficult part of any program, plan, or project is the beginning. How often have all of us made elaborate preparations or plans for something and then failed to begin, failed to initiate the action to carry out the plan? It is important to discriminate between two kinds of planning activity, long-range plans and *action plans*. Long range plans unaccompanied by action plans, while important, can constitute a trap. Such plans can be subtly transformed into cop-outs. They can become a basis for self-deception. They can lead us to believe that we are at last doing something to transform our aspirations into realities, when in fact, we have simply found a more sophisticated form of procrastination.

Planning without action is procrastination. If we really have a plan as opposed to a pipedream, that plan must have one or more *action steps* that we can begin to implement now, on our own, without waiting, seeking someone else's permission, or otherwise having to postpone action. The best test for the existence of an action plan is to determine whether you can begin implementing it now. In this book we often couple the words action and planning. While planning without action is procrastination, action without planning is purposeless.

Action Planning

We earlier defined planning as intelligent cooperation with the inevitable. If we want to gain some degree of direction and control over our own lives, if we want to get out of the reactive, passive-aggressive way of living, we need to set goals, make commitments, and translate those goals into *action through planning*. A plan is a strategy through which we attain a goal. Since goals are usually ends that we hope to achieve over some considerable period of time, we need to develop a plan to guide our step-by-step, day-by-day actions as we move toward them.

How Do We Make Action Plans? We make action plans by breaking down our long-term goals into short-term objectives, or mini-goals, that we can begin to work on immediately. A mini-goal may be but one step in the process of attaining a long-term goal, but it is a step that we can take now. By setting and publicly affirming our mini-goals, we are making a contract or commitment to ourselves and others. We begin by:

1. Getting together with a partner or group or thinking our situation through alone.
2. Carefully studying our goals and long-range plans.
3. Thinking through possible immediate strategies to move closer to our goals.
4. Thinking through all of the steps in a strategy.
5. Organizing our resources to implement our strategy.

Writing Out Your Action Plan There are four parts to an action plan:

1. *The Mini-Goal Statement* The first part of an action plan is a statement of the short-term goal or mini-goal, to be pursued. That statement should be as specific as possible so that it can lead to the consideration of appropriate strategies.

2. *Action Strategies* The second part of an action plan is developing and describing the immediate strategy or approach that will be used to attain the mini-goal. For example, if our goals require further training or education, an action strategy will be needed to guide us in getting that training. If we need to pass some kind of entrance examination to enter training, then we may need an action strategy to prepare to meet that hurdle, and so on. An action strategy involves steps that are within our control. It is something that we can do for ourselves, and something that we can begin immediately.

3. *Action Objectives* The third part of an action plan is the action objective. It is what is to be accomplished, and it is worded explicitly so that we will know when it has been accomplished. For example, action objectives to prepare for a graduate or professional school entrance examination might be to (a) identify and obtain the appropriate study materials, and (b) demonstrate knowledge of the material by passing a sample or practice examination.

4. *Action Progress Records* The final part of an action plan involves the charting of progress within a specific timetable. With an action progress chart we mark off the attainment of specific objectives and set targets for the accomplishment of the next objectives. The action progress chart helps to encourage us by recording our movement toward goals and helps us be honest with ourselves about our motivation and commitment. Action progress charts should be made public to those with whom we live or work. By making our plans and progress public, we help ourselves to be accountable. Exercise 9.1 will take you through this process.

Managing Our Behaviors to Achieve Our Goals

Often when we fail to carry out our responsibilities or follow through on our commitments, we indulge in a little orgy of self-recrimination and blame. In the course of this generally unproductive exercise, we usually bewail our lack of willpower or self-control. Self-control to most of us means diligence, sacrifice, dedication, duty, responsibility, persistence, industriousness, self-denial, maturity, buckling down, strength of character, self-discipline, and gratification deferral. Just reading this list without skipping items requires self-control! More than 80 years ago psychologist William James wrote that all of our impressive terms for willpower and self-control could be reduced to one simple term: a good set of *habits*. Thinking of willpower and self-control as being simply the outgrowth of good habits takes some of the fun out of our feelings of self-righteousness and superiority when we do accomplish a difficult task. It has the tremendous advantage, however, of placing what we like to call willpower within the reach of all of us. A term that captures James's notion of building willpower through good habits is the concept of *self-management*.

What Is Self-Management? One of the serendipitous findings that has arisen out of the last 30 years of research on the behavior of people is the surprising fact that to some degree people can and do use reward and punishment to manage their own behavior. Self-management of behavior seems to require two necessary elements: *Awareness* of the specific behavior to be changed, and an understanding of the presence of a *contingency* between that behavior and some significant rewards or punishments in the present or near future.

What Is the BDA Method of Self-Management? As we just noted, one dramatic way to improve self-control is simply to increase self-awareness. An even more effective way to approach self-management involves what is sometimes called the BDA (or "Before, During, and After") method, which involves systematically monitoring, analyzing, and rewarding our own behavior as a means of acquiring good habits. Basically the BDA method of self-management consists of four steps as described in the following paragraphs.

1. **Pinpoint** The first step in the method is to select the target behavior or behaviors that you want to manage more effectively. The more specific and concrete your target behavior is, the easier and more effective your self-management program will be. You may choose target behaviors that you want to increase or strengthen (that is, "good habits") or target behaviors that you want to decrease (that is, "bad habits"). You must define a target behavior so that it is (a) recognizable, (b) quantifiable (countable), and (c) within your own control.

In this step, you must pinpoint or zero in on, an actual movement, statement, or act that you associate with a problem or goal. Whatever behavior you decide upon, remember that it must be something you *do;* that is, it must be observable and countable. Thus you wouldn't pinpoint things such as time spent, pounds gained or lost, or grades obtained. You must, instead, pinpoint your behaviors. For example, suppose that your problem involves discouraging statements that you say to yourself when you are faced with challenging situations or opportunities. You would pinpoint the exact things that you say to yourself or others in such situations, Such as, "I've never done that," "I couldn't do it, I'd be sure to fail," and "I'd make a fool of myself."

2. **Record** Every time you make any of these kinds of self or public statements record the incident. You may do this in a daily diary or even use a counter such as a golf scorekeeper. Every day, start from zero and count again. Then every evening before bedtime, chart the number for the day on a piece of graph paper.

> Monday—five can't do's
> Tuesday—three can't do's
> Wednesday—six can't do's etc.

3. **Alter** It is generally best to record for at least 10 days before trying to alter a behavior. By the time 10 days have passed, you will find that you are thoroughly aware of both the behavior and the situations in which it occurs. Sometimes this awareness alone produces a desirable change in the frequency of the target behavior. At the end of 10 days, however, a "systematic change" will provide an extra "push." The systematic change involves attaching a small but significant reward or punishment to the target behavior. For example, You might "fine" yourself a dollar for each time you say a "can't-do" statement and give the proceeds to a charity. You might reward yourself for a day without "can't-do" statements with a movie, a favorite TV show, or a small luxury that you've wanted.

4. **Try Again** If the first attempt at changing behavior doesn't work or seems to "wear out" in a few days, try again. Keep on recording and graphing your target behaviors. Try some new rewards or punishments.

Then take away the rewards or punishments. When you do so, you will see whether you have succeeded in acquiring, changing, or eliminating the target habit. Keep on recording for at least 2 weeks after eliminating the systematic rewards and punishments.

If you backslide after 2 weeks, resume the reward or punishment schedule and try again. If the rewards or punishments seem to be a crutch, try rewarding yourself for a week of reduced or eliminated "can't do's." Try planning a major reward for a week or month of successful change.

The BDA method, or self-management in general, is a way to actualize your good intentions in the service of your real goals and aspirations. "Is it a way to help yourself stay on track in meeting your goals?" It puts the control and responsibility for your own life back where they belong: within yourself. Self-management is the path to responsible freedom.

What is Self-Contracting? Both simple observation and systematic research have shown that an important way in which we can establish control over our own behavior and accomplish the things that we want to achieve is to make specific, *public commitments* to the tasks confronting us. This is the process of "self-contracting," and it is an important part of self-management. In a self-contracting situation, we make a firm, specific commitment to dedicate ourselves to a goal or task that has eluded us in the past because of procrastination, poor work habits, or some other problem in self-management.

Prior to writing a self-contract, we need to analyze the situation carefully and honestly so that we will be able to specify the task to be accomplished in a precise and comprehensive way. We also need to analyze our previous attempts to accomplish the task and think about the forces or problems in ourselves, others, and the situations that have prevented our successful accomplishment of the task. In addition, we need to think about and list the forces or factors within ourselves, others, and the situation that will help us accomplish the task. These forces may include our own good feelings about accomplishments, public commitments to others whose opinions and respect we value, specific rewards that we promise ourselves, positive consequences that flow from accomplishing the task, and so forth. We may make notes where necessary to remind us.

After completing this analysis, we would write out the self-contract in very specific and precise terms, citing the people, places, tasks, outcomes, and times involved. We would sign the contract and share it with one or more significant people whose respect and good opinions we value. We might actually ask them to witness the contract. By doing so, we would have made a firm public personal commitment. Exercise 9.2 will help you write a self-contract.

Managing Time

One of the most important factors influencing whether we will achieve the results we want from planning is how well we use time. No matter how well chosen our goals are or how carefully crafted our plans are, they will generally not amount to much unless we make a careful investment of our time and energy in them. In a very real sense, time is not only our most important resource, it is our *only* resource. As living beings, time is really all we have. When we run out of time, we run out of everything.

Why Can't We Save Time? There is a popular song by the late Jim Croce that begins, "If I could save time in a bottle." This thought has been echoed by everyone at some time or other. Time, or lack of time, is the element that plagues all of us all of our lives. As children at play, the call for bed comes all too soon. As students, we are faced with the term paper that has to be completed for tomorrow's class. On the job, there are due dates, travel schedules, weekly meetings, annual reports, and a thousand other commitments that have to be met on time.

If all the hours lost in waiting to get started, waiting for transportation, waiting for phone calls, or simply waiting for others to be ready could be saved in that bottle and poured out when needed, think how easily most of our tasks could be accomplished. Time, unfortunately, cannot be stored, because it isn't tangible. What we experience as time is a form of measurement. Seasons, years, months, days, hours, and minutes are only the measurements and milestones that we have created to control and organize the activities and actions in our lives.

Managing time really involves maintaining effective control of the flow and direction of our lives. Often we seem to be playing catch up; we feel out of control, unable to order or organize our lives. But time *is* controllable. We can't arrange to save time or borrow time, but we can learn to manage what we have. How well we manage time ultimately determines how well we live our lives. Our greatest enemy in managing time is our tendency to want to "keep busy," to go through the motions, doing things in a mindless and ritualistic way without thinking of results or priorities.

Why Do We "Run Out" of Time? All of us lose, or rather *misuse,* time. Each of us has one or more personal habits or idiosyncrasies that result in wasted time, time that we would like to have used differently. Surprisingly, however, people who have studied time management problems in business, industry, and education have concluded that up to 80% of the time wasted by busy people in all walks of life can be accounted for by a relatively few categories of activity. More important, most of these time-wasting habits can be eliminated or at least significantly reduced when we become aware of them and committed to eliminating them.

According to these experts, most of the really significant time wasters that afflict busy people both at work and in other parts of their lives center around the following activities:

1. Trivial telephone calls
2. Unneeded meetings
3. Unexpected and uninvited visitors
4. Unnecessary conversation
5. Responding to phony crises or emergencies
6. Procrastination
7. Failure to say "No!"
8. Routine and unproductive trivia

When we recognize that most of the really flagrant time wasters in our lives involve commonplace daily activities that are actually easily controllable, we can begin to eliminate them and to "save time" that can be used to advance our highest priority goals.

SUMMARY

In this chapter we have examined the process of generating commitment to our goals, reality testing our goals and then taking action to bring them to fruition. We have also looked at the process of mobilizing our most important resources—that is, those that lie within ourselves—on behalf of our most cherished aspirations.

CAREER PLANNING 109

Exercise 9.1
Action Planning

Step 1: In the action planning guide that follows step 3, state one of your career actualization goals.

Step 2: Think of immediate strategies for achieving your goal. For some goals this is more easily done than for others. You can use three resources:

1. What you have thought of doing in this situation, or what you have successfully done in similar situations in the past.
2. What actions you have observed other people taking in similar situations.
3. Suggestions given by others who have special expertise or experience.

Step 3: Identify at least three specific actions you will take to implement your goal. Ask yourself these six questions, translated into specific terms applicable to your strategy:

1. By doing what?
2. How often?
3. For how long?
4. Where?
5. With whom?
6. How will I know it is accomplished?

Action Planning Guide

Specific Goal	Immediate Action Strategies	Action Objectives
	The Approach I Must Take to Move Toward My Goal	Specific Actions I Must Take
To pass the foreign services officer test, (pass the CIA test?)	turn 21, sign up, study? somehow, take it until I pass	**By doing what?** Studying **How often?** once a week **For how long?** however long it takes — about 1 yr **Where?** home, library, before **With whom?** phone Dad **How will I know it is accomplished?** pass

Step 4: For one week observe the progress you make in your action plan. To do this, you must first decide whether you have taken appropriate action toward your goal (discovery phase); second, record and chart your progress (recording phase); third, evaluate your data (evaluation phase).

Design a chart to record the progress you make in taking actions toward your goals.

Action Progress Record

When Set	Objectives Target Date	Date Accomplished	If Not Accomplished, Why?

not really something I am working on taking action towards right now

Evaluate your progress chart in the light of the goals, strategies, and objectives you have set. Did you meet the objectives you set for yourself?

Exercise 9.2

Self-Contract

Below is a sample form of a self-contract. Work through the criteria below to write a contract relevant to one of your goals or one that has been especially difficult for you to work on.

It must be *conceivable*——capable of being put into words.

It must be *believable* to the person setting it.

It must be *achievable*.

It must be *controllable*.

It must be *measurable* in time and accomplishment.

It must be *desirable,* something "I want to do."

It must be stated with *no alternatives* (no either-or, yes, but).

It must be *growth facilitating* to self and/or others.

I want to:

pass the foreign services officer exam

Signed

Witnessed

CHAPTER 10

Taking Care of Yourself, So That You Can Take Care of Business

CHAPTER OVERVIEW

This chapter helps you to examine three highly related concepts: self-care, social support, and balance. Self-care is the process of keeping yourself in the best possible shape physically, mentally, and spiritually, which is always important but is especially so when you are going through a stressful and challenging time in your life. The second concept, social support, refers to the network of friends and family with whom you have surrounded yourself who can provide you with affirmations and enhance your feelings about yourself during stressful times. Balance, the third concept, is the ongoing process of striving to maintain a proper perspective on all that you are doing. This chapter will help you develop specific strategies to take better care of yourself, make appropriate use of friends, and, in the process, learn not to let the demands of one task get the best of you when you really must stay involved with many.

Listen for a moment to the words of John and Sharon as they describe how self-care and social support are lacking in their lives:

"I feel so burned out on all this resume' writing and informational interviewing and constantly feeling like I need to search the Web for another opening. I haven't been sleeping well. I feel too rushed to fix a decent meal, and I can't tell you the last time I went out with friends." —John

"Every time I bring up going into the Peace Corps to my friend, she says things like, 'How can you even think about going into the Peace Corps and being overseas? You can't even find your way to the grocery store' or 'You are so naive to think you can do anything to change other people's lives. What have you done to change your own.'" —Sharon

The career and life planning process requires work. It is also a process that many people experience as stressful. It requires putting yourself on the line to be accepted or rejected. The process itself can be time consuming, and it rarely comes at a time when you have nothing else to do. Thus, while career and life planning can be very challenging and exhilarating, it can also be exhausting, both physically and emotionally. It is vitally important that you think about how you are caring for yourself and what support you are getting from others to help you through this process.

THE IMPORTANCE OF SELF-CARE

Self-care is a relatively new term that reflects a growing awareness of our need to take responsibility for our own health and wellness. While the last generation was reaping the benefits of a highly advanced, and some thought omnipotent, medical establishment, the present generation is seeing its shortcomings as well. We are learning that medical care has its place but that there is no substitute for an active approach to our own health and well being. A generation ago people often viewed health in a one-dimensional and rather passive manner: You get sick, you go to the doctor, the doctor gives you medicine, and hopefully you get well. There was little appreciation that the lifestyle that was lived had anything to do with the health of the individual.

While these attitudes are clearly changing, numerous influences in our society still promote unhealthy living. For example, advertisements still link cigarette smoking with being cool, having friends, and relaxing despite the fact that we know that smoking is a leading cause of suffering and death in the United States. Similarly, drinking is portrayed as a way to get close to friends, control stress, and celebrate important occasions. Yet we know that alcohol contributes to a host of medical problems ranging from cancer to diabetes. In the same women's magazines that have heart-wrenching articles about the eating disorder anorexia we see advertisements featuring malnourished-looking super models and advertisements for fat-laden, tempting desserts. Thus, while our society is making some positive changes to enhance our health and well-being, there remain many conflicting messages.

People today are also recognizing more and more that health is not restricted to the physical part of our lives. Compelling research is showing us that there is a mind, body, spirit connection and that if one area of our life is out of sync, the others more than likely are following suit. Whereas much of current medical practice is designed to treat an already sick person, the emphasis of self-care is prevention, trying to live in such a way that we can avoid the need for remedial treatment through our active self-care. The self-care model places a great deal of responsibility on the individual to become knowledgeable and aware of his or her own needs. It calls on each of us to be informed about harmful and healthful ways of living.

The issue of our spiritual health and its effects on our physical health is a particularly recent awareness. Until recently, most authors in the health and wellness field shied away from the issue of spirituality fearing that the concept would be interpreted as formal religion or some fringe New Age movement. Today, however, spirituality has become a mainstream topic. Often broader than a formal religious affiliation, spirituality involves recognition of the importance of finding meaning and mission in our daily lives and feeling connected in a broader way to nature and the universe. Not only does this connection to others and our planet feed our spiritual well-being; it is being shown to have important mental and physical health benefits as well. In our work with individuals who are struggling to find their vocational selves, we are witnessing a growing sense of awareness of the spirit. We see individuals wanting their vocation to be one of mission and meaning rather than simply a means to receiving a paycheck.

Like physical and spiritual health, mental or emotional health is also clearly linked to our overall wellness. We know that when people feel depressed, anxious, sad, angry, guilty, and so forth and do not understand or express these feelings, their physical health suffers. Many of us have come from homes and families that were not emotionally healthy, and thus we have not had role models for appropriate emotional understanding and expression. This does not mean that we cannot change our patterns of dealing with emotion; it just means that it will take some work to do so.

The Role of Self-care in Effective Career Planning

Why are we writing about the importance of eating right and exercising in a book about career planning? We believe that in order to make truly good choices and have the energy you need to conduct an effective career planning process, you must be healthy in body and mind. We believe that your body, mind, and spirit are all connected and that if any one of these areas is being ignored, the others will suffer. Here are just a few of the many comments made by people we have worked with over the years that support our viewpoint:

"I was stressing out so much about getting a job that I really didn't think about how I was taking care of myself. I must have gained 20 pounds during my job hunt, and by the time I actually got an interview, I was feeling fat and really down on myself. I know that was reflected in my interviews."

"I know that these things are all related, but I feel like I am in a vicious cycle. The more stressed out I feel about my future career, the less likely I am to really get out and exercise. The less I exercise, the more depressed I feel. The more depressed I feel, the less likely I am to go out and network with people and do the kinds of things I know I need to do to find a job I will like."

Remember that exploring occupations and thinking about your future career can be stressful. Keeping yourself in optimal health through self-care activities can greatly aid you in this process. In the following sections we will ask you to take an inventory of your emotional, spiritual, and physical health and think about ways of enhancing your life in all three of these important areas.

We will discuss ways of taking responsibility for your own health, the first step of which is developing an awareness of the patterns in your life that are health enhancing and those that are health defeating. It is only with such an awareness that you will be able to begin to change those patterns that are hindering your health. After helping you to develop such an awareness, we will offer some suggestions of ways you might increase your wellness. Fully realizing and respecting the fact that we are each unique, we offer these suggestions with the intent that you simply try them out to see how they fit your own needs.

Physical Self-Care

In the past many people seemed confident that medicine could solve their major health problems. Today we are becoming increasingly aware of the role that diet and exercise both play in mental and physical health. Improper diet has been linked with almost every major disease, including cancer, heart disease, and strokes. Diet has also been linked to stress and mental illness. Thus, it is critical to become aware of how your diet may be harming and helping you.

Given today's increased focus on health, most Americans know that a healthy diet is high in fruits, vegetables, and fiber and low in saturated fats. And yet research continually indicates that even when we know what we should be eating, we tend to make poor choices. We tend to eat foods high in fat, processed foods, and foods with high sugar contents. Very few Americans actually get the recommended daily requirements for fruits, vegetables, and fiber.

As we noted earlier, the first step in changing any part of your self-care routine is to become aware of your strengths and weaknesses in that area. Thus, we encourage you to think about your diet. We recommend that you keep a diary of your food intake for a 1 week period. What are you putting into your body to nourish you? Analyze your dietary intake to determine what you are doing that is healthy and where you might improve. Some questions to think about as you conduct this self-analysis are:

- Are you getting enough protein in your diet?
- How about carbohydrates?
- Are you eating too much sugar, salt?
- Are you eating too much processed food?
- How much fat are you consuming, and what kinds of fat do you primarily consume?
- Are you getting the vitamins and minerals you need?
- How about water? Are you replenishing your body with the water that is so vital to your overall health?

By conducting this type of diet audit, you might find that you are doing a lot right. You will also likely find areas in which you can improve. If you find that your diet is not what you want it to be for optimal self-care, you need to develop an understanding of the purpose your poor food choices serve for you and then develop action steps to change your detrimental food routines. Understanding the "why" behind your choices is important, because oftentimes your choices are clues to broader emotional and spiritual issues in your life. Sometimes, the "why" is simple: You are rushed and don't take the time to think about what you are eating, someone else is preparing your meals and you feel that you have little control over them; you had simply lost track of the importance of your diet, and this reminder is enough to put you back on track.

Other times, the "why" is more complex. Food intake may have become associated with other psychological and spiritual issues in your life. Perhaps you are under stress, feeling anxious, fearful, or depressed, and eat in unhealthy ways because you perceive food as being a comfort and a way of avoiding pain. Perhaps food is taking the place of other forms of security that you need. Oftentimes, the foods we choose during stressful times are not ones that would be considered healthy. Rather, they are comfort foods: high in fats and sugars. Although these foods may provide immediate relief from pain, take our mind off worries, or relieve boredom, they do not nourish our bodies and improve our well-being. Often, in fact, they have just the opposite effect.

Changing food routines is not an easy thing to do. Some of us have developed these routines over many years. Thus, be gentle with yourself. Take baby steps. Change one thing at a time and learn to integrate that change into your life. If your first step is to eat more fruits and vegetables, make a conscious effort to buy your favorite fruits and vegetables at the grocery store so that they are readily available to you. Integrate these changes into your daily routine, and note how they make you feel about yourself.

In addition to food, exercise is another critical element in physical self-care. We know that exercise creates stronger bodies, reduces the chance of disease, reduces stress, increases mental acuteness, improves circulation, increases stamina, and promotes better sleep, lessens depression, promotes higher self-esteem, and lessens use of drugs, alcohol, and high-fat foods. But again, even though we know that exercise is important to our overall well being, the majority of us live as if these overwhelming data do not exist. We have become a nation of sedentary individuals. Our work lives have increasingly put us in front of computer terminals using our minds as opposed to using our bodies in our day- to-day work. Survey after survey indicate that Americans are overweight and under exercised. We take cars or public transportation rather than walking ; we insist on parking close to our destinations; we insist on remote controls for our televisions so that we do not have to get up off the couch to change the channel; we orchestrate our lives in ways that allow us to expend the least possible energy.

The following are just a few of the excuses we use to avoid exercise:

- I don't have time.
- I don't have the money to buy equipment or join a health club.
- When I get through with school, I am going to start a new routine.
- I have no friends who are interested in joining me in sports.
- I have to lose some weight before I would be caught dead in exercise gear.

As with diet, more than likely, you've used some of these excuses yourself, the first step to change is awareness. The following method will help you to become more aware of your exercise habits. Over the next few weeks make note of exactly how many times you exercise. You might put a star on your calendar each time you exercise to help you keep track of your schedule. Note the kind of exercise you did and how long you did it. Also note any difference in how you felt or slept following exercise. Then analyze your data to determine:

- How much exercise you are getting.
- What types of exercise you are getting.
- How you felt when you exercised and when you didn't; and
- Whether you slept better, felt less depressed or stressed, and so forth, after exercise.

If you have been a sedentary individual, you will experience more success in adding exercise to your life if you start slowly and reinforce yourself for small steps. Exercise will eventually become reinforcing in and of itself—you will feel better and look better, and you will miss your exercise routine on days when you are unable to exercise. But at the start exercise may not be reinforcing. Thus, think of ways to make it more so. You might, for example, exercise with a friend or buy yourself something special if you stick to your exercise goals for a week.

Mental or Emotional Self-Care

Particularly during times of stress, such as when you are making important life decisions (like finding a meaningful career!), it is important to audit your mental health. You may be experiencing a host of emotional or psychological issues, such as anxiety, the "blues," mood swings, irritability, or becoming discouraged easily. Having these emotions can be quite normal, and it is important to not be hard on yourself if you are experiencing them during this time. This is a time to be gentle with yourself and remind yourself of your good qualities.

One effective way of reminding yourself of your good qualities is to make a list of your most positive assets. Your list might include, for example, "I am a competent person," "I am well liked," "I have a creative mind," "People trust me," and "People have told me they view me as a person of integrity." Post your list in a place where you will see it frequently.

Remind yourself of these traits daily. Such an exercise has been shown to be very effective in driving away negative thinking. Similarly, making a list of everything you are grateful for can put the struggle of your career planning in a different perspective. Your list might include, "I am grateful for my health, for my good friends and family, for being privileged enough to go to college, for having a warm home and plenty to eat, and for feeling stimulated and challenged intellectually." When you really consider how much you have that you can be grateful for, the struggles of your job search or career transition will become the small stuff.

Although feeling some anxiety or depression during times of stress will often not be a problem, things that those emotions drive us to do can become a real problem. Oftentimes, people find that anxiety and depression lead them to self-defeating behaviors, the behaviors that keep us from doing, being, and growing in the ways we would like. Self-defeating behaviors are constantly whispering in our ear telling us we can't do something or be something.

Psychologist Albert Ellis developed a model for conceptualizing how a stressful event, such as a career transition, affects our feelings and how these feelings in turn affect the way we act in situations. Called the ABC method for analyzing responses to a challenging situation, it involves consideration of the *activating* situation (the "A" in ABC); the *beliefs* (the "B" in ABC), both rational and irrational, values, and expectations that we hold and the things we say to ourselves; *consequences* of the situation (the "C" in ABC), or what we feel and the action we take.

It is important to recognize how much control we have of our beliefs and the things we say to ourselves. Although situations happen, the consequence of those situations is very much a product of our beliefs and self-statements. Consider the following two cases:

John is trying to decide on a college major. He has pretty much decided he wants to major in chemistry and perhaps go on to medical school. He has just gotten an exam back, however, on which he received the lowest B in the class. He starts believing that he can't do the work, that he is not cut out for medical school, that perhaps even college is not for him. He feels depressed and tells his parents that he wants to drop out of college for a while.

Merissa has much the same goal as John. She's in the same chemistry class, and she gets even a lower grade than John does. She tells herself: I need to apply myself more. I partied the night before this test, and I knew I wasn't prepared. I know this grade doesn't reflect my true ability. I need to apply myself more, but I can do it.

While John and Merissa's situations were very much the same, their beliefs and self-statements were very different and led to very different outcomes. John's beliefs could be labeled self-defeating; they served to stop him from reaching an important goal or, at the least, slowed his progress.

There are numerous ways in which we defeat ourselves. The three self-defeating behaviors that we have seen most frequently in our work with students doing career planning, are avoidance, impulsivity, and irrational beliefs. These are illustrated in the following cases. Do you see yourself in any of them?

Avoidance: *Jason knew he needed to get going with his job search. Graduation was just 3 weeks away, and he had done nothing. He knew what he needed to do, but somehow other things always got in the way. He had planned to make an appointment for this week at the career center on campus, but he ended up going out of town to help a friend instead.*

Impulsivity: *Jamaica was feeling anxious about her career choice. Even though her parents told her to take her time and make a good decision, Jamaica really wanted to be set in a major. She* *felt that picking a major, any major, would make her feel better. But which one to pick? She went to a party and started talking to a woman who had just transferred to Fisheries and Wildlife. The woman seemed so happy and resolved. Jamaica had always kind of liked the outdoors. The next day she declared the same major.*

Irrational beliefs: *Whenever Angela tried to think about choosing her major, she would freeze. She would tell herself, "Whatever decision I make I will need to stick to for the rest of my life." She would remind herself of all the bad decisions she had made in her life. She remembered her dad's voice as he lectured her about her ineffective decision making style. She became more and more anxious and less able to do the work she needed to do to move ahead in the career planning process.*

Awareness as you might have guessed, is the first step in changing self-defeating behavior. You need to recognize what you are doing that may be keeping you from your goals so that can make the changes you need to make. We have found that the best way to become aware of what you are doing is to listen to the voice within—your self-talk. What are you telling yourself about your career planning? Listen hard for self-defeating thoughts, and try to alter those that you hear. Self-defeating thoughts are like audiotapes that are being played over and over again. Reprogram your tape with positive affirmations and self enhancing rather than defeating dialogue. You may find the following lines helpful for altering your self-defeating thoughts:

"I have made other important decisions in my life. I can make this one too."

"This decision isn't the last career decision I will ever make. I want to make a good decision, but it doesn't have to be perfect. People change careers all the time."

"I am going to take one small step today toward getting clearer on what I want to do—Then I am going to reinforce myself for making that step."

"I am not alone. There are a lot of people who care about me and can help me."

Remember that it is normal to feel some emotional distress, anxiety or depression during this time of transition But also bear in mind that you can take control of those feelings and stop them from creating consequences that you do not want.

Spiritual Self-Care

Often it is at times of transition that issues of meaning come to the fore. Transition, such as entering the work force, marriage, divorce, or the death of an important person in our lives, tend to push the issue of meaning into our daily awareness. We get a lot of our meaning and identity from our relationships, work, the important roles we play in our lives (e.g., being a sister, parent, or best friend), or our religious beliefs—the very things that transitions affect. When these things are altered, we may be left feeling not quite sure of who we are and what the meaning or purpose of our lives really is. We may start asking ourselves questions like:

Who am I?

Why am I here?

What is my purpose, my mission, in this world?

How do I find my place?

Where am I going?

What do I want?

What will I ultimately find satisfying?

Finding meaning and mission—that is, nurturing our spiritual selves—is a very personal journey. It is a journey of self-reflection that can be extremely gratifying. It can also be scary and hard. A large part of this journey involves looking within ourselves and trusting what we find there, trusting our own feelings, values, and heart. Many people avoid this journey altogether. They get caught up in the day-to-day details of life and never really question the big picture of why they are here and what difference they want their lives to make in the world. Socrates said, "The unexamined life is not worth living." We tend to agree. We can say with certainty that the unexamined life is often less rewarding and fulfilling than a life of purpose and meaning.

There are a host of ways to get started in the process of self-reflection, of finding meaning and purpose in life. The following are two of our favorites. We hope they will help you to focus on what you find most meaningful.

The first method is to close your eyes and picture yourself at 80 years of age. You are sitting on a front porch in the fall. It is about dusk, and the last traces of the sun are leaving the western sky. You start reflecting back on your life. All of the various things you have been involved in—your work, relationships, travel, the time you have spent building a home, the status you have achieved in your profession—all of these things come rushing through your mind. You sift through it all, and you ask yourself, "What, out of all of this, has really been important and meaningful in my life? What is the thing that I most value?"

The second method is to think about those activities that you get so caught up in that you totally lose track of time. Perhaps you were creating something, reading certain kinds of books or travel brochures, or working for a social cause you feel strongly about. There are important clues in this information about the things that you value. And it is information that can greatly inform your career planning process.

Social Support: Developing a Powerful Network

> We all need somebody to lean on.
> I just might have a problem that you'll understand,
> We all need somebody to lean on.
> —Bill Withers, Interior Music Corporation, 1972/73

A healthy support system is important at all times in our lives, but at times of transition it is crucial. A social support system can provide emotional support, help us master emotional burdens, provide us with tangible help, or offer guidance on handling difficult situations. It can be made up of friends and family; it also can include people who have shared similar life experiences to ours and thus provide answers to some of our life dilemmas. Further, our support system can include resources; such things as libraries, religious organizations, pets, or hobbies.

With each new venture, our support system may need to be reorganized or expanded. Especially at times of transition, we need to identify our existing support system and access additional members.

The need for a support system is not an issue of dependence versus independence. Although many times weakness is associated with dependence and strength is associated with independence, we all need our social support systems. There are times in our lives when we may be independent, times when we may be dependent, and times when we may be both. The goal is to achieve a balance between the two and strive for interdependence.

Think about various needs you have in your life. Many people mention things like acceptance, self-esteem, personal connections, work connections, stimulation and challenge, role models, guidance, comfort, and assurance. How many of these needs do you have, and what support do you have in meeting them? Exercise 10.1 provides a visual way for you to explore the nature and extent of your social support network. Take some time now to complete Exercise 10.1.

Maintaining Balance in Life

When we look carefully at our lives, we often realize that, for one reason or another, things are out of balance. A task has presented more obstacles than we anticipated, or we have taken on too many tasks, and we find ourselves overwhelmed. We reach the weekend and think we will catch up, but we don't. Soon we realize, that we not only are behind, but our lives are out of balance! While it may have been necessary to take on the tasks that we did, we know we have to work hard to get our lives back in balance. We also know that doing so may be stressful. Indeed, we know there may be serious consequences to our health, our relationships, and so forth, for living our lives in this way. We know it isn't right, it isn't even efficient, but all too often it seems to be the only way. Striving to find balance is a constant preoccupation for most of us. Indeed striving to find balance is more the norm than actually finding it.

It is important to develop a scheme for periodically looking at ourselves and quickly doing two things: identifying what has us out of balance, and taking steps to reestablish a better sense of balance. In the best of worlds, we would learn to do these things as easily and naturally as our body brings itself back into balance physiologically. If only we could control our thoughts and actions in a similar manner when under stress.

We obviously can't do that, but we can take the following steps. First, we can accept that we will constantly strive to attain balance but that we must live with the fact that balance is an ideal often not achieved. That doesn't mean we should give up striving for it, but it does mean that we should not be too hard on ourselves when we don't always find ourselves where we want to be. Life is a struggle, but it should be a pleasant struggle; and striving to meet the demands of the life we create for ourselves should be strenuous but satisfying.

Second, we can strive to find personal satisfaction, while not allowing our life to get out of control, and work to not let it get the best of us. This may mean for example, maintaining an attitude that nothing is so important that it should damage your health. When a cold, a pulled muscle, a stressful or demanding week at school, a few days of snow or rain, or particularly bad news of some sort throws us off our schedule, we can't get discouraged. We need to make a new plan. Maintaining balance requires a constant plan! We must accept that and make it part of the challenge—a challenge that energizes us. Even highly successful people find themselves out of balance during particular periods of their lives. No matter who we are, responding to the demands of a new job or starting any new venture may upset us . The underlying message is that there is always a need to bring ourselves back into balance. You might say this is a long-range goal, since immediate goals may make balance unreasonable for a time.

So how do you go about attaining this goal? What do you do when you don't get enough sleep or exercise or you find yourself always with people and never alone (as may be the case when you turn completely into finding work for yourself)?

Think back to times in your life when you clearly were out of sorts, and think about how you managed to regain your center. Perhaps there was a person you talked to, a place you went, an activity you turned to, or even something quite unconventional that made the difference. Now, while you are centered, assess whether that strategy would work again as you surely will be out of balance still another time.

Many people find that turning to friends is their first recourse for regaining balance. It is important to note that not all friends are equally good at helping in this regard. Some may be struggling themselves and not in a position to do anything more than commiserate. You may end up feeling like you have to help *them*! Other friends may seem to always be calm and collected and respond in creative ways. They are the ones you should turn to.

You have options about what to do when you are out of balance. Use the ones that work best for you, so that your time out of balance is minimized. You don't want to be too off kilter when you approach the task of looking for work, since, if you are like most people, being uncentered probably doesn't bring out the best in you.

SUMMARY

The purpose of this chapter was to give you an opportunity to think about how you take care of yourself. Self-care is a lifelong skill. If you start developing good self-care habits, attending to your body, mind, and spirit, these habits will serve you well for a lifetime.

Building an effective network of friends and colleagues as a support system is an important part of self-care. It, too, is a lifelong skill and an ongoing process. By periodically examining your support system, you may find that you need to add to it. It is important to put time and energy into developing a healthy and affirming support system.

Your social support network can help when you are striving to find balance. Balance is necessary for your health, and health is necessary as you negotiate the many stressful transitions that will continue to come your way.

Exercise 10.1

Analyzing Your Support System

This exercise is designed to help you take a look at your own support system and see how it is meeting your needs. In it, you will be asked to draw a visual model of your social support system. Below is a diagram to guide you as you develop your model.

Part 1: Creating Your Model

1. At the center of a blank sheet of paper, draw a symbol to represent yourself. It can be simply, a circle with "Self" written inside.
2. Next think about the significant people in your life. They could be friends, relatives, coworkers, religious figures, a spouse or partner, and so forth.
3. Now draw the symbol for each of these people on your paper. Use a larger symbol for these people who have a larger impact (either positive or negative) on your life and a smaller symbol for people with a smaller impact. Draw the symbol close to your "self" symbol if you frequently see this person or connect with him or her by, for example, phone or e-mail. If you rarely see the person, draw the symbol close to the perimeter of the page. To keep track of the people your symbols represent, note their first names or initials within the symbols. It is sometimes helpful to also indicate whether these people are male or female.
4. Next, connect each symbol to your symbol with two lines, one representing energy you put out and the other representing energy coming in to you. If the energy is positive, use a straight solid line. If it is neutral, use a dashed line. If it is negative, use a squiggly line. You may be surprised to realize that you are putting a lot of positive energy into a relationship but receiving only neutral energy in return. You may find that there are people with whom you continue to interact even though both the energy going out and that coming in are neutral or even negative.
5. Now write a few words next to each set of lines indicating the needs each particular individual meets in your life (e.g., acceptance, self esteem, personal connections, work connections, stimulation and challenge, role models, guidance, comfort, assurance, tangible help).

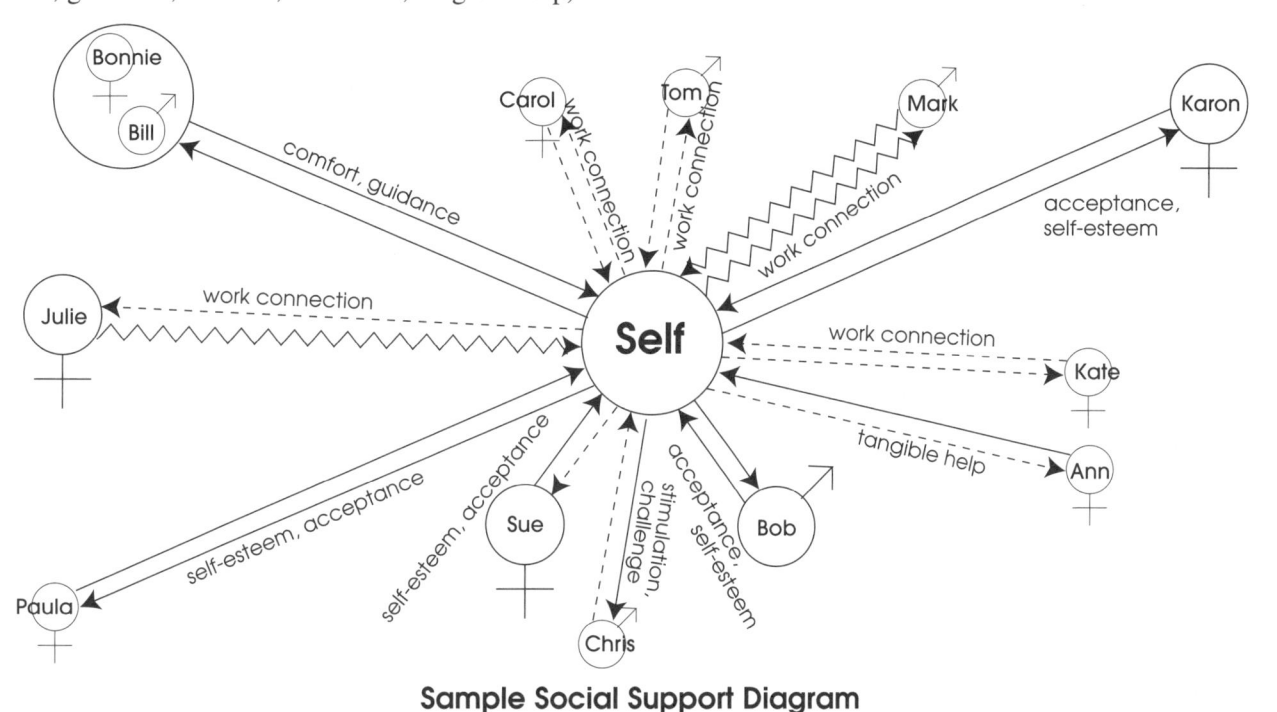

Sample Social Support Diagram

Part 2: Examining Your Support System

The model you have drawn provides important information about your support system. Carefully examine your model as you respond to the following questions.

1. In looking at the number of people symbolized on your model, do you feel that you have sufficient people who can meet your needs for social support? If not, in what areas do you need to shore up your network? What needs do you have that could use more support?

   Yes, I have many ppl that care about me and I aren't utilize them enough

2. Look at the lines you have drawn to depict the energy you expend and receive. Are there any themes that you can draw from them? For example, are you getting and giving positive energy most of the time, or do your relationships seem unbalanced in some way? Examine your individual relationships. In the spaces below, jot down some of the themes you see and insights you gain when you examine the lines that flow to and from your symbol on the model.

   give a lot, get a lot but don't ask for it enough

3. Examine the size of the symbols and their distances from your symbol. What do you see? Are some of the people you consider to be positive and important to you also people that you don't get to spend much time with? In the spaces below, note the patterns you detect in the size and distance of the symbols.

   Yes, I don't see very many people like good friends from hs and the fam. I talk to them a bit, & should more.

4. Based on the analysis you have just made, what changes, if any, would you like to make in your social support network?

   Talk to friends more often, be more patient with mom and dad

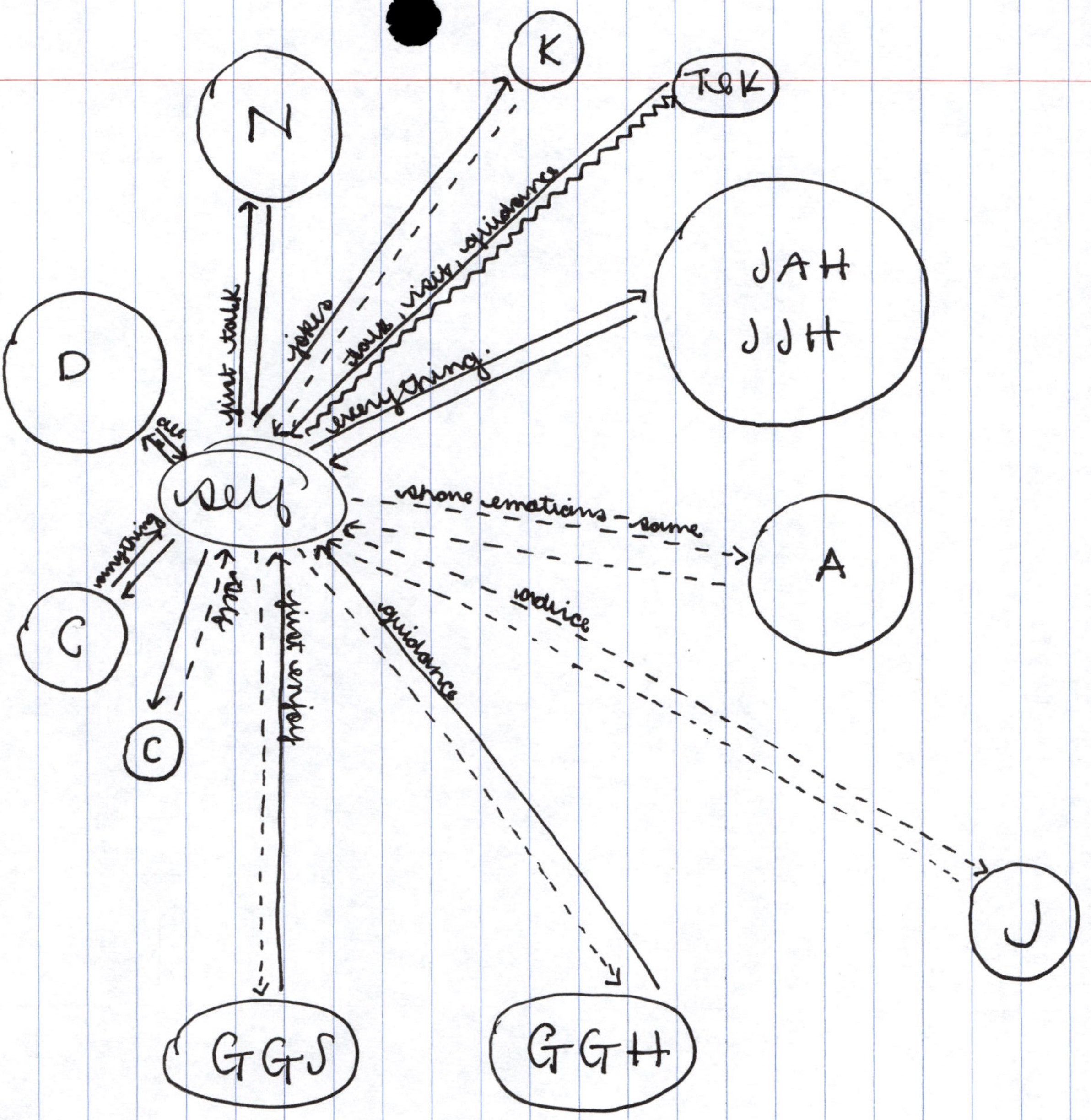

N
K
T&K
JAH
JJH
D
self
just talk
jokes
talk, visits, guidance
everything.
phone emotions—same
A
advice
guidance
just enjoy
self
anything
C
C
GGS
GGH
J

CHAPTER 11
Confronting Obstacles

CHAPTER OVERVIEW

This chapter discusses ways to deal with the obstacles that will inevitably confront you as you pursue your career goals. Effective problem-solving processes are described, as are ways to understand, assess, and manage the stresses you will encounter as you move toward your goals.

How are you dealing with obstacles in your life right now?

A word that is frequently used to describe effective successful people is resilience, the ability to bounce back after taking a blow. Resilience is probably more important to attaining a life of achievement and goal attainment than intellectual brilliance and raw ambition put together. Resilience is just as important to a career as it is to a nose tackle or a prize fighter.

The proverbial road to hell may well be paved with good intentions, but the road to success is usually full of potholes. Almost anything worth going after lies beyond one or more obstacles.

Fortunately, most of the obstacles that block our efforts to reach our goals are amenable to problem solving. Unfortunately, many human beings react ineffectively to problem-solving situations. At times they may react emotionally with blaming or guilt-evoking responses that accomplish nothing. At other times, they may jump at presumed solutions to yet undefined problems.

Sometimes we are paralyzed in the face of obstacles and withdraw in fear of failure. But obstacles are an inevitable part of life. No matter how thorough and well thought out our plans are, it is almost certain that we will encounter unforeseen obstacles that must be overcome.

Problem Solving

Probably the most important area of human thinking involves problem solving. Schools try to prepare students to think critically and to be successful problem solvers. Employers constantly tell us that they are looking for good problem solvers. Unfortunately, people who can consistently react to problems in rational, careful, and systematic ways seem to be the exception rather than the rule.

One of the reasons for the relative scarcity of effective problem-solving behavior is that there is no single, easy to define, and simple to teach general problem-solving skill or technique. Instead, problem solving is a complex process that involves many separate and discrete skills. Further, problem solving has a strong emotional component in addition to its more rational aspects.

We know that much of the difficulty that people have in solving problems stems from relatively few sources. First, people tend to distort or deny crucial factors in themselves and in problem situations because of the strong emotional components that tend to be involved. Second, people tend to move precipitously to "grab" solutions without thoroughly examining and analyzing the problem situation. Finally, people tend to stifle their creative abilities and respond mechanically and in old ways to new challenges and opportunities.

What Is Involved in Problem Solving?

There are several distinct aspects to any effective problem solving process. We must *locate* the problem. We must *define* the problem. We must *find* and *examine* alternative solutions to the problem. We must *implement* one or more of those solutions. Finally, we must *evaluate* the results of our solution. Each of these functions involves one or more specific steps, and each of these steps requires its own set of skills, understandings, and attitudes. In the following sections, we examine these functions and some of the specific steps involved.

Locating the Problem The first phase of the problem-solving process involves developing an awareness and understanding of the problem situation. Although this phase sounds simple, it doesn't occur naturally and automatically. Many people are not even really aware of what a problem is. A problem is an *obstacle* that prevents us from meeting a need or reaching a goal. The first indication of the existence of a problem is the inability to attain a desired goal. The symptom of the presence of a problem is always *frustration*.

In this sense, then, all problems have an emotional aspect. Whenever we are frustrated, we experience some degree of emotional arousal. Consider a hot day in summer. You have just come from 3 hours of exercise in the hot sun. You put your last coins in a soft drink machine that malfunctions. You very quickly experience emotional arousal, the extent of which is likely to be clear to any interested observer.

Although it may seem that people who feel frustration would immediately engage in problem-solving behavior, this is not the typical reaction. The reaction of many people in many situations to frustration is immediate and explosive rather than rational and systematic. One very common reaction to frustration is aggression. When we are frustrated, we tend to strike out at some other person, group, or organization—to "kick the Coke machine," so to speak. When we vent our emotions on someone who is conveniently available, we may feel better, but we have probably not done much to solve our problem.

The most common error in problem solving that results from the frustration aggression reaction involves slipping into a blaming stance. In this unproductive way of reacting to problem situations, we begin to look for someone to blame rather than for a way to overcome the obstacle to our goal. Blaming someone else may result in a temporary reduction in our emotional arousal, and may make us feel, better but it seldom eliminates the real obstacle.

Further, blaming often assigns the *ownership* of the problem inappropriately. When we react by blaming, we often attempt to place the ownership of *our* problems on others. We typically say things to ourselves and others like, "I am upset because *they* have a problem in being punctual, or responsible, or truthful." While such statements may temporarily assuage our feelings, or even make us feel comfortably superior for the moment, we have simply deceived ourselves and rejected an opportunity to engage in problem solving.

The ownership of any problem is always with the person who is frustrated. *When I am frustrated, I have the problem.* The only way I can get rid of the problem is by overcoming the obstacle to my own need satisfaction—that is, by problem solving.

The first step in the problem location phase of the problem-solving process, then, is called *problem sensing*. The effective problem sensor is aware of his or her own needs, goals, and objectives and monitors his or her feelings continuously. Such a person is aware of feelings of frustration before they reach explosive proportions. The problem sensor is then able to accept the ownership of a problem by acknowledging the presence of an obstacle to his or her *own* goal attainment or need satisfaction. The problem sensor resists moving into a blaming stance and immediately recognizes the need to establish a problem-solving strategy.

The second step in the problem location phase is *problem identification*. This step involves establishing the nature of the goal-blocking situation. Essentially, this step consists of asking and answering a set of basic questions about the frustrating situation. Answers to such questions as "When?" "How often?" "Under what circumstances?" "With whom?" and "What resources do I have to intervene?" provide information that pinpoints the most important characteristics of the problem situation. Identifying the problem situation in an accurate and thorough way is a necessary condition for proceeding with the next phase of problem solving.

Defining the Problem The most important phase in the entire problem-solving process is *problem definition*. Most failures in practical problem-solving situations arise out of an incorrect definition of the problem. The definition of a problem has two essential components. First, the problem definition must suppose a *cause-and-effect* relationship between the two key elements in the problem situation: (a) the identified obstacle, and (b) the goal-blocking effect. After the problem has been defined, all of the proposed solutions represent attempts to remove or reduce the obstacle. If we define the problem incorrectly in terms of the cause-and-effect

Have you ever found it difficult to own a problem? When? Why?

Have you ever had someone lash out at you in frustration?

In haste, have you ever defined a problem inaccurately? What was the result?

relationship between the obstacle and the goal blocking, we cannot hope to achieve an effective solution.

The second crucial element in satisfactorily defining a problem is that the problem must be defined in a way that gives us some degree of possible control over the important factors. If I define the relationship between my goals and a given set of obstacles as totally outside my control, then I have defined the wrong problem. If the events that frustrate me are totally uncontrollable, my problem is not what to do about it but how to live with my lack of control. This concept is well expressed in what is called the Serenity Prayer, which goes like this "God grant us the serenity to accept the things we cannot change, the courage to change the things we can, and the wisdom to know the difference."

A satisfactory problem definition, then, is one that describes a set of potentially controllable factors that cause and maintain a goal-blocking situation. Only when we have developed such a problem definition, are we ready to move to the phase of finding possible solutions. Considerable time, care, and information must be given to problem definition. When we are thoroughly frustrated, we too often tend to leap over this step and define the problem in a hasty and superficial way with disastrous consequences.

Finding and Examining Alternative Solutions As we begin this phase, we have moved into the creative aspect of problem solving. We know quite a bit more about this phase in problem solving than the earlier ones because most studies have given subjects ready-made or predefined problems and examined problem-solving strategies from this point on.

Research and simple observation point clearly to the fact that the crucial task in this phase is to conduct a thorough, comprehensive, and flexible search for possible alternative solutions. Research has also shown that there are several major difficulties that people experience in this phase that diminish their problem-solving ability. The first and most important of these difficulties lies in the tendency to quickly select one of the alternatives without completing a thorough and systematic search for other possibilities.

As we noted earlier, when people encounter problems they experience frustration. That frustration and accompanying anxiety often lead us to act impulsively and irrationally. Even when we avoid the blaming trap and identify and define the problem rationally, our strong feelings of frustration and anxiety may prompt us to be hasty and superficial in our search for alternatives. We may feel that the "action" involved in implementing any solution is preferable to the waiting involved in searching.

There are other sources of error at this phase as well. One is our tendency to not respond flexibly and creatively in our search for alternatives. Very often we don't really examine and "play with" all of the aspects of the problem in an effort to search for novel or unusual possibilities. A classical laboratory situation called the "two string problem" illustrates this difficulty. A person is brought into a large room in which two strings are hanging from the ceiling. The task is to tie the strings together. They are too far apart for the subject to take one in hand and walk to the other. A number of objects are in the room, and the subject is told that he or she may use any of them in any way he or she chooses.

The situation is structured so that the only solution is for the subject to tie one of the available objects to one of the strings and then swing it toward himself or herself, creating a pendulum effect, while holding the other string. The only object suitable is generally one not usually used in this way, such as a pair of pliers. This problem is fairly difficult, and many subjects are unable to solve it after 15 minutes.

The problem illustrates the fact that all too often we are unable or unwilling to search for alternatives that utilize the objects available to us in novel or unusual ways. Many times, we simply do not take the time to look past obvious and familiar approaches to consider creative or unusual possibilities.

Still another limiting factor in our search for alternatives is our tendency to use only approaches that we have successfully utilized in the past. We know, for example, that if a person is given three problems that can be solved in a particular way and then a fourth problem that must be approached in an entirely different way, the fourth problem becomes more difficult to solve than if it had been the only problem given. People tend to persist in the approach that worked with the prior problems even though that approach is completely ineffective in the fourth situation.

We all acquire a number of these hindering strategies as we solve problems in the course of our lives. When we are faced with novel and perhaps more complex problems later in life, our biggest challenge may be to throw off our old approaches and begin the search for alternatives with a fresh and open mind.

In summary, then, an effective search for alternative solutions to a problem is systematic and thorough, and avoids hasty or impulsive action. It is flexible and creative in attempting to seek out novel and unusual relationships and approaches. And it uses a variety of approaches rather than relying on a single, traditional, or familiar format. Once we have completed an effective search for alternative solutions, our next step is to examine and compare the possible solutions, as discussed in the next section.

Examining Alternatives When we examine alternative solutions to a problem, we are really trying to predict how well they will work. In other words we are comparing the probable effectiveness on solutions. This is sometimes called doing a "feasibility study." Unlike when we were thinking in fresh and new ways to generate a list of possible solutions, when we are examining and comparing the alternatives we very much want to rely on our prior experience and the experience of others who have been in similar situations. Since our best predictions about the future are usually based on a thorough understanding of the past, we want to review all of our relevant experiences. At this point in the problem-solving process, experience is especially valuable. Essentially, we are trying to predict the probable cost, effectiveness, and payoff for each of our alternative solutions. The accuracy of our predictions will have a strong effect on our ultimate problem-solving success.

Choosing a Solution The phase of choosing one of the alternatives involves decision-making. Our goal is to choose the most effective and efficient strategy, the one that will work best with the least cost in terms of time, energy, money, and relationships.

Implementing the Solution Obviously, no amount of thinking, analyzing, or planning will, by itself, solve a problem in the real world. After we have developed a problem-solving strategy, we must act on it if it is to make a difference in our lives. This stage of the problem-solving process involves implementing an *action plan*. As we saw in Chapter 9 the key elements in following through on any action plan are:

1. To organize the plan into a sequence of specific, discrete action steps.
2. To establish a firm and definite timeline with target dates for the completion of each step.
3. To make an open, public, and explicit commitment to the action plan with those whose respect we value.
4. To develop a series of check points for measuring progress.
5. To attend to our good feelings about our progress and/or to reward ourselves in other ways for making progress.
6. To begin action *now*.

Evaluating the Results of the Solution
If we define a problem appropriately, our problem definition should tell us when the problem is solved. That is, when we remove an obstacle to our goal attainment or need satisfaction—the end result of problem solving—we should be able to

see some specific changes or results. Sometimes however, when we are working on complex problems, we need to have a fairly elaborate way of evaluating the effectiveness of our strategy as we carry it out. It is often useful to build into our strategy a number of evaluation points at which we can determine the effectiveness of our strategy and add to or modify it to obtain optimal results.

Putting Problem Solving to Work in Our Lives

Thus far, we have discussed problem solving in abstract terms, presenting a general model or framework that can be used in many different ways. However, the kind of problem-solving processes that make a real difference are those that relate to us in very real and personal ways. No matter how well conceived our plans are and how realistic our goals are, we are bound to encounter obstacles along the way. Sometimes those obstacles are within ourselves; sometimes they are outside in the real world. Always, we must confront them honestly and challenge them courageously if we are to overcome them.

Take some time now to think carefully about your typical reactions to past problem situations. Then rate your typical past responses as honestly as you can on the scale provided in Exercise 11.1. From your responses you will likely see important ways in which you can strengthen your problem-solving skills.

COPING WITH STRESS

How do you deal with stress and tension?

When we confront obstacles, we must engage in problem solving to determine how to proceed, but we must also deal with the stress that we feel when we encounter obstacles. Dealing with stress is the focus of the remainder of this chapter.

Many people fail to take advantage of important opportunities for career actualization because they fear the effects of the stresses they may encounter if they move into demanding situations. Of those who do move into new and responsible positions, some thrive whereas others experience tension and stress that is sometimes more than they can handle. These latter individuals may fail, retreat before the tensions, or suffer physical or psychological damage when they are unable to cope effectively. As we saw in Chapter 10 the first step is protecting your own physical, emotional, and spiritual well-being.

What is Stress?

In the field of metallurgy, *stress* is used to indicate the amount of force a material can take without breaking. The concept translates well to human situations.

Psychologists define the term *stress* very broadly, describing it as a perceived threat to any important or fundamental human need. According to this definition, we experience some degree of stress almost every day of our lives. An argument that threatens a cherished relationship, the loss of a chance for job advancement, or a difficult but important examination in school may provide relatively high levels of stress.

Not all stress is generated purely by external circumstances. Whenever we fail to achieve an important goal or to fulfill what we see as our potential for success, we face a threat to our need for self-esteem and respect. However, when we avoid external stress or resign ourselves to a passive, fatalistic kind of life, we may be condemning ourselves to a lifetime of chronic stress borne of feelings of inadequacy and failure. Such low-level chronic stress often is, as we will see, more destructive in its consequences than is more intense but short-term exposure to tension.

Stress is by no means always harmful. Some stress actually triggers and motivates learning and growth. Each time we face a problem—a situation that represents an obstacle to our need satisfaction—we experience stress. We also, however, experience a new opportunity to master the environment and gain a greater degree of control in our lives.

Each new venture into the unknown, every calculated risk that we take to achieve our goals, arouses some apprehension or anxiety. A life without stress would be a life of boredom and monotony, devoid of challenge, opportunity, or adventure. Healthy development and career actualization involve the art of managing and regulating stress levels in ways that allow us to succeed, grow, and enjoy while at the same time preventing physically or psychologically damaging consequences.

Some Prevailing Myths About Stress

Stress or the prospect of experiencing stress is often very frightening. But, as noted earlier, when people are so afraid of stress that they avoid stressful situations, they can actually help to create long-term problems that will eventually produce chronic and potentially more dangerous levels of the very conditions that they were so anxious to escape. Much of the fear and confusion that we experience in regard to stress management is borne of a set of popular myths about the nature of tension. Let's look at some of these myths.

Myth 1: Only Unhappy Events Can Cause Severe Stress This is contrary to the facts. Many happy events are at least as stressful as those that we perceive as sad or tragic. Marriages, the birth of children, promotions, holiday celebrations, and even vacation trips can be stressful. Generally, any situation that creates high levels of novelty, emotional intensity, complexity, or uncertainty may be stressful. Obviously, a life without these elements would be dull, monotonous, and boring. Here and in many other ways we see that the potential for stress is very closely rooted to the potential for growth and satisfaction in our lives.

Myth 2: Tranquilizers or Other Drugs Including Alcohol Are a Guaranteed Way to Relieve Stress No chemical really relieves stress. Drugs may help to suppress or mask certain symptoms, but they do nothing in helping us cope with the sources of the stress itself.

Myth 3: Relaxation and Meditation Are the Most Effective Ways to Cope With Stress Practicing some forms of relaxation can be helpful, but they are effective only within limits. Our basic attitudes, outlooks, and goals and the way these interact with forces in our environment are the basic sources of stress. Improving our ways of thinking about and coping with the environment is the most effective form of stress management.

Myth 4: Financial Pressures and Economic Problems Are the Biggest Sources of Stress This is also not true. The most stressful and destructive situations in life are caused by chronic interpersonal conflicts with those with whom we share close, long-term relationships. The surest way to be damaged by stress is to do nothing about an intimate, chronically disturbed interpersonal relationship.

Myth 5: Most of Us Know When We Are Experiencing Excessive Stress The facts fail to support this myth, as well. Many people become so used to living in stressful conditions that they fail to connect physical or emotional symptoms with the actual sources of stress. Thus, they continue to live in stressful situations that threaten their health and well-being. Many others refuse to face the stressful factors in their lives and tend to blame trivial or peripheral sources of dissatisfaction for their symptoms.

Myth 6: The Best Way to Relieve Stress Is to Escape From the Stressful Situation Because part of the source of stress in any situation lies in our attitudes and cognitions, we can never really run away from stress. Many people spend a good part of their lives running away from stressful jobs or stressful relationships. For them, the same scenarios are often played out in situation after situation. It is important to remember that the seeds of stress and the formula for coping with stress usually lie

How do you maintain a balance between being stressed out and bored stiff?

within ourselves at least as much as in the environment.

Myth 7: Variety and Change Are Stress Reducers To the contrary, major life changes such as new marriages, new living conditions, major geographical changes, and new jobs, regardless of the emotional tone attached to them, all include factors that raise stress levels. Having too much change at one time is a sure recipe for aggravating stress reactions.

Major Dimensions of Stress

People who study stress and stress reactions point to three basic factors that determine how we react in stress situations and what the consequence of the situations will be for us. These are (a) the intensity of the stress, (b) the duration of the stress, and (c) the state of health of the individual.

Intensity of Stress The most immediate factor that determines our reaction to any stressful situation is the intensity of the stress. When any of us encounters an intensely stressful situation, we tend to react in an obvious and immediate way. If we accidentally touch a hot stove or a live electrical wire, for example, we generally react loudly and forcefully. No one watching us will likely have much doubt about what occurred.

Studies of reactions to stress indicate that the level of intensity of stress is an important determinant of how well we learn or perform in a stressful situation. Mild levels of stress actually facilitate learning. Intense levels of stress, conversely, almost always inhibit learning.

Similar effects can be seen regarding how well we perform in other tasks as well. Actors, athletes, and performing musicians, for example, often testify that a mild nervousness, or "butterflies," prior to an important performance is usually a positive sign. It seems to help them mobilize their energies and resources and motivates them to do their best. Extreme nervous reactions or panic generated out of intensely stressful situations is almost always detrimental to the quality of learning or performance. Under extremely stressful conditions we may experience *panic*.

Panic generally arises out of sudden and unforeseen exposure to an intensely stressful situation. Panic is not, of course, an effective way of coping with any situation, and it is seldom accompanied by positive learning. Panic can usually be avoided by practice, training, or rehearsal of effective ways of coping with the stressful situation.

One of the difficult things about judging the intensity of stress is that the level of stress experienced by an individual is a product of both the *objective* characteristics of the external situation and of how that particular individual *interprets* the situation and thinks about it. Two different people facing the same obstacle—for example, climbing out of a deep ditch—may experience very different levels of stress. One may be able to summon up the energy to make a powerful and effective effort, while the other may panic. The difference in their reactions may have little relationship to their actual physical capabilities or circumstances.

Perhaps the most important factor that determines an individual's reaction to a stress situation is how he or she thinks about it. Our thoughts about a stressful situation are like a powerful but irregular lens that can magnify and distort what we are viewing. Indeed, confused and chaotic thinking is generally the principal cause of panic. The process of magnifying and distorting stressful situations in our minds is called *catastrophizing*. This is, perhaps, the surest way to induce panic and ensure failure.

Duration of Stress The second important factor in determining our reactions to stressful situations is the duration of the stress. Most of us are very much aware of our reactions to short periods of relatively intense stress. When a speeding taxi careens around a corner missing us by a few inches, we tend to react with increased perspiration and pulse rate, some butterflies in our stomach, and perhaps

How have you experienced stress in the midst of change?

some nervous laughter. If the stressful situation is even more intense, such as a serious injury to a loved one, we may experience nausea, crying, trembling, or other physical symptoms. Such incidents of acute stress are called *traumas*.

When we experience relatively low levels of stress over a long period of time, our reactions are different. We may not remain aware of either the nature of the stress or our reactions to it. Contrary to what we might believe intuitively, exposure to chronic, low-level stress for a long period of time is much more dangerous and destructive both physically and psychologically than are the isolated, traumatic incidents that we are much more apt to remember.

We learn ways of coping with short-term and intense stress situations earlier in our development than we learn ways of coping with prolonged stress. In most cases, the key ingredient to recovering from acute stress is to simply put ourselves safely back into the environment in which the stress was encountered. After an auto accident, for example, we may be anxious about driving. Given a few hours behind the wheel, however, our anxiety dissipates. Coping with chronic stress is much more complicated.

State of Health The third and perhaps most important factor in how we react to stressful situations lies in our individual physical and emotional condition. To some degree, our reactions to stress are governed by our sense of self-confidence and self-esteem built out of previous successful encounters with similar situations. That is, our reactions are governed by what has been called our *general security factor*. An illustration of this point would be athletes going into a Super Bowl game. Those athletes who will likely perform best will be the ones who have been in a Super Bowl before. Prior success is the best preparation for future success and for coping with stress.

Other factors that are of great importance in coping with stress are related to good general health. Almost all studies of successful people across all fields report that the factor most frequently related to success is *good health*.

Changing life situations may make it difficult or impossible to approach all stressful situations with a solid experience of success behind us. We can, however, do much to ensure that we approach challenging and stressful opportunities in good health. The best preparation for any encounter with stress is a history of good eating, sleeping, and exercise habits combined with abstinence or moderation in the use of alcohol, tobacco, or other drugs. The greatest asset anyone can have in coping with stress is a *healthy, relaxed, well-rested and well-conditioned body*. We discussed this factor in Chapter 10 and provided some basic suggestions about protecting one's health.

Learning to Deal With the Factors That Cause Stress in Everyday Life

Given that we encounter stressful elements in almost every phase of life, our best way to cope is to learn how to understand the factors that cause stress in our environments. These factors include *novelty, intensity, ambiguity, complexity*, and *involvement*. Let's examine these elements and see how we can learn to appraise them realistically and develop coping strategies to manage them.

Novelty The most common element that produces stress is novelty. Most new and therefore unfamiliar situations produce a certain amount of stress. Meeting new people, entering a new job, fulfilling a new role in a group—all of these introduce some degree of stress. When we view the unknown elements as potentially harmful or dangerous, the level of threat, and therefore of stress, escalates. We may be rejected by the new people we meet. We may fail in the new job. We may be ridiculed in our new role.

Yet, without some degree of novelty, our lives would be dull and monotonous. The important thing is to learn to manage novelty, and we can do that in several ways. First, we can consciously try to

How have you reacted to intense stress?

How have you seen people break down under chronic stress?

How have you handled highly stressful situations in the past?

Have you felt stress in new situations? When?

relate the new situation to other situations in our lives in which we have coped successfully. Often, once we search, we can find many common elements between the new and the old. Second, we can observe others who are familiar with and successful in the new situation and develop a plan or model for coping. Finally, we can consult with others or obtain information from other sources about the new situation so that we remove much of the unknown. When we are confronted with a new situation, we need to learn about it, analyze it and engage it rather than withdraw from it or try to ignore or avoid it!

Intensity Highly intense stimuli, such as extremes of noise, light, or temperature, are obviously stressful. Intense expressions of emotions, such as anger, grief, or despair, are also stressful to those at whom they are directed or even to those who are observing. Uncontrolled expressions of emotion are "contagious" in this sense.

In dealing with intensity of a physical or an emotional nature, the first step is to assess the situation and establish some tolerance limits of either duration or proximity—that is, to determine in *advance* the point at which we will act to withdraw or reduce contact. Knowing our own tolerance limits is an important part of this appraisal. In physical situations we may have a pretty good idea of our limits. When we are confronted by intense emotional situations, however, we may be less aware of our tolerance limits.

Consider the following scenario: You are faced with dealing with a particularly difficult, emotional, and unreasonable person in a face-to-face confrontation. You do not want to lose control of yourself, but you also do not want to bottle up painful or even health-threatening emotional upheaval. In such a situation, it is helpful to appraise the stress level by thinking about which internal reactions will tell you to disengage from the situation. You might determine that when you begin to raise your voice, feel your hands shaking, or feel your face flush, you will acknowledge that a tolerance limit has been reached and that a disengagement strategy should be used. One or more such strategies should be planned in advance. For example, you could terminate the interview, postpone it, or take a recess. The point is that you must remain in *control* of the situation and operate to avoid unreasonable levels of stress that push you past your own tolerances.

Ambiguity Highly ambiguous situations will also result, quite often, in stress. Ambiguity is essentially a lack of structure in a given situation that makes it difficult or impossible to interpret expectations, choose alternative courses of action, or predict eventual outcomes. When we are faced with extremely high levels of ambiguity and the threat level is vague or unknown, we sometime project our worst fears and immature fantasies on the situation. It is in this kind of situation that the greatest danger of catastrophizing exists.

We can best cope with ambiguity by trying to reduce it. We can search for clues or indicators that may give us some idea of what to expect or how to cope. We may observe or confer with others who seem to understand the situation. Generally, in a highly ambiguous situation our best strategy is to be tentative and experimental in our behavior or strategies. We may, for example, carry out limited low-risk experiments with strategies or approaches that will give us some relatively immediate feedback about the result.

Suppose for a moment that you are in a new work group. The nature of the relationships within the group is unclear. The relationships between the senior members and the others are especially ambiguous. At times the atmosphere seems relaxed and very democratic; at other times it seems almost impersonal and authoritarian. At a session in which the group is supposed to react to an important new project, you sense that the senior people are very much advocates of the proposed program. You are asked by the boss to present your views on the project to the group, but you are uncertain as to whether the senior members really want your critical analysis or personal opinion.

In such a situation, a tentative, experimental strategy may be to give a brief and balanced outline of the pros and cons of the project. Then, if a genuine invitation to proceed with a critical analysis of the risks or deficiencies of the project were extended, you could proceed, having reduced ambiguity about the expectations regarding your role. If, however, the senior members appeared really uninterested in hearing such an analysis, you could proceed in a relatively neutral way to discuss the project without risking an unwanted confrontation. In either event, you would have reduced some ambiguity regarding role expectations, relationships, and group climate. You also would have developed a plan or strategy.

Complexity Yet another element that produces stress is complexity. We've all experienced the stress that can accompany extremely complex situations, especially those in which we have to sort out relevant factors for decision making or problem solving. In such situations, dealing with complexity may induce fatigue and tension very quickly.

Complexity is generally managed best by adopting conscious, thoughtful strategies or plans. With this approach, when we are faced with an extremely complex task or problem, our first step could be to carefully list all of the factors involved in solving the task or problem. This task analysis would help us to appraise the true level of complexity. After developing this list, we could estimate the real significance of each factor and eliminate the least important factors from further consideration, thereby reducing the complexity. We could also combine closely related or similar factors. This technique, called *chunking,* reduces the total number of factors to a more manageable level. Finally, we could organize the remaining crucial factors into a set of relevant forces or influences that must be addressed.

Another important approach to managing complexity is to appraise our tolerance limits. When we are aware of our limits in working with highly complex problems, we can arrange our work schedules to intersperse complex tasks with more simple tasks. Further, we can arrange to deal with complex tasks early in the day or early in the week while we are relatively fresh.

Involvement A factor that can increase stress in any situation is our level of involvement, or the level of material or psychological stakes or values that we feel are at risk in the situation. When we feel that important outcomes are at risk, our involvement in the situation is naturally very high. The higher the stakes and the greater the risk or uncertainty, the greater is our involvement and, consequently, the level of stress involved.

We can manage involvement by trying to distribute our important values and risks across a variety of situations, much as an insurance company spreads risks across many policyholders. When much of our material and emotional security is concentrated in a single situation or relationship, we are dependent on that situation, and consequently we feel very vulnerable when it is threatened. In this interdependent world, none of us is really independent. To be genuinely independent would be to be truly alone, isolated, and very largely helpless. However, we can develop a feeling of independence and security by distributing our dependence across situations and relationships—that is, by putting our eggs in several baskets, so to speak. When an Olympic champion was asked what he thought about immediately prior to a gold medal dive, he said, "I thought that my mother will still love me whether I miss this one or not." He had distributed his involvement so that it didn't rest completely on athletic competition.

Using Our Resources to Manage Stress

Any accurate and full appraisal of a difficult situation should include a careful assessment of our resources for coping

When are you most effective in dealing with complicated situations or problems?

How do you try to handle ambiguous situations?

How are your needs distributed across relationships and situations?

with it. Among the resources that help us to manage stress emotionally and practically are our support systems and our use of structure.

Support The most important element in managing stress is the utilization of a good support system. Supportive relationships are those marked by warmth, empathy, and caring. It is mostly when we feel alone, isolated, and alienated that we feel vulnerable to threat and panic. We discussed the importance of support in Chapter 10.

Support systems help us to manage stress in at least two distinct ways. First, they give us emotional support. Simply knowing that others understand our situations, care for us, and respect our struggles gives us a real emotional lift. Second, when we have supportive relationships, we are able to discuss our fears and doubts with others. We can also reality test our perceptions of situations and use our energies to deal with what is real and practical rather than with imagined, fantasized, or exaggerated threats.

A vital skill in stress management is to learn how to mobilize our support systems. When we begin to feel stress, it is critical to reach out to others rather than close up. Reaching out to others and talking through fears, doubts, and uncertainties are signs of strength; clamming up is not. The myth of the "strong, silent type" is precisely that—a myth. In most cases the strong, silent type is really the "broken and brittle type."

Structure A second major resource in managing stress is the use of structure. We have already mentioned the importance of putting a rational perspective on situations. Systematic planning, decision-making, and problem-solving approaches are very useful in helping us to deal with difficult situations in rational, logical and thorough ways.

There is, however, another sense in which structure is very important in stress management. When we are coping with stressful situations, we need the stability and security of structured and routine patterns of daily living. When we are under stress, we need, for example, comfortable and familiar home surroundings. We need regular, palatable, and nutritious meals eaten in cheerful surrounding. We need regular and sufficient times for restful sleep in a comfortable, familiar, secure environment. We need the routine and stability provided by our normal and regular social and recreational activities.

A major mistake that people make in managing stress is to allow the stressful situation to disrupt the structures and routines that provide stability and security in their everyday life. Whenever possible, changes in place of residence, basic eating and sleeping habits, and social and recreational routines and activities should be avoided during periods of extreme stress. When we disrupt many of our basic living patterns to fixate and focus solely on a stressful situation, we make ourselves more vulnerable to anxiety, physical breakdown, or other reactions that will actually reduce our overall level of performance in coping with the stressors. We seldom gain much by drastically disrupting the health-maintaining functions of sleep, nutrition, exercise, and relaxation that enable us to operate effectively.

Learning to solve problems and manage stress will take you a long way toward removing the obstacles that separate you from your most cherished goals and aspirations. Managing the inevitable stress that comes into every active and committed life is an important part of career actualization.

Take some time now to complete Exercise 11.2. It will help you to think through the ways in which you can better manage stress in your life.

SUMMARY

This chapter looked at confronting obstacles in two ways. One was to use effective problem solving for removing the obstacles. The other was to develop ways to manage the inevitable stresses encountered as we deal with the obstacles.

Exercise 11.1
My Typical Problem-Solving Behavior

Think about your typical behavior in past problem situations. Then rate your typical *past* responses as honestly as you can on the scale provided.

1. When I feel frustrated, I try to analyze the situation and my responses to it before acting.

Never					Always
1	2	3	(4)	5	6

2. When I am thoroughly frustrated, I look first for the person whose fault it is.

Never					Always
1	2	3	(4)	5	6

3. When I am the one who is frustrated, I know I have the problem.

Never					Always
1	2	(3)	4	5	6

4. When I am frustrated, I ask *why* the problem exists and what the causes are.

Never					Always
1	2	(3)	4	5	6

5. I take time to really study or define the problem I am working on.

Never					Always
1	2	3	4	(5)	6

6. I propose answers without really having thought through the problem and its causes carefully.

Never					Always
1	(2)	3	4	5	6

7. I make sure that I consider the pros and cons of several alternative solutions to a problem.

Never					Always
1	2	3	4	(5)	6

8. My strategies tend to be vague regarding what they are and how I will carry them out.

Never					Always
1	2	(3)	4	5	6

9. I develop definite criteria to determine how my strategies are working out.

Never					Always
1	2	3	(4)	5	6

10. I know for sure if the results of my problem solving are worth the effort.

Never					Always
1	2	3	4	(5)	6

Exercise 11.2
Stress Situation Analysis

Think about a situation in your life that is highly stressful. Then, using the ideas discussed in this chapter, develop an action plan to manage the stress more effectively. Use the following outline as a guide.

1. Describe a stressful situation that presently exists in your life. It may involve work, family, or social relationships. Remember that a stress situation is one that you see as threatening an important need or goal that you have and one that you typically experience with some degree of discomfort, fear, or anxiety.

    figuring out what I'm going to do next year

2. Identify the basic goals or needs that you see threatened in the situation.

    Satisfaction
    Happiness
    Home
    Support

3. List:
    The *worst* probable outcome of this situation:

    I stay in Morris
    (I go Montana and hate it)
    and I and I freak up

The *best* probable outcome of this situation:

I go to Montana (and love it) and P and I stay together

The *most* probable outcome of this situation:

I go to Montana and love it (& and I maybe break up but its okay)

4. List the kinds of information you could obtain to understand the stressful situation better.

*good school
PJY major
accepted (scholarships?)
golf, music ✓
parents
money   credits — transferring, funding   graduating correctly*

5. List your reactions to the stressful situation, including your emotional reactions, self-statements, level of tolerance for the situation, and present way of coping.

6. List the resources that you have available to help you cope. Include supporting relationships, expert advice or information, physical health, relaxation, rest, recreation and leisure, and so on. Analyze your general well-being outside of the stressful situation.

Mom & Dad
Daniel
Jenn
Advisors/Admissions here
Buddhism → meditation, yoga
working out
OBOE

7. Develop a strategy for dealing with the situation that will allow you to better manage the stress involved. It may include steps aimed at gaining control of the situation, steps for keeping your reactions within tolerable limits, ways of utilizing your resources to help you cope with your reactions, and so forth.

continue doing research, list pros and cons of both schools, examine all the info, present all info to mom and dad, talk about, do what's right for me → what I really want to do, heart, work on plan for career/future

CHAPTER 12
Putting It All Together

CHAPTER OVERVIEW

While this may be the last chapter, it is really only the beginning. Clearly, if you have come this far, you have done much to better understand yourself and what you want out of life. In particular, you have explored—and maybe even decided on, some career opportunities that appeal to you. Now it is time to be less introspective and more focused on how we can best represent ourselves to people who have jobs or opportunities that we want. We know they want to hear from us! We could well be the people who will change their lives or reenergize their organizations, but how will they find us? This chapter should give you ideas about how you can take the next step toward going where you say you want to go.

Representing Yourself to Others

How do you best represent yourself to others? You know what you want and what you have to offer, and maybe you even know a place where you would like to work (or go to school), but how do you represent yourself to that opportunity? Not too long ago, you would have thought first to phone and ask about opportunities that might be available where you wanted to work or study. Today, you might first think of using the Internet to view what is available, but in either approach, you would quickly find need to represent yourself well on paper and eventually in an interview.

An employer is apt to represent him/herself with a business card. Once employed, it may be all that is needed to get an appointment or leave some record of a visit, but you don't have a business card until you are employed. So you need a more elaborate and dependable way of representing yourself to others until you get the job. You need a résumé. Everyone should have one, but most of us don't take the time to compose one until it becomes an onerous task. Like a lot of things, once you get down the basics, the rest comes easy. The hard part is getting started and gathering the relevant details and information about yourself and putting it all on paper so it best represents you and your experience. It is, however, as essential as the business card, and once completed, it is relatively easy to add to it or modify it, as your situation requires.

There have emerged in recent years, a number of conventions about what belongs on the résumé. We now find, for example, some kinds of information that once were standard on the résumé are no longer appropriate. So before you get started, take the quiz that follows that will test your knowledge of these conventions. Where you don't mark the right answer, the author prompts you as to why it is not correct. When you can score high on the quiz, you are ready to begin the writing of your résumé.

To summarize, then, the résumé is a one, maybe two, page document that represents you. On it, you list your (a) skills, (b) training, (c) education, (d) professional affiliations, (e) publications, (f) out-of-classroom activities, (g) honors and awards, and other information that indicates your ability to learn through inquiry, ability to acquire knowledge, and ability to make good decisions based on evidence, analysis, and reflection.

The general process for creating a good résumé includes learning some basic rules which you've done in this chapter, reviewing some good résumé examples, applying good writing skills, being concise but complete, reviewing, revising, and getting constructive feedback followed by more reviewing and revising.

Because your life is a dynamic process, your résumé should be updated regularly. As you have new experiences, develop new skills, complete training programs, conduct research, volunteer, join organizations, receive honors or awards, or the like, your résumé should be revised to reflect these events. Attending to your résumé regularly will not only keep it current but will also allow you to reflect on how much you have grown and changed.

You have, or are in the process of attaining, a college degree, an accomplishment that takes a considerable amount of time. On average, it will now take you about 4 hours to create and refine your résumé. So let's review. It takes about 4 years to get a degree; it takes about 4 hours to develop a good résumé, and it takes about 40 seconds for a hiring professional reviewing your résumé to determine your employment fate. Given those facts, your résumé could be one of the most important documents that you will ever create. Take the time required, get help if needed, and do it right!

With the information you now have about writing your résumé, you can begin the task knowing that your efforts will be in line with current conventions. You will want to get help with the task, from someone familiar with résumé writing but not before you gather some basic information and format it on a page or two. Think of writing your résumé as a creative and eventually collaborative effort but one in which you, on your own, need to gather the basic information, such as dates of time in school, dates of employment, honors and accomplishments, references, and the like.

Types of Résumés

We next discuss two commonly used résumé formats: one is the chronological format and the other is the functional format. You will have to decide which best fits your situation.

The chronological format, as you learned in Exercise 12.1, attempts to account for all of your work-related experience from the most recent to the earliest. The format is easy to follow and may be valued by an employer who wants to easily account for what you have done. With this format, you need to list *all* of your work-related experiences in chronological order. In addition to listing jobs and dates of employment, you will need to account for any gaps in employment, which means that time out raising children or a leave of absence from a job need to be shown. The wording of such events is important and is one area in which getting a second opinion is valuable.

A functional résumé highlights the skills you have and does not necessarily list the jobs you have held in chronological fashion. Some people find that this format allows more flexibility and permits them to focus on particular skills or experiences that are most relevant for the direction in which they want to go, as opposed to where they have been. A disadvantage is that some employers who are used to looking at careers in an ordered manner may look negatively at a functional résumé. Many recent graduates, however, find a funtional résumé easier to create and more representative of them as they may have little past experience to highlight.

You may want to look at sample résumés, which are usually available in college career centers and in your local library, to help you pick an appropriate style. There is no one style that is best, and it is generally agreed that people should choose the format that best reflects them. You might think of selecting a résumé style as picking a greeting card; you need to choose the one that best reflects you and your message. In the next section, you will find a number of guidelines to help you get started on your résumé. Perhaps the best advice we can offer is to read the guidelines and get started writing. Leave the fine-tuning until later. Once you have something in hand—basic information that only you can provide—others will usually be more than willing to help. As you write, bear in mind that all résumés require you to be accurate as to dates of employment, job responsibilities, skills, references, phone numbers, and the like. While the résumé is not the place for modesty, it is the place for honesty. Anything less than honesty will haunt you later.

Résumé Guidelines and Sample Résumé

What follows is a set of guidelines for preparing your résumé. These are the guidelines used at the Career Center at the University of Missouri, where students from all colleges and disciplines come for help in preparing their résumés. You can quickly see the usual format: personal data, professional objective, education, work history, related professional information, and references. Read these guidelines carefully and then review the sample résumé provided, which is typical of a résumé presented upon graduation. If you are preparing your résumé before graduation—for example, to use in finding a part-time job or an internship earlier in your career—we applaud your effort. Later, you'll find that you can simply add on to your résumé rather than having to begin from scratch.

Note. The résumé guidelines and sample résumé are adapted from ones used as examples at the Career Center at the University of Missouri. Used by permission.

Résumé Guidelines The following are the topic areas often included in résumés. These are typical headings but not the only ones you can include. Use them as guidelines in developing a first draft. Career specialists can help critique your résumé and help tailor it to best suit your unique background.

Personal Data

- Always include your name, *local and permanent* address, and phone number(s) (make yourself *optimally* accessible by phone—this is how employers will typically contact you for an interview). Also, include your e-mail address if you can check your e-mail regularly!
- Evaluate all other personal information in terms of its job relevancy. Information regarding height, weight, etc., is irrelevant to your candidacy for most positions and should not be offered. Also, information about your marital status, sexual orientation, gender, race, religion, and any disabilities *may not be requested by an employer* unless it is job related, so do not include it on your résumé.

Professional Objective

- Make a concise, positive statement about your work goals. Indicate (a) the position or job you want, (b) the skills you will bring to the job, or (c) a combination of position and skills. The more focused you are the better.
- If you are aiming at a diverse group of jobs, you might want to leave the objective off the résumé and explain your interests in your cover letter instead.

Education

- Name of school, city, and state.
- Degree and major, date of graduation (month and year) or expected date of graduation.
- Minor and/or area of concentration.
- GPA (Generally, include if it's a 3.0 or above. This may be cumulative or in your major.).
- Relevant course work. List courses that you feel will add to your qualifications and are not implied by your major or minor.
- Other colleges (same format as for school of graduation). This is optional. Students who transfer from one school to another normally list only the school they graduated from.
- Accomplishments (e.g., financed 100% of education through . . . , consistently worked 20–25 hours per week while full-time student, graduated in 4 years, etc.).
- Do not include high school information if you have had substantial postsecondary education or training.

Work History

- Include job title, place of employment, city and state, dates (list most recent job first and work backward in time).
- Describe job in a way that clearly highlights relevant skills (this can be done through a brief paragraph or through several short concise statements that are set off from the rest of the text with bullets, asterisks (*), or the like).
- Use high impact verbs, adverbs and qualifying adjectives.
- Quantify when possible (e.g., supervised a staff of 10, increased sales by 15%, handled up to $15,000 daily, etc.).
- Describe your experience as it relates to the position or field of interest.
- Use headings, if necessary, to separate experience that is most directly related to your objective. Examples include: Computer Experience, Sales Experience, Financial Experience, Writing Experience, Retail Experience, Banking Experience, Foreign Travel.

Related Professional Information

Any of these can become a separate category if your background warrants:

- Licenses, certificates currently held.
- Honors, scholarships, awards, fellowships earned.
- Professional organization memberships and offices held.
- Publications.
- Affiliations with civic and community groups.

- Special skills such as fluency in a foreign language, computer skills, etc.
- Extracurricular activities/leadership.
- Internships/externship experiences.

References
- References can be handled in a variety of ways. Currently, the most preferred method is listing your references' names, addresses, and phone numbers on a separate sheet of paper. On your résumé you may indicate that references are available upon request, but this is not necessary. Make sure each of your references has agreed in advance to write reference letters or answer phone calls concerning your candidacy. Professional references from work or school tend to carry more weight than personal character references.

When you have a draft of your résumé, you will want to solicit reactions from others. Invariably we make mistakes or are not as clear as we think we are being, and friends or professionals can now provide valuable input. Getting others involved may also be a way of letting them know you are looking for a job or internship, and they can help with that as well.

NETWORKING AND COVER LETTERS

The Importance of Networking

With your résumé completed, you need to think about how you are going to let others know you are available. Two means are networking and cover letters. Frankly, most jobs aren't advertised but rather come to your attention through friends or acquaintances. It is important to remember that most of your friends are probably not aware of your decision to seek a given opportunity, so you must begin the important process of telling them, or reminding them, that you are seriously looking for something. You need to help them understand what that "something" is, as it may not be obvious to them.

Hence, an important step in finding employment is networking: making appropriate use of your friends to find opportunities that are out there that may be known to them but not to you. We can't overstate the importance of the role your friends and acquantances can assume at this point in your life. However, they need to know you are looking and what you are looking for. You need to coach them so they can do what friends want to do as friends—help one another. Not only can your friends help you find jobs, but they can also help counter the feeling that you are out there looking all by yourself. As important as receiving their leads is receiving their support. Being turned down for a job will likely be a part of your job search. You should not take being turned down personally, but you are apt to, and that is where you'll appreciate your friends.

The All-Important Cover Letter

When you send your résumé to an employer, as when you are talking with a friend, you need to convey that you are seriously looking for something and explain what that something is. That's where your cover letter comes in. You need to create a cover letter that specifies the particular position you are applying for and how you see yourself uniquely qualified to fill it. You can practice the wording with friends: Tell them in your own words about the position and remind them of skills and experiences that make you qualified. Your friends will be able to help you polish the essence of your cover letter.

Let us talk a bit more about what makes a good cover letter. A cover letter should be short and to the point. It should be addressed specifically to the person who is in charge of the search or is most likely to know about an opening. It should be personal, positive, attention getting, and speak clearly to the position for which you are applying. Even though you will be enclosing your résumé with your cover letter, you may want to call attention in the letter to some relevant experience or skill mentioned in the resume that makes you a

Sample Résumé

Truman T. Tiger

Current Address
50 Faurot Field
University of Missouri
Columbia, Missouri 65211
(573) 882-CATS
tiger@mizzou.edu

Permanent Address
6 Column Drive
Fish, Missouri 65000
(573) 828-2000

EDUCATION

Bachelor of Science in Accounting
University of Missouri-Columbia
Minor: History
Anticipated Date of Graduation: May 2002
GPA: 3.5/4.0

WORK EXPERIENCE

Sales Associate, Breaktime Service Station, Columbia, Missouri
September 1999–Present

- Served customers in a timely and courteous manner.
- Ordered and displayed various merchandise.
- Performed closing procedures nightly.
- Received Employee of the Month Award based on performance.

Internal Auditor, Davis Internal Auditing, Kansas City, Missouri
June 1999–August 1999

- Participated in audit teams to review internal controls within various departments.
- Assisted in the completion of labor accounting and asset management audits.
- Reviewed audit findings with various levels of management.

Camp Counselor, Camp Arcadia, Lee's Summit, Missouri
June 1999–August 1999

- Supervised a co-ed group of children ages 8 to 10.
- Created weekly curriculums and projects related to given themes for children.
- Communicated with parents about children's progress in the camp setting.

VOLUNTEER EXPERIENCE

Volunteer, Humane Society, *September 1999–Present.*
Publicity Co-Chair, Habitat for Humanity, *January 1999–May 2000.*
Student Representative, Ronald McDonald House, *August 1999–December 1999.*

HONORS & ACTIVITIES

Dean's List, 7 out of 8 semesters	Student Athletic Board
President, Chi Alpha Theta, 1999–2000	Society of Professional Accountants
Joe Phillips Scholarship	Missouri Student Association
Missouri Bright Flight Scholar	Amnesty for Animals

REFERENCES (Put on separate page) (You may choose to simply say Available on Request)

Dan Williams
Manager
Breaktime Service Station
203 South Providence Road
Columbia, Missouri 65201
(573) 886-7851

Jeff Dare
Audit Manager
Davis Internal Auditing
110 Salisbury Drive
Kansas City, Missouri 66821
(816) 442-0256

Vera Thomas
Director
Camp Arcadia
499 West Avenue
Lee's Summit, Missouri 66345

James Mason
Regional Advisor
Chi Alpha Theta Fraternity
568 Calloway Lane
Hundred Acre Woods, Nebraska 68970
(645) 284-6904

uniquely qualified applicant. Be sure to close your letter in a way that conveys your intent to follow up the letter with a phone call in a few days. You want to let the recipient know in a polite way that you are seriously interested in the position and that yours is not simply a casual inquiry. Some specific cover letter tips and a sample cover letter follow.

Cover Letter Writing Tips

The Purpose of the Cover Letter

- To serve as a business letter for transmitting your résumé to a prospective employer. The cover letter is a good way to highlight points on your résumé.
- To introduce yourself and your background to the employer.
- To serve as a sales letter, intended to convince the prospective employer that you have something valuable to contribute and that it would be worth his or her time to interview you.

Organization of the Cover Letter

- *Paragraph 1: Why you are writing.* Mention the contact person (who told you about the job) in the first sentence.
- *Paragraph 2: Why the organization should hire you.* This paragraph takes the most work, because you need to "hook" the reader. You could begin with wording like, "As indicated on the enclosed résumé . . ." and then mention two or three things that are central to your qualifications, such as your degree, specific course work, work experience, or extracurricular activities.
- *Paragraph 3: Why you want to work for the organization.* (This is an optional paragraph.)
- *Paragraph 4: The close.* Be assertive. Use wording like, "I will call you (be specific about when) for an appointment (not 'interview'). Do not hesitate to call me at (phone #)." If you say you

---

Note. The cover letter writing tips and sample cover letter are adapted from materials used at the Career Center at the University of Missouri. Used by permission.

will call, be sure to do so. Telephone skills are very important.

The Cover Letter Needs to Be:

- Typed
- Original
- Addressed to a specific person (put every effort into finding a contact name!)
- Upbeat and confident
- Not repetitious of the résumé
- Written on stationery that matches the résumé
- Short and to the point
- PROOFREAD!!

More Tips . . .

- Do not exceed one page.
- With regard to addressing the letter to a specific individual, call to request the name and title of the person in the organization who is responsible for hiring college graduates in your career area. "Dear Sir or Madam" is no longer considered proper in professional correspondence. Further, some women are offended by being called "Madam." Contemporary literature suggests that the salutation should be omitted if you do not know to whom the letter should be addressed. Another option is to direct the letter to a specific job title, such as Director of Editorial Services.
- Sound positive and confident. Your cover letter should motivate the recipient to find out more about you, that is, to read your résumé and maybe even interview you.
- Write an attention-getting introduction. Remember the three basic functions of an opening: to invite, inform, and entice.
- State the position for which you are applying and point out your relevant qualifications. Tell why you are uniquely suited for the job you are seeking. Avoid using "I" to begin every sentence.
- Focus on certain qualifications you wish to emphasize, but do not merely repeat the contents of your résumé. Select specific experiences relevant to the job and talk about details. Fill in the blanks your résumé leaves open.

Sample Cover Letter

May 3, 1998

5020 Glencairn Drive
Columbia, MO 65203

Ms. Evelyn Smith
Environmental Design Associates
210 Grand Avenue
St. Louis, MO 63017

Dear Ms. Smith,

While attending an ASID seminar in St. Louis last week, I learned that your firm may be hiring an additional designer to assist with residential design projects. I am writing to inquire further about this potential position.

I am currently enrolled as an Interior Design student in the Department of Environmental Design at the University of Missouri in Columbia. Although I do not anticipate graduating until June 1999, I feel that my current creative and technical skills, as well as my interest in residential design, would qualify me to do the type of design work you require. As outlined on my enclosed résumé, I have had experience with computer-aided design, am proficient at drafting and rendering, and am comfortable making presentations. In addition, I place a high priority on client/user involvement and the application of behavioral designs in the design process, a quality that could make me a valuable addition to your firm.

I am impressed by the reputation of your firm and feel confident that my qualifications would enable me to perform the job well. I am excited about the opportunity for growth and learning that would be afforded me by working with your team of design professionals, and I believe that I possess unique qualities that would enhance the team. I would appreciate an opportunity to meet with you to discuss my qualifications and to learn more about this job opportunity and your firm. I will call you the week of May 10th to see if a meeting can be arranged. In the meantime, I may be reached at (314) 443-9507.

Thank you for your consideration. I look forward to meeting with you.

Sincerely yours,

Leslie D. Martin

Enclosure

- Tailor your letter to the needs of the company and the requirements of the position. How will the employer benefit by employing you? Want ads and company publications offer clues about what to stress. Get inside information about the workings of your chosen industry by reading trade publications and business magazines and contacting trade associations.
- Inform employers of your intention to contact them within the next few weeks. Make a follow-up call a few days after you have sent your résumé and letter.
- Use matching paper for your cover letter and résumé. Traditionally, they are printed on white, off-white, ivory, or light gray 8½" x 11" paper that is at least 24 pound bond weight.
- Take time to create a letter that demonstrates your enthusiasm and creativity. Remember, the cover letter is an important part of your total sales pitch for the job.

Finding Information on the Internet

On-line Job Hunting

In today's technological world, you may find yourself being asked to submit your résumé electronically. In an article in the July 5, 1999, issue of *Fortune Magazine*, Jerry Useem estimated that 2.5 million résumés had been posted on the Internet. He noted that there were, at that time, 28,500 Websites that offered job postings. Further, he indicated that 45% of the FORTUNE Global 500 companies were actively recruiting on the Internet. That figure has probably increased dramatically since then, as more and more companies are seeing the Internet as an important means of recruiting. Thus, you need to know how to represent yourself on-line as well as in the more traditional résumé fashion.

Many schools actively prepare students to write on-line résumés and to post them on the Internet. The following are some important tips for writing electronic résumés:

- **Think Nouns, Not Verbs.** If you emphasize nouns (i.e., key words), your résumé will be more likely to be selected when employers search from a résumé database.
- **Less Is More.** Use a straightforward font—nothing fancy that could turn into squiggles when downloaded. For the same reason, avoid underlining, bold, and italic. Stick to a white or beige background and avoid graphics and shading (computers are set to read text).
- **Use Lots of White Space.** Gaps between text sections allow the computer to recognize where one topic ends and another begins.
- **Use Common Language.** To maximize "hits," use language everyone knows, and don't use abbreviations.
- **Keep It Short.** New graduates, 1 page max; senior executives up to 3.

To appreciate the extent of the career-related activity that is evolving on the Internet, you need only look at some of the specific sites that are available. If you are looking for jobs, for example, in government, you should try http://www.jobs fed.com. The following list provides a sampling of these helpful Websites. Take some time now to access a few of these helpful sites.

Internet Informational Career Sites

Guides to the Internet
- **Newbie's Guide to the Internet:** http://ug.cs.dal.ca:3400/newbie.html
- **Learn About the Internet:** http://www.clark.net/pub/lschank/web/learn.html
- **The Argus Clearinghouse (subject search):** http://www.clearinghouse.net/index.html
- **Charm Net Learning:** http://www.charm.net/learning.html
- **EINet's Galaxy (subject search):** http://galaxy.einet.net/

- **Purdue University's Virtual Reference Desk (subject search):** http://thorplus.lib.purdue.edu/reference/index.html

Famous Job Sites
- **Career Mosaic:** http://www.careermosaic.com.cm/usenet.html
- **Online Career Center:** http://www.occ.com
- **Monster Board:** http://www.monster.com
- **Career Resource Center:** http://www.careers.org/01_jobs.html
- **Career Web:** http://www.cweb.com/ jobs
- **E-Span Job Search:** http://www.espan.com/job
- **America's Job Bank:** http://www.ajb.dni.us
- **Job Web:** http://www.jobweb.org

Other Job Sites
- **Riley Guide:** http://www.dbm.com/jobguide
- **Job Hunt:** http://www.job-hunt.org
- **Magellan:** http://www.mckinley.com/magellan/Reviews/Business/Jobs/index.magellan.html
- **Best Bets From the Net:** http://www.lib.umich.edu/chdocs/employment
- **Yahoo! Employment:** http://yahoo.com/business_and_economy/index.html
- **JobBank USA:** http://www.jobbankusa.com/search.html
- **SEARCH.COM:** http://www.search.com
- **Career Resource Homepage:** http://www.rpi.edu/dept/cdc/homepage.html
- **Career Path:** http://careerpath.com
- **Career Magazine:** http://www.careermag.com/db/cmag_postsearch_form
- **JobTrak:** http://www.jobtrak.com

Job Listings for Specific Career Areas
- **Government:**
  Federal Jobs Digest: http://www.jobsfed.com
  FedWorld: http://www.fedworld.gov/jobs/jobsearch.html
- **Academia:**
  Academe This Week: http://chronicle.merit.edu/ads/links.html

  Galaxy Employment: http://galaxy.einet.net/GJ/employment.html
- **Graduate Schools:**
  Peterson's Guide: http://www.petersons.com
- **Business:**
  Infoseek Guide: http://guide-p.inforseek.com/business
  University of Iowa: http://www.biz.uiowa.edu/recruiters.html
  Ohio State University: http://www.cob.ohio-state.edu/~fin/osujobs.htm
- **Conservation:**
  Student Conservation Association, Inc.: http://www.sca-inc.org

Other Career-Related URLS
- **Action Without Borders:** http://www.idealist.org
- **America's Talent Bank (résumé bank):** http://atb.state.mo.us
- **Career Xroads:** http://careerxroads.com
- **Ecola Newstand:** http://ecola.com
- **Eresumes (résumé bank):** www.eresumes.com
- **Four11:** http://fur11.com
- **Job Smart:** http://www.jobsmart.org
- **Missouri Works!:** http://www.works.state.mo.us
- **NationJob Network:** http://www.nationjob.com
- **Needle in a Cyberstack:** http://home.revealed.net/albee
- **Occupational Outlook Handbook:** http://stats.bls.gov/ocohome.htm

Career Center Home Pages
- **University of Missouri-Columbia Career Center:** http://career.missouri.edu
- **Pennsylvania State University Career Services:** http://www.psu.edu/cdps/index.html
- **Arizona State University Career Services:** http://www.asu.edu/career/
- **University of Arizona Career Services:** http://w3.arizona.edu/~career/careerservices.htm

The activity on any of these sites may astound you if you haven't searched this way for a job before. We turn our discussion now to organizing your Internet job search and Internet job search strategies. With some companies, the Internet may, in the not too distant future, be the only way you will be able to access their personnel office. For that and many other reasons, if you are not yet conversant with the Internet, or not yet comfortable with it, we urge you to get some help in this area. Many opportunities will soon be available only through the Internet.

Organizing Your Internet Job Search

Define Your Search Terms Search terms are the terms you will type into the computer to begin your job search. Some helpful terms are *employment opportunities, job announcements, job listings, job openings, job resources, job vacancies, labor, position announcements, positions available, resume postings,* and *staff openings.*

Determine if the Database is Searchable When you access a Website, it is helpful to determine if its database is searchable. Sometimes using a backslash (/) will give you a search prompt, which will allow you to specify what you are looking for, such as "advertising positions available" or "computer job listings."

Make a Schedule for Looking for Jobs and Keep to It It is important to establish a routine for regularly checking your job resources. You might, for example, check your job resources daily for an urgent search, two or three times a week if you have a job but have mentally left it, and once a week if you are just fishing for new opportunities. Some resources, such as the *Chronicle of Higher Education,* are updated every week, so keep track of the schedules for the resources, as well, so that you can be sure to get the new listings "while they're fresh."

Keep Good Job Records Use a system to keep track of whom you have contacted and where your résumé is posted. Since you are already using the computer, you may want to use a spreadsheet program to create your own job search tracking forms. One way to organize information is to list the databases (Websites) you are using on one page and the employers you are targeting on another.

Find a Good Newsgroup Newsgroups can be a valuable source of information about current opportunities and possibilities. When you first sign up for a newsgroup, it is important to take the time to read the posted messages to learn what type of dialogue is acceptable. Most contain a FAQs (frequently asked questions), file which should help you in this process. After you have familiarized yourself with the group, you need to become a "recognizable presence" by participating in ongoing discussions. Letting people know what type of work you are doing is an important way to get your name out there. When you mention that you are job seeking, do so clearly and politely. If you identify someone you think can assist you in your job hunt, approach the person privately via his or her e-mail address. If you post a message to everyone in your group about your search, be tactful. Instead of saying that you are looking for a job, ask questions that will help identify valuable contacts. For instance, you might ask, "Does anyone know of any newsletters for accountants?" Then you could follow up by asking if the newsletters suggested are a source of job listings, because you are looking for a new position.

Find Some Good Bulletin Boards When you locate a relevant bulletin board, it is important to determine if a fee is required to participate as a job seeker. Many commercial Bulletin Boards (BBSs) charge employers but not job seekers. Keep a list of BBS addresses in a job search log book or diary that allows you to summarize information and frame new questions to be answered as you learn more.

Find Some Good Listservs Listservs enable you to receive important notices and announcements. If you have a "presence" (by subscribing) in the right mailing lists, you will be in the "right place at the right time" when job openings are announced. Keep a list of Listservs in your job search log book.

Contact Employers Posting Ads When you are able to determine a postal address ("snail mail") for an employer you're interested in, follow up your electronic résumé with a paper résumé. If you know the fax number, you may, instead, want to send a faxed résumé. This may seem like overkill, but something as important as making your presence known to a prospective employer should not be left to chance.

Network With Employers Via E-Mail Via e-mail avoids secretaries and human resource personnel who may screen you out and allows you to directly contact the person with the hiring power. You can use Internet location-finding tools such as Whois and Finger to obtain the e-mail addresses. Once you have established an e-mail contact, you can ask for a personal interview. Aldea Publishing's NetPages is another good resource for obtaining e-mail addresses. This printed directory is free; the only cost is shipping.

Post Your Résumé On-Line As noted earlier, in today's world it is extremely valuable to post your résumé on-line. To do so, you should use one or more of the many résumé databases available. These are located in BBSs, newsgroups, mailing lists, the World Wide Web, and commercial on-line resources. Tips for writing an electronic résumé were provided earlier in this chapter.

Follow Up With A Phone Call Tenacious job hunters follow up with a phone call to make sure their résumés have arrived safely. Even in this high tech job searching process, the personal touch is still the most effective.

Internet Job Search Strategies

You've got a major, you have a career goal, you even have a graduation date—all you need now is a *job*. Welcome to the newest way to locate the job of your dreams: the Internet. You've used it to e-mail your friends, turn in your assignments, even catch the local movie listings. Now you need to turn your computer skills to the task of job seeking, the 21st Century way. This section offers a few suggestions to help you get started.

You are undoubtedly familiar with these facilities. The next time you are at your favorite lab, check out the attached job search sites. Once you know which job sites are appropriate to you, drop in daily to check your e-mail or send electronic résumés.

Access Providers Serious job seekers often want to plunge into the Net itself, some of which is not yet available through membership with the commercial on-line services. The Internet reaches the business and governmental sectors, as well as scientific and medical research institutions, universities, and the Library of Congress. It is also linked by e-mail to many independent bulletin boards. Navigating is not always simple, but, fortunately, companies are springing up all over to help you get onboard. They are most commonly called Internet access providers and connectivity providers.

The electronic version of community bulletin boards posted at the local supermarket, these often cater to special interest groups and offer a way for people to instantly get in touch with one another. Any computer on a BBS uses a special program that allows other computers to call it over standard phone lines. Some BBSs are free; others charge an access fee.

These services include such household names as America Online, Prodigy, and Compuserv as well as not-so-well-known names, including Delphi, Genie, ZiffNet, and The Well. These services are the "middlemen" between you and the Internet. By using them, you can access the world's libraries, newspapers, encyclopedias, bulletin boards, travel agencies, and banking services, to name just a few resources.

Telnet, FTP, and Gopher connect you to other computers on the Internet. Resources are presented on menus so you don't need to know addresses or special commands. You just highlight an area of interest, select it, sit back, and wait for the item to fill your screen. Making these tools even more effective is the fact that they are interconnected. Some tools allow you to search "gopherspace" by using key words. Jughead, for example, will search for words in the directory of the gopher server you are connected to, and Veronica will search for words in all gopher directories anywhere in the world. Telnet allows you to get information from all over the world through remote login. To access information, however, you must first have an exact Internet address. Archie helps you search anonymous ftp (file transfer protocol) sites, or computers where files are kept around the globe, to locate a specific file. You use the login name "Anonymous" followed by your e-mail address.

World Wide Web The World Wide Web (www) is a spectacular Internet tool that took off in 1993 when Mosaic, a browser software, that presents information in a point and click format, was released. Mosaic is free to anyone. Other popular browsers include Netscape, NetCruiser, and enhanced NCSA Mosaic. Websites are linked through hypertext hot buttons, which, when clicked, propel you to a different address. In function, the www is like a CD-ROM encyclopedia that allows you to access data through text, soundclips, video, and pictures.

Wide Area Information Servers Pronounced "ways," WAIS search the Internet by using key words and phrases that index the contents of documents rather than document titles. In other words, you can search for files based upon what is in its title.

Netiquette tips . . .

- Remember, you are addressing people, so be courteous.
- Check spelling, grammar, and punctuation before posting.
- Using capital letters is considered shouting. Don't.
- Don't use emotions, or "smileys" (a colon followed by a closing parentheses). Keep it professional.

INTERVIEWING

We next include some tips on interviewing, the logical next step in your job search. You've sent a résumé and cover letter, and the recipients were impressed with what they read. Now they want to meet you. Can you represent yourself well in an interview? The following interview tips, drawn from the University of Missouri Career Center Website, are also helpful.

Interviewing Tips

- *Be on Time.* We recommend arriving at least 10 to 15 minutes before the scheduled interview time.
- *Be Prepared.* Know the interviewer's name and how to pronounce it (including proper title: Mr., Mrs., Dr., etc.). Know the company's major products or services, the organization of the company, and its major competitors.
- *Bring a Spare Copy of Your Résumé in a Briefcase or Folder.* This demonstrates that you are prepared. It also gives the interviewer something to take notes on.
- *Expect to Spend Some Time Developing Rapport.* Personal chemistry is a main ingredient in the hiring process. Try to relax and become comfortable with the interviewer.
- *Watch Your Nonverbal Communication.* Maintain an open body posture and appropriate eye contact. Seat yourself at a reasonable distance from the other person.
- *Don't Be Embarrassed by Nervousness.* Interviewers are human, and they often become nervous too. In fact, nervousness is a good sign—it shows that you

are taking the interview seriously. However, avoid nervous mannerisms such as tapping your fingers or feet or playing with pens.
- *Don't Play Comedian or Try to Entertain the Interviewer.* It is important to be personable, but do not overdo it.
- *Don't Exaggerate or Lie.* You might be tempted to embellish your achievements in the interview, but lies will come back to haunt you on the job!
- *Follow the Interviewer's Lead.* Don't try to take over the interview. Stick to the main subject at hand, but do not dwell too long on one point. It is better to deal with many questions than just one or two in-depth questions, unless that's where the interview leads.
- *Be Prepared for Personal Questions, Even Some Inappropriate Ones.* Anticipate how you will handle personal questions without blowing your cool. Some interviewers may not be aware of what they can and cannot legally ask you. For example, questions about religious or political beliefs or ethnic origins.
- *Be Sure You Understand the Questions Asked.* It is okay to ask for clarification.
- *Emphasize the Positive.* Be frank and honest, but never apologize for lack of experience or weaknesses. Be self-confident but not overconfident or cocky.
- *Wait for an Offer to Bring Up Salary.* Let the interviewer bring up this subject.
- *Pay Attention to the Timing of Answers.* Use silence and intentional pauses to your advantage. Time is occasionally needed to think and to reflect.
- *Emphasize What You Can Do for the Organization.* This means emphasizing your transferable skills. Employers are concerned most with what you can do for them. Focus on your ability to learn, communication skills, interpersonal abilities, analytical thinking talents, and other skills developed while in college.
- *Don't Try to Give the "Answer He or She Wants."* Most employers know a "set answer" when they hear one.
- *Avoid Debate.* Arguing with an employer will shorten the interview and lessen your chances of employment.
- *NEVER Slight a Former Employer, Colleague, Teacher, or Institution.* Even if there were problems with your previous experiences, try to put your answers in the positive rather than the negative. If you slight a former employer, the interviewer may assume that you will someday do the same to him or her.
- *Try to Be as Specific as Possible.* Never say "I'll do anything!" Take charge of your own life or someone else will take charge of it for you.
- *Watch Your Grammar.* Employers are interested in candidates who can express themselves properly. Even if you have to slow down to correct yourself—do it!
- *Be Prepared to Ask Questions.* When asked for comments or questions, have some ready. This shows that you are prepared and interested.
- *Do Not Bring a Pile of Exhibits or Samples Unless Asked.*
- *If You Are Applying for a Job in a Place You Cannot Easily Commute to, Suggest a Half Hour Telephone Interview.* A preliminary telephone interview can help you assess whether it would be worth your time and expense to travel for a personal interview.
- *Don't Expect an Offer on the Spot.* Offers usually follow the interview, sometimes 2 or 3 weeks later. If, by a fluke, you are offered a position on the spot, it is appropriate for you to ask for 1 or 2 days of thinking time before responding.
- *Be Careful With the Closing.* Do not linger; end quickly and courteously.
- *BE YOURSELF!* You do not want to get hired on the basis of something you are not. You want to be hired for who you are: *you!*

It is important to know that while there are things you can do to prepare for an interview, you have been preparing to represent yourself for years. In preparing for an interview, don't focus too much on yourself. Instead, focus on finding out all you can about the organization—its history, its management style, how others feel about working there, the work norms, expectations, particular things the company might be looking for in this position, and perhaps who previously held the job if it is not a new position. This kind of knowledge is likely to impress your interviewers, showing them that you did your homework and prepared for the interview. Armed with this knowledge, you'll feel more confident in the interview as you, too, will have an agenda—impressing the interviewer for sure, but also learning information that will better assure you that you are a good fit for the job. Most people find themselves more confident in an interview when they have some control of the content or agenda. It helps you present yourself in a more comfortable manner.

Interviewing, like much of the job search process, is stressful. You are putting yourself on the line, and that often is not a comfortable position. You also are likely to be told more than once that you are not the one being offered the job, and you may take that personally. Recall what stress does to you. For some, it brings out the best; for others, it brings out the worst. Think about how you handle stressful situations, and don't lose sight of that as you move through the career search process. It helps to recall as often as necessary that you are looking for one job and only one and that it is usual to interview for many before finding *the* one.

Getting help from your friends is important both for support and for job leads, but you can also get help from college career centers, from high school guidance offices, and from public libraries. These resources can provide examples of good résumés, cover letters, job openings, and the like. At the same time, their staff can become part of your support network. Let them be part of the team that helps you find what you are looking for in a job. That is what makes their job personally satisfying. Good luck with your search!

SUMMARY

We have discussed in detail preparing résumés and beginning the actual job search. We gave particular attention to the use of the Internet as a key resource in obtaining information and actually locating and seizing career opportunities. Utilizing the many suggestions that are provided here will get you started on the path to career actualization.

Exercise 12.1

Test Your Résumé Knowledge

This instrument was designed to test your knowledge of the basic information you should know prior to developing a résumé.

The developer realizes that some very specific types of employment might require you to include information that is not normally acceptable on a traditional résumé. This instrument was not designed to take into consideration all of those variables. For information on different types, styles, and other résumé do's and don'ts, visit your local college or university career center.

For this test, you are to assume that you are a college student or recent college graduate and select answers using that as your frame of reference. Please choose the best answer or answers for all questions.

1. Which of the following does/do not belong on a résumé?
   a. Work experience
   b. Letters of reference
   c. Education
   d. Honors and activities
   e. Hobbies

2. Which is/are not normally appropriate to use on a résumé?
   a. Abbreviations
   b. Personal pronouns (i.e., "I")
   c. Action verbs
   d. Pictures
   e. Personal information (date of birth, religion, gender, national origin, etc.)

3. What type of information should be included in the Professional Objective statement?
   a. Type of position sought
   b. Desired geographic location
   c. Salary requirements
   d. Duration (part-time, internship, full-time, etc.)
   e. Information about what you have to offer

4. What length should a traditional résumé be for a recent graduate?
   a. 1 page
   b. 2 pages
   c. 2 to 5 pages
   d. 5 to 10 pages
   e. As long as needed to include everything

Note. Adapted from a quiz developed by Robert M. McDaniels, Career Center, University of Missouri. Used by permission.

5. Work experiences should be described as:
   a. Narrative description
   b. Bulleted phrases that begin with action verbs
   c. Bulleted phrase that begin with action adjectives
   d. Bulleted sentences
   e. Any of the above

6. How much time might the average employer spend reviewing a résumé?
   a. 3 to 5 minutes
   b. 2 to 3 minutes
   c. 1 to 2 minutes
   d. 30 to 60 seconds
   e. 15 to 45 seconds

7. What should be included in the Personal Data section?
   a. Address
   b. Phone number
   c. Home page
   d. Date of birth and place of birth
   e. E-mail address

8. What color paper should your résumé be printed on?
   a. Depends on your major
   b. Blue, green, or red
   c. Depends on who is receiving the résumé
   d. White, light gray or off-white
   e. Any color

9. What other information sections are appropriate for a résumé?
   a. Skills
   b. Honors
   c. Hobbies
   d. Professional affiliations
   e. Publications

10. What is the purpose of a résumé?
    a. To get a job
    b. To get an interview
    c. To represent yourself in writing
    d. To deceive the employer
    e. All of the above

11. What are the different types of résumés?
    a. Functional
    b. Chronological
    c. Electronic
    d. Alphabetical
    e. Vitae

12. Which of the following are important aspects for a résumé?
    a. Overall appearance
    b. Paper color
    c. Length
    d. Organization
    e. Absence of typos and spelling and grammatical errors

13. A Professional Objective statement is most useful when:
    a. You are submitting your résumé for a specific position
    b. You are changing career paths
    c. You are a recent graduate with little hands-on experience
    d. Your career history or major alone do not present an easily identifiable "fit" for the position being targeted
    e. All of the above

14. Who should review your résumé before you submit it?
    a. Just you
    b. As many people as possible
    c. People who know you and your skills
    d. Professionals in the field
    e. None of the above

15. What documents should accompany your résumé?
    a. Application
    b. Portfolio
    c. Picture
    d. Reference list
    e. Cover letter

Answer Key

The answers provided are meant to communicate general rules of résumé writing. There are, of course, exceptions to most rules, but only the most common exceptions will be mentioned here. With résumé writing, it is best to start with some basic knowledge and then address the exceptions as needed.

1. Which of the following does/do not belong on a résumé?
   a. Work experience
      - Work experience is considered a required field on a résumé.
   b. **References**
      - References do not belong on a résumé but can be attached to a résumé on a separate sheet as an accompaniment.
   c. Education
      - Education is considered a required field on a résumé.
   d. Honors and activities
      - Honors and activities, although not considered a required field on a résumé, can add substance and strength to a résumé.
   e. **Hobbies**
      - In general, hobbies do not belong on a résumé unless they are directly related to the position that you are seeking.

2. Which is/are not normally appropriate to use on a résumé?
   a. **Abbreviations**
      - Abbreviations are not appropriate on a professional document.
   b. **Personal pronouns** (e.g., "I")
      - Personal pronouns are not appropriate on a professional document.
   c. Action verbs
      - Action verbs are appropriate and should be used in a past-tense form at the beginning of all phrases describing previous jobs and activities.
   d. **Pictures**
      - In general, pictures are not appropriate on a résumé, unless you are applying for a position that requires specific physical characteristics or you have been asked to supply evidence of acquired skills. In such instances, pictures can be included as attachments or in a portfolio.
   e. **Personal information (date of birth, religion, gender, national origin, etc.)**
      - Personal information is not appropriate on a résumé, as it is not legal for an employer to use this information in hiring. It can be discriminatory information.

3. What type of information should be included in the Professional Objective statement?
   a. **Type of position sought**
      - The type of position sought should be included so that the prospective employer will know what type of position you are seeking.
   b. Desired geographic location
      - Desired location should not be included in your objective as it might eliminate you from being granted an interview. It may be included, however, if you are limited as to where you can work.

c. Salary requirements
- Salary requirements should not be included in your objective. Salary requirements are usually discussed near the end of the interview process.

d. **Duration (part-time, internship, full-time, etc.)**
- Duration should be included so that the prospective employer will know the length of the position that you are seeking.

e. Information about what you have to offer
- What you have to offer to an employer is important information, but it should not be included in your objective. What you have to offer should be a part of your cover letter and the interview.

4. What length should a résumé be for a recent graduate?

   a. **1 page**
   - The length of a résumé for most recent college graduates should be one page. Exception: If you have extensive related experiences (e.g., several internships, co-ops, or part-time or summer jobs) and related skills, your résumé might be two pages. Education majors, for example, will frequently have two-page résumés due to their numerous field experiences.

   b. 2 pages
   - The length of a résumé for most recent college graduates should be one page. Review answer "a" to see why.

   c. 2 to 5 pages
   - The length of a résumé for most recent college graduates should be one page. Review answer "a" to see why.

   d. 5 to 10 pages
   - The length of a résumé for most recent college graduates should be one page. Review answer "a" to see why.

   e. As long as needed to include everything
   - The length of a résumé for most recent college graduates should be one page. Exception: If you have extensive related experiences (e.g., several internships, co-ops, or part-time or summer jobs) and related skills, then your résumé might be two pages.

5. Work experiences should be described as:

   a. Narrative description
   - Narrative descriptions can be too wordy and do not clearly identify your skills and responsibilities.

   b. **Bulleted phrases that begin with action verbs**
   - Job descriptors should be in the form of phrases beginning with action verbs in the past tense. They should be bulleted and listed in order of importance, beginning with the most important descriptor. This is the substance of your résumé, so make sure that your skills, abilities, and responsibilities are demonstrated.

   c. Bulleted phrases that begin with action adjectives
   - This is a trick answer. "Action adjectives" should be "action verbs."

   d. Bulleted sentences
   - Bulleted sentences can be too wordy and do not clearly identify your skills, abilities, and responsibilities.

   e. Any of the above
   - Only one of the above is correct: bulleted phrases that begin with action verbs. Review answer "b" to see why.

6. How much time might the average employer spend reviewing a résumé?

    a. 5 to 10 minutes
    - The answer is "e." Review it to see why.

    b. 3 to 5 minutes
    - The answer is "e." Review it to see why.

    c. 2 to 3 minutes
    - The answer is "e." Review it to see why.

    d. 1 to 2 minutes
    - The answer is "e." Review it to see why.

    e. **15 to 45 seconds**
    - Although there are some slightly different thoughts regarding the exact amount of time employers generally spend reviewing résumés, most believe that it is in the range of 15 to 45 seconds. The important thing to realize is that hiring representatives generally spend a very short amount of time initially perusing your résumé. If in that short time something interesting does not catch their attention, your résumé and you may be eliminated from consideration.

7. What should be included in the Personal Data section?

    a. **Address**
    - Although there are concerns about security and safety, the prospective employer must be able to contact you easily, so include any address that may assist an employer in finding you (campus, permanent, etc.).

    b. **Phone number**
    - Although there are concerns about security and safety, the prospective employer must be able to contact you easily, so include any phone numbers that may assist an employer in finding you (campus, permanent, etc.).

    c. Home page
    - The inclusion of a home page is optional. If you include one, it should contain information that is relevant to the type of position you are seeking and should be professional.

    d. Date of birth and place of birth
    - Date of birth and place of birth are information that could be used to discriminate and should not be included.

    e. **E-mail address**
    - Although there are concerns about security and safety, the prospective employer must be able to contact you easily. You should include your e-mail address on your résumé if you check your e-mail regularly. The name that you use in your e-mail address should be professional.

8. What color paper should your résumé be printed on?

    a. Depends on your major
    - Although you might want to demonstrate to a prospective employer your ability to be creative or innovative or to have your résumé stand out from the others, colored paper is not considered appropriate for a résumé. If you need to demonstrate your skills through colors or graphics, you should do that via attachments or in a portfolio. Review answer "d" to see why.

b. Blue, green, or red
- Although you might want to demonstrate to a prospective employer your ability to be creative or innovative or to have your résumé stand out from the others, colored paper is not considered appropriate for a résumé. If you need to demonstrate your skills through colors or graphics, you should do that via attachments or in a portfolio. Review answer "d" to see why.

c. Depends on who is receiving the résumé
- Although you might want to demonstrate to a prospective employer your ability to be creative or innovative or to have your résumé stand out from the others, colored paper is not considered appropriate for a résumé. If you need to demonstrate your skills through colors or graphics, you should do that via attachments or in a portfolio. Review answer "d" to see why.

d. **White, light gray, or off-white**
- Résumés will be copied, scanned, or otherwise made available to others to review, so it is important that the copies look as good as the original. Good quality white bond paper is considered the best choice.

e. Any color
- Although you might want to demonstrate to a prospective employer your ability to be creative or innovative or to have your résumé stand out from the others, colored paper is not considered appropriate for a résumé. If you need to demonstrate your skills through colors or graphics, you should do that via attachments or in a portfolio. Review answer "d" to see why.

9. What other information sections are appropriate for a résumé?
   a. **Skills**
   - Skills can be included on a résumé to help a prospective employer quickly identify things that you have learned.
   b. **Honors**
   - Honors can be included on a résumé to show how you have excelled academically.
   c. Hobbies
   - In general, hobbies do not belong on a résumé unless they are directly related to the position that you are seeking.
   d. **Professional affiliations**
   - Professional affiliations demonstrate your interest and desire to connect with others in your chosen career field and to keep abreast of current issues and new developments.
   e. **Publications**
   - Publications, although not a part of most undergraduate degree requirements, should be included in your résumé if they relate to the field or position that you are seeking.

10. What is the purpose of a résumé?
    a. To get a job
    - Although this is a logical answer and a résumé can lead to a job offer, it is not the purpose of a résumé.
    b. **To get an interview**
    - The purpose of a résumé is to get an interview. The résumé is the document that is used to screen applicants. If the hiring personnel identify characteristics that are compatible with their hiring objectives, then the next step is the interview.
    c. To represent yourself in writing
    - The résumé is indeed a document that represents you, your skills, your education, and your career objectives, but representing yourself is not the most important purpose of the résumé.

d. To deceive the employer
- Although this is a no-brainer, many people have tried to use their résumés to represent themselves in less than honest ways. If you are caught being deceptive or dishonest on your résumé, you can be sure that your chances of getting the job are zero.

e. All of the above
- Review answers "a," "c," and "d" to see why this is not the right answer.

11. What are the different types of résumés?

   a. **Functional**
   - This is one of the two major types of résumés. (The other is the chronological résumé.) The functional résumé lists positions you've held that are related to the type of position you are pursuing rather than just listing all positions in chronological order. This type is typically used by job seekers who have a variety of experience in many different settings and want to be sure the relevant experience and information stand out so that the hiring personnel can see it easily.

   b. **Chronological**
   - This is one of the two major types of résumés. (The other is the functional résumé.) The chronological résumé lists positions in chronological order, from the most recent to the oldest. This is the most common type of résumé used.

   c. Electronic
   - This résumé is simply an electronic version of the functional or chronological résumé.

   d. Alphabetical
   - Another trick answer

   e. Vitae
   - A vitae or curriculum vitae is not typically thought of as a résumé. It does, however, have some of the same characteristics as a résumé listing, for example, education, work experience, honors, etc. Job seekers who are pursuing academic positions use this document most often. It usually contains sections on publications, papers, presentations, conferences, grants, and so forth.

12. Which of the following are important aspects for a résumé?

   a. **Overall appearance**
   - Overall appearance affects first impressions. If the overall appearance of your résumé is not good, the hiring personnel may not look any further. Remember, there are sometimes hundreds of résumés for a single position, so hiring personnel are looking for reasons to eliminate.

   b. **Paper color**
   - The résumé is a professional document and must be easy to read, copy, and scan, so use good quality white bond paper.

   c. **Length**
   - Hiring personnel are looking for reasons to either eliminate your résumé or further consider you, so it is important to describe yourself and your experience clearly and concisely.

   d. **Organization**
   - If your résumé is not organized in a way that makes it easy to follow, hiring personnel may stop reading it and eliminate you as a candidate. A disorganized résumé might also reflect on your ability to organize and prioritize, which could be an important hiring consideration.

e. **Absence of typos and spelling and grammatical errors**
   - Once the hiring personnel really look at your résumé, they will react negatively to typos, misspellings, and grammatical errors. After all, you are a college graduate, and they expect you to produce error-free work. A résumé with such errors can also be construed as a sign that you do not attend to detail, which might be an important hiring consideration. So proofread, proofread, proofread, and have others do the same for you.

13. A professional objective statement is most useful when:
    a. You are submitting the résumé for a specific position
       - All answers are correct. If you are applying for a specific position, that position should be clearly reflected in your objective statement.
    b. You are changing career paths
       - All answers are correct. New college graduates typically will not be in this situation, unless they have returned to school to get a degree that is different from the field in which they have been working or is in a different field from their first degree.
    c. You are a recent graduate with little hands-on experience
       - All answers are correct. Recent graduates would typically use an objective statement for this reason. They are usually seeking some type of entry-level position in a field or area.
    d. Your career history or major alone do not present an easily identifiable "fit" for the position being targeted
       - All answers are correct. The objective statment provides an opportunity for someone without career history or a major in a particular field to be considered for a position in that field. The statement would identify the candidate's career interests and desires for prospective employers.
    e. **All of the above**

14. Who should review your résumé before you submit it?
    a. Just you
       - Even people who consider themselves expert résumé writers will ask others to review their résumé. Many times others can see important things that you have missed, including information, omissions, typos, and the like.
    b. As many people as possible
       - This is a better answer than "a," but you need to consider what the people know about writing a résumé, how well they know you and what you have done, whether they have any expertise in the profession that you are pursuing, and whether they have good English language skills.
    c. People who know you and your skills
       - This is a better answer than "a" and "b," but it does not address what the people know about writing a résumé, whether they have any expertise in the profession that you are pursuing, and whether they have good English language skills.
    d. Professionals in the field
       - This is a better answer than "a" and "b," but it does not address what the people know about writing a résumé, how well they know you and what you have done, and whether they have good English language skills.

e. **None of the above**
      - Ideally, the best people to review your résumé would have some current knowledge of and experience with writing a résumé, knowledge of you and what you have done, expertise in the profession that you are pursuing, and good English language skills. Given that it is difficult to find several people, let alone one person, who meet all four of these criteria, you may find that you will need to ask several people who meet one or more of the criteria and try to cover all four areas with the people you select.
15. What documents should accompany your résumé?
    a. Application
       - An application should accompany your résumé only if it is specifically asked for as part of the process.
    b. Portfolio
       - A portfolio should accompany your résumé only if it is an important part of demonstrating your skills.
    c. Picture
       - A picture should accompany your résumé only if it is specifically required for the position that you are seeking.
    d. **Reference list**
       - There is some debate about whether to include your reference list with your résumé. The general consensus among practitioners is that the inclusion of a reference list will not hurt you. In fact, many believe that if you have an inside contact, a recognized authority or someone in your network who will or might be recognized, it usually works in your favor to include a reference list. Remember to choose your references carefully and ask if they can give you a good recommendation. It is better to ask upfront than to find out later that you did not get the position because of a less than positive recommendation.
    e. **Cover letter**
       - A cover letter should always accompany your résumé. The cover letter is your opportunity to identify how you found out about the position, state what makes you a good candidate, clarify your career goals, show enthusiasm for the position and organization, and ask for an interview.

Give yourself one point for each answer you got right. There are 30 possible points. How many points did you earn?

27–31 points = Excellent

24–26 points = Very Good

21–23 points = Good

The main purpose of this exercise was to prompt you about the information you will need to put together the best possible résumé. Even if you received an "Excellent" score, the question(s) you missed might have a profound impact on your résumé. Review the questions that you missed so that you will be sure to include appropriate information and not include inappropriate information on your résumé.

EPILOGUE

"Do Whatever You Want, But Do It With Your Whole Heart": Some Final Thoughts on Dreams, Passions, and Finding Your Own Path

We begin with a story of a life-changing conversation. "When I was a teen-ager shortly before my grandfather died, we had a talk. He asked me about my future plans, what I hoped to spend my life doing. I replied in the sex-role stereotypic manner in which I had been raised that I thought I would be a secretary or an elementary school teacher. He thought for a moment, and then in his usual gentle and nonjudgmental style he said: "Do whatever you want, but do it with your whole heart." He went on to say that life is too short to not spend it doing activities that engage your heart, stimulate your mind, and nourish your soul.

We hope that the information and exercises in this book have provided the stimulation for you to think about your life plan and analyze the type of career and lifestyle that will best engage *your heart,* stimulate *your mind,* and engage *your soul.* Our goal was to help you to take the first steps on this journey toward self-understanding. We hope that we have given you many things to think about as you prepare to take the next steps on that path.

As we have emphasized, the skills that you have learned by reading and digesting the ideas in this book are ones that you will use over and over again in your life planning process. Especially today, with the dynamic nature of the job market, the chances that this will be the only time you choose a career field are very slim. Instead, you will most likely make career changes a number of times throughout your life. The Chinese proverb "Give a man a fish, and he will eat for a day. Teach a man to fish, and he will eat for the rest of his life" is of particular relevance here. The ideas you have learned in this book should have provided you with new awareness, knowledge, and skills to use over and over again in your life.

Specifically, we hope that you have heard some of the following messages:

- Career planning is a lifelong journey of self-awareness and discovery, not a one-time event.
- Work can and does provide deep meaning and satisfaction for some people, and it can do that for you as well.
- Control and involvement are key ingredients in the quality of one's life, and becoming truly involved in this journey of self awareness and discovery can lead to happiness and career actualization.
- Effective career planning requires a great deal of self-awareness. Really knowing your values, your interests, and your skills is essential to choosing the best path for yourself.
- Part of this self-awareness is understanding the role that both gender and cultural diversity have played in helping to shape the person you are and will become.
- Effective career planning also requires a thorough knowledge of the changing world of work and the skills and values most relevant to various career fields.
- An important part of career and life planning involves learning to take care of yourself, developing active social support networks, and achieving a healthy balance in the various aspects of your life.
- Learning to solve problems and managing stress is necessary to overcome obstacles and develop resilience along the bumpy road to success.
- Career planning also requires learning the specific skills of networking, résumé writing, interviewing, and setting effective short- and long-term goals and plans.

Most of all, we hope that you have heard our message about the need to hold onto your dreams and devise creative ways to turn them into reality.

We realize that even though this book has given you a good start at career and life planning, you may still have a long way to go. We have some recommendations for you about the road ahead:

First, there are numerous resources in your environment to help you in this process of career planning—don't feel like you have to do it alone. There are career centers in many towns, especially those with community colleges or universities. These can be excellent resources for you to find out more about yourself and the world of work.

Second, you may want to consider completing additional assessment measures or using computerized career information programs. We recommend using these measures as "tools of discovery" and trying to get the most you can out of each one. How do the results of each measure fit with how you see yourself and with the information you already know from assessments you have taken as part of this book? What is congruent? What seems contradictory? How can you put these pieces of the puzzle together?

Third, try to surround yourself with people who are affirming of you. A bumper sticker recently sighted read, "People who don't have dreams step on yours." It is important to seek out people who will help you to restore and nurture your dreams rather than discourage them.

In addition, the internet is a source of valuable career information that you should not overlook. The sites recommended in Chapter 12 of this text are a good starting point. You must of course be careful of the information you receive from the Web, but there are many sites that offer a wealth of information about career fields and specific jobs that may be of help in your career planning process.

Although you can gain a great deal of assistance in your career planning process through interacting with others, the decisions you make will ultimately be just that—*your* decisions. We have found that the more you can reflect about who you are and what is important to you, the better your decisions will be. As we have discussed in the text, reflection can happen in a number of ways. Some individuals use a journal to help them reflect on their experiences and what their reactions might be about eventual career paths. Others find it helpful to use exercises, such as thinking about what they would want said about them at their life's end and what these thoughts and feelings might tell them about what they most value. However you do it, thinking and reflecting about your own life is the most useful source of career information available to you.

We encourage you to continue on your career planning journey. As we noted at the beginning of this book, most people expect too little from their lives—especially their work lives. We hope that we have helped you to expect more, to reach high and to stretch out to achieve the dreams you have for yourself.

Appendix A

Missouri Occupational Card Sort

Cut out the cards and laminate them for more functional usage.

Appendix B
The Strength Audit

Complete this audit when you have some time to yourself and freedom from distraction. This is not a test that you can "pass" or "fail." Try to think on the horizontal dimension! Make your experience with the audit one of fun and self-discovery.

PART 1: ASSESSING YOUR STRENGTHS

The audit taps 15 strength areas. Each area is listed, followed by a number of specific items, and to the right of each item are four lines for indicating "None," "Little," "Some," or "Much" with regard to your strength or strength potential. Think about your level of strength for each item listed and place an "S" on the appropriate line. Then consider your potential in this area, and place a "P" on the appropriate line. You may find that you've put the "S" and "P" on the same line for some items.

Mark each item as you see yourself. Remember that *if there has been evidence of strength in the past, this may still be a potent force able to affect your present or future functioning.* Remember also that most people tend to underrate themselves and to deny or ignore their strengths.

You are also asked to list specific information under some strength items. Complete the blanks provided for this purpose. List any additional strengths or potentials you know or feel you have in the spaces provided at the end of each area.

It may be helpful to have a person who knows you well go through the completed audit with you. This person might use a different color pencil to mark the items in the light of his or her knowledge of you. You then may wish to take over the marking and revise your earlier assessment.

Note. Adapted from Herbert Otto, *The Inventory of Personal Resources.* Class handout from a course in human potential, University of Utah, 1967. Used by permission.

CAREER PLANNING 199

1. **Appreciation Strengths**

Strengths in This Area

	None	Little	Some	Much
a. Periodically attending football games, basketball games, or similar sports events during the year			S	P
b. Attending plays, movies, and lectures or watching "good" TV plays and educational programs			S	P
c. Reading books, fiction, plays, poetry, biography, history, or books on contemporary issues a number of times during the year		S	P	
d. Reading a variety of magazines: news magazines, family magazines, or literary magazines a number of times monthly	S	P		
e. Reading daily newspapers or listening to news broadcasts to keep abreast of events	S		P	
f. Enjoying trips to museums, art exhibits, etc.				SP

Other appreciation strengths

g. _____
h. _____
i. _____
j. _____
k. _____

2. **Sports Strengths**

Strengths in This Area

None Little Some Much

a. Actively but intermittently participating in sports or games during the year

List Major Sports	How Often
_____	_____
_____	_____
_____	_____

b. Consistently and throughout the year participating in sports or games

List Major Sports	How Often
golf	5 d/w
volleyball	2 d/w
dodgeball	1 d/w
_____	_____

c. Actively but intermittently enjoying nature and participating in outdoor activities such as camping, hunting, fishing, hiking

List Major Activities	How Often
walking	
fishing	
hunting	
camping	

d. Consistently and throughout the year enjoying nature and outdoor activities

List Major Activities	How Often
walking	
sitting	

e. Doing body-building exercises or having a "gym workout," massage, and so on, actively but ☐ intermittently ☐ consistently (check one) throughout the year

List	How Often
gym	3/wk

f. Wishing and desiring more active participation in sports, nature and outdoor activities, body-building exercise, massage, and so on

List Which	How Often
massage	
hunting	
[pilates]	

Other sports strengths

g. golf

h.

CAREER PLANNING   201

3. **Leisure Strengths**

Strengths in This Area

	None	Little	Some	Much

a. Showing interest in one or more hobbies

List Which

knitting   SP
movies   SP
walking   S   P
reading   SP
music   SP

b. Spending a great deal of time and effort on one or more hobbies

List Which

knitting   SP
reading   SP
music   SP

c. Making products that are praised and admired

List Which

d. Receiving instructions, or training, in crafts such as furniture making, weaving, pottery, jewelry making

List Which

e. Having special knowledge or interests to which you give time or effort

List Which

_JD_   SP
movies   SP
books   SP
music   S P

f. Having possible hobby(ies) or craft(s) that you would enjoy but for which you have had little opportunity

List Which

_____

_____

_____

_____

Other hobbies or crafts that you enjoy

g. _____

_____

h. _____

_____

4. Artistic Strengths

Strengths in This Area

	None	Little	Some	Much

a. Actively and periodically participating in social dancing — Little: SP

b. Having special skill in social dancing and knowing several types of dances such as rhumba, square dancing — Some: SP

c. Doing modern or interpretive dancing — Little: SP

d. Participating in plays or dramatic productions — None: SP

e. Writing stories, essays, articles, or poetry — Little: S; Some: P

f. Having one or a number of writings sold or printed in any source — None: SP

g. Doing painting in oil, water color, etc., or sketching and drawing — Little: PS

h. Doing sculpture in clay, stone, or other media or doing wood carving — None: S; Little: P

i. Making pottery, mobiles, or other art objects — Little: S; Some: P

j. Having sculpture, wood carving, pottery, or other art object admired, used in interior decorating, or bought — None: SP

k. Having a definite feeling for music and rhythm or "can pick out a tune" on some musical instrument — Much: SP

l. Being able to improvise or make up own tunes or compose music — Little: S; Some: P

m. Playing a musical instrument in a band or entertaining people or having skill in playing an instrument

n. Appreciating music—listening to popular or classical music or singing

o. Appreciating music—studying and learning about music

p. Wishing or desiring or would enjoy participating in the expressive arts

List Which

_____
_____
_____
_____

Other artistic strengths

q. _____

r. _____

5. Health and Physical Fitness Strengths

Strengths in This Area

	None	Little	Some	Much

a. Being able-bodied and capable of hard physical labor

Check one: Heavy labor _____

Light labor _____

Occasional labor _____

b. Being in general good health

c. Being in top physical condition and health

d. Having an active interest in maintaining health by periodic physical examination and regular monitoring of health

e. Fostering health through regular physical exercises, gym workouts, or sports

f. Maintaining health through proper nutrition or a diet designed to meet activity level and age requirements

g. Seeking medical attention or treatment and psychiatric or other professional help *at once* when needed _____ _____ _√__P__ _____

h. Being full of energy and vitality most of the time _____ _____ __SP__ _____

i. Maintaining and continuing an immunization program _____ _____ _____ __SP__

j. Using and enjoying all senses—hearing, smell, sight, taste, touch _____ _____ _____ __SP__

Other fitness strengths

k. _____
   _____ _____ _____ _____ _____

l. _____
   _____ _____ _____ _____ _____

6. Educational Strengths

a. Grade school and/or some high school education

   List years of school completed __2009 — graduated high school_____

b. Graduation from high school and/or some college education

   Years of college __graduated college — 3 years_____

c. Graduated from college

   Degree _____ Year _____ Institution _____

d. Postgraduate education, professional education, and/or graduate degree

   Graduate Degree _____ Year _____ Institution _____

e. Vocational, trade, or technical training with completion of a course of training or certification

   Training Course   Completed

   _____   _____
   _____   _____
   _____   _____

f. Some vocational, trade, or technical training

   Training Course   Months

   _____   _____
   _____   _____
   _____   _____

CAREER PLANNING   205

g. High marks, grades, scholastic honors, or superior achievement at any time during education or training

List High Grades, Achievement — good grades, AP award, Spen. ton. luci.

Where

h. On-the-job or other training leading to a skill salable on the labor market

List Training

Where

i. Enrollment in special courses, classes, evening classes, institutes, or workshops

List Courses — summer classes

When — summer

j. Self-education in specific or general areas through extensive study and systematic reading of books and other sources

List Areas of Study

Any education or training that you have offered others as teacher, coach, leader

k. _____

l. _____

m. Having the education and training for work, job, position, or to earn a living — s p

n. Having the necessary education or training to achieve vocational goals or advancement in job or position

o. Having education or training as a means to better understand life, living, and the world — s p

p. Having education as a means of enjoying life and living more fully — s p

q. Having education as a tool to achieve more vital, spontaneous, and emotionally satisfying life experiences _____ _____ _____ _SP_

r. Having education as an aid in understanding yourself or other persons _____ _____ _____ _SP_

s. Having education as a source of stimulating intellectual curiosity—an eagerness to learn and find out more _____ _____ _____ _SP_

t. Being definitely interested in obtaining more education or training _____ _____ _____ _SP_

List Areas

_____
_____
_____
_____

7. Personal Strengths

Strengths in This Area

	None	Little	Some	Much

a. Having hunches or a sense of intuition that usually turns out to be right _____ _____ _____ _SP_

b. Usually following through on sense of intuition or hunches _____ _____ _____ _SP_

c. Having a "green thumb" or the ability to make things grow _____ _____ _____ _SP_

d. Having mechanical ability _____ _____ _SP_ _____

e. Having ability in mathematics, physics, chemistry, or others _____ _____ _____ _____

List Which

f. Having sales ability _____ _____ _____ _SP_

g. Having the ability to instruct or teach children or adults _N_ _____ _____ _SP_

List Areas

_____
_____
_____

h. Making a good impression on people through physical appearance—having a good physique, face, figure _____ _____ _____ _SP_

i. Having manual dexterity _____ _____ _____ _SP_

j. _____

k. _____

8. **Family and Friendship Strengths**

                                                   Strengths in This Area

	None	Little	Some	Much

a. Having a husband or wife who gives love, attention, and understanding

b. Having a husband or wife who is interested in things you are doing and who listens and gives support

c. Having relationships with children as a source of satisfaction, stimulation, and growth for you

d. Having close relationships with parents or in-laws as a source of strength

e. Having close relationships with other relatives   *SP*

         List Relatives

_____

_____

_____

_____

_____

f. Having access to family unity, loyalty, and cooperation   *SP*

g. Having close friends on whom you can rely in a crisis as a source of strength; list number of friends 4/3   *SP*

h. If single, having close relationship(s) with others   *SP*

Other family/friendship strengths

i. _____

j. _____

9. Intellectual Strengths

Strengths in This Area

	None	Little	Some	Much
a. Being able to apply reasoning processes to problem solving				S P
b. Having intellectual curiosity—wanting to know the why and wherefore of things or doing critical reasoning				S P
c. Being able to stimulate or develop intellectual curiosity in others				S P
d. Formulating and expressing ideas verbally or in writing			S	P
e. Being receptive to new ideas from people, books, or other sources				S P
f. Working on extending your intellectual horizon through extensive reading, discussion, sharing of ideas				S P
g. Doing original and creative thinking			S	P
h. Working to improve your ability to concentrate on being engaged in any course, program, or activity designed to improve your intellectual strengths				S P
i. Having the ability to learn and enjoy learning				S P

Other intellectual strengths

j. _____

k. _____

l. _____

10. Aesthetic Strengths

Strengths in This Area

	None	Little	Some	Much
a. Recognizing and enjoying beauty in nature				S P
b. Recognizing and enjoying beauty in art or things				S P
c. Recognizing and enjoying the physical beauty of people				S P
d. Recognizing and enjoying the beauty expressed through the personality of people				S P

e. Using a sense of beauty or aesthetic sense to enhance home and physical environment

f. Making an effort to develop, sharpen, and extend the range of your aesthetic sensibilities and perceptions

Other aesthetic strengths

g. _____

h. _____

i. _____

j. _____

k. _____

11. **Organizational Strengths**

Strengths in This Area

	None	Little	Some	Much
a. Assigning and carrying out priorities or doing first things first				S P
b. Thinking through problems or projects to make plans, then taking concrete steps to carry out such plans			S	P
c. Developing and planning realistic short-range and long-range goals			S	P
d. Organizing resources, energy, and time to achieve short- or long-range goals			S	P
e. Being able to carry out or direct detailed jobs or projects requiring much detail work			S P	
f. Having the capacity to coordinate the efforts and productivity of people or other factors in an organization, business, industry			SP	
g. Carrying out as well as giving orders			SP	

h. Having experience in organizing enterprises or projects

   List Major Experiences   When

i. Having experience in organizing clubs, social organizations, political work, or others

   List Major Experiences   When

j. Having held leadership position(s) in organizations (include social or church groups)

   Major Position Held   Organization   When

Other organizational strengths

k. _____

l. _____

m. _____

12. **Creative Strengths**

Strengths in This Area

None   Little   Some   Much

a. Using creativity and imagination by thinking up new and different ideas (or things to do, fun projects) in relation to home and family

b. Using creativity and imagination by thinking up new and different ideas in relation to work

c. Using creativity and imagination in social relationships and situations ___ ___ __S__ __P__

d. Working on developing and extending your imagination and creative abilities through any means ___ __S__ __P__ ___

e. Using imagination to make up stories for children, inventing new games for them, and so on ___ ___ __S__ __P__

f. Exercising the capacity for original and independent thinking in private and in company

g. Expressing creativity and imagination through writing, painting, sculpting, dance, music, or any other expressive arts (underline which) ___ ___ __S__ __P__

Other creative strengths

h. _____

i. _____

j. _____

13. **Relationship Strengths**

Strengths in This Area

	None	Little	Some	Much
a. Feeling comfortable meeting people, making them feel comfortable, or having ability to talk freely with strangers				S P
b. Enjoying being with people most of the time				S P
c. Having good relations with neighbors			S	P
d. Willing to help others or do for others without expectation of return				S P
e. Being kind or loving to people			S	P
f. Treating people with consideration, politeness, and respect				S P
g. Being able to really listen to what others have to say				S P
h. Being sensitive to the needs and feelings of others				S P
i. Understanding why people behave the way they do and helping them to grow through this understanding			S	P
j. Having real patience with children or adults			S	P

k. Having the capacity to "stand up to people" when necessary, to "get through when needed," or to say no _____ __S__ _____ __P__

l. Being able to help others become more mature, loving, and productive human beings _____ __S__ _____ __P__

m. Helping others to be aware of their strengths, potentialities, and abilities as well as their shortcomings or problems _____ _____ __S__ __P__

n. Relating to people as individuals regardless of sex, creed, or race _____ _____ _____ __SP__

o. Conveying the feeling to people that you understand them _____ _____ _____ __SP__

Other relationship strengths

p. _____

14. Emotional Strengths

Strengths in This Area

	None	Little	Some	Much
a. Being able to give warmth, affection, love				SP
b. Being able to receive warmth, affection, love				SP
c. Being able to openly express anger to others		S		P
d. Being able to "take" anger or hostility from others				SP
e. Being able to *feel* a wide range of emotions				SP
f. Being able to *express* a wide range of feelings and emotions			S	P
g. Being sensitive to the feelings of others				SP
h. Having the capacity for spontaneity—to do or express things on the spur of the moment				SP
i. Using feelings and emotions productively				SP
j. Exercising emotional honesty—for example, *not* saying, "No, I'm not mad," when you are angry		S		P
k. Having the ability to "put yourself in the other person's shoes," to feel empathy			S	P
l. Understanding the role of your feelings and emotions in everyday living				SP

Other emotional strengths (include ability to handle stress or pressure in specific situations)

m. __stress_____

_____ _____ _____ __S   P__

n. _____

o. _____

15. Other Strengths

Strengths in This Area

	None	Little	Some	Much

a. Using humor as a source of strength in social relations, at home, or at work

b. Being able to laugh at yourself and having the ability to take kidding at your expense

c. Having the ability to "stick your neck out," to risk yourself with people and in situations

d. Liking to adventure or pioneer—to explore new horizons or try new ways

List Examples

_____

_____

_____

_____

e. Having the ability to grow through defeat, crisis, or adversity or by turning a reverse to advantage

f. Having perseverance or sticking to a task or goal despite obstacles or discouragement

g. Having a strong drive to get things done and doing them

h. Taking the initiative in situations or with people

i. Being self-critical, self-evaluative—being able to look at yourself and your actions and beliefs critically

j. Having the capacity to dissent—to take a stand different from the crowd or people

k. Having the ability to manage financially, evidenced by investments, savings, and so on

l. Being able to tell stories, poems, anecdotes, or jokes to adults or children or being able to keep a crowd entertained

m. Being "handy around the house"

n. Knowing languages or knowing other cultures through travel or reading (underline which) _____ _____ _____ *SP*

o. Speaking publicly or being able to get up in front of people and express your views _____ _____ *S* *P*

p. _____

q. _____

r. _____

s. _____

t. _____

u. _____

Part 2: Reviewing Your Assets, Possibilities, and Goals

The purpose of the Strength Audit is to stimulate you to a better understanding of your personal strengths. Reexamine your completed audit now. As you examine *each area,* ask yourself the following questions. Then jot down notes about your strengths and potentials in each area listed in the chart below. From these notes, list your assets, possibilities, and possible goals.

1. What new strengths have I discovered?
2. What strengths have I confirmed?
3. What potentials have I discovered that I would like to develop more fully?
4. What assets have I found that I can build on for greater success, greater personal satisfaction, greater contributions to others?
5. What new possible goals are suggested by my strengths?

Work Life

Notes: _____
_____
_____
_____

a. Assets

b. Possibilities

c. Possible Goals

Leisure Life

Notes: _____
_____
_____
_____

a. Assets

b. Possibilities

c. Possible Goals

Contributions to Others

Notes: _____
_____
_____
_____

a. Assets

b. Possibilities

c. Possible Goals

Describe Below

What are some strength situations that you can engage in that would help you to further assess and affirm some newly discovered strengths and strength potentials?

Describe Below

What are some ways of exploring new areas and possible goals that tie into your strengths?

Vocational Situations and Areas

Leisure Situations and Areas

Appendix C
Reality Testing Goals and Plans

If your goals are to be worth committing yourself, they must fit with your needs, desires, abilities, and experience.

PART 1. NEEDS FIT

Below is a list of needs. On the left, check whether they are true of you. On the right, decide if they would be satisfied if you accomplish your present goals.

True	Not True	Doubtful		Certain	Possible	Unlikely
____	____	____	1. I need to function where I would be *by myself most of the time.*	☐	☐	☐
____	____	____	2. I need to function where I would be *by myself part of the time* and *with people part of the time.*	☐	☐	☐
____	____	____	3. I need to function where I would be *with people all of the time.*	☐	☐	☐
____	____	____	4. I need to function where I am involved *with familiar people most of the time.*	☐	☐	☐
____	____	____	5. I need to function where I am involved *with new people most of the time.*	☐	☐	☐
____	____	____	6. I need to function where I am involved *with new people some of the time* and *familiar people some of the time.*	☐	☐	☐
____	____	____	7. I need to function where I would *not meet* new people.	☐	☐	☐
____	____	____	8. I need to function where I would be able to *meet new people.*	☐	☐	☐
____	____	____	9. I need to function where I would have the *authority to tell people what to do.*	☐	☐	☐
____	____	____	10. I need to function where I could *influence and persuade people.*	☐	☐	☐
____	____	____	11. I need to function where I would have a great deal of *independence* and *freedom.*	☐	☐	☐
____	____	____	12. I need to function where I am *free of pressure.*	☐	☐	☐
____	____	____	13. I need to function where I feel *some amount of pressure.*	☐	☐	☐
____	____	____	14. I need to function where I am *free from personal conflict with others.*	☐	☐	☐
____	____	____	15. I need to function where I am involved in *some or considerable personal conflict with others.*	☐	☐	☐
____	____	____	16. I need to function where I am the *center of attention.*	☐	☐	☐

Note. © The Carroll Press, Cranston, R.I. Used by permission.

True	Not True	Doubtful		Certain	Possible	Unlikely
_____	_____	_____	17. I need to function where I would *contribute* directly or indirectly *to the welfare of others.*	☐	☐	☐
_____	_____	_____	18. I need to function where I would *not have to contribute* directly *to the welfare of others.*	☐	☐	☐
_____	_____	_____	19. I need to function where I work mostly with *ideas.*	☐	☐	☐
_____	_____	_____	20. I need to function where I work mostly with my *hands.*	☐	☐	☐
_____	_____	_____	21. I need to function where I work with both my *mind and my hands.*	☐	☐	☐
_____	_____	_____	22. I need to function where I use my mind in a *practical* way to see tangible results of my efforts.	☐	☐	☐
_____	_____	_____	23. I need to function where I use *theories* to solve problems.	☐	☐	☐
_____	_____	_____	24. I need to function where I *organize logical* facts or figures.	☐	☐	☐
_____	_____	_____	25. I need to function where I *prepare charts and graphs* to solve problems or to draw conclusions.	☐	☐	☐
_____	_____	_____	26. I need to function in *routine* or repetitive work most of the time.	☐	☐	☐
_____	_____	_____	27. I need to function where I do a *variety* of different things.	☐	☐	☐
_____	_____	_____	28. I need to function where I do a *variety* of things some of the time and *routine* things some of the time.	☐	☐	☐
_____	_____	_____	29. I need to function where I can *work with ideas* to create new processes or products.	☐	☐	☐
_____	_____	_____	30. I need to function where it is important to understand *how and why things work.*	☐	☐	☐
_____	_____	_____	31. I need to function where I can usually *see the results* of my efforts.	☐	☐	☐
_____	_____	_____	32. I need to function where I have time to *think through a problem* before I must make a decision.	☐	☐	☐
_____	_____	_____	33. I need to function where I *must think in very accurate and precise ways.*	☐	☐	☐
_____	_____	_____	34. I need to function where I can *use my hands and fingers to create things.*	☐	☐	☐

True	Not True	Doubtful		Certain	Possible	Unlikely
_____	_____	_____	35. I need to function where I can *use my hands and fingers to build or to repair things*.	☐	☐	☐
_____	_____	_____	36. I need to function where I *use tools or machines* most of the time.	☐	☐	☐
_____	_____	_____	37. I need to function where I am able to move about and be *on the go most of the time*.	☐	☐	☐
_____	_____	_____	38. I need to function where I work *outdoors most of the time*.	☐	☐	☐
_____	_____	_____	39. I need to function where I work both *in and out of doors*.	☐	☐	☐
_____	_____	_____	40. I need to function where my *surroundings are beautiful*.	☐	☐	☐
_____	_____	_____	41. I need to function where I use *considerable* amounts of *physical energy*.	☐	☐	☐
_____	_____	_____	42. I need to function where I use *some physical energy*.	☐	☐	☐
_____	_____	_____	43. I need to function where I have a *high status and prestige*.	☐	☐	☐
_____	_____	_____	44. I need to function where I earn a very *large amount of money*.	☐	☐	☐
_____	_____	_____	45. I need to function where I earn at least an *average amount of money*.	☐	☐	☐
_____	_____	_____	46. I need to do work that I enjoy; *money that I earn is not all-important*.	☐	☐	☐
_____	_____	_____	47. I need to function where my *hours are regular*.	☐	☐	☐
_____	_____	_____	48. I need to function where my *hours are flexible*.	☐	☐	☐
_____	_____	_____	49. I need to function where my *job is secure*.	☐	☐	☐
_____	_____	_____	50. I need to function where I am *part of a team*.	☐	☐	☐

Part 2. Desires Fit

How do your goals fit with the lifestyle you want? Think about your future as you really want it to be. Complete each of the following sentences about the present and the future.

1. I am now living in (city, rural, suburban, region) _____
2. I would like to be living in_____
3. I now live with (mate, parents, alone, etc.) _____
4. I would like to be living with_____
5. I now live in (type of house, apartment, etc.) _____
6. I would like to live in_____
7. I now work as (occupation, student, etc.) _____
8. I would like to be working as _____
9. I now work in (office, shop, store, etc.)_____
10. I would like to be working in_____
11. My working hours are _____
12. I would like my working hours to be_____
13. I now travel _____
14. I would like to travel _____
15. The people I work with now _____
16. The people I would like to work with _____
17. In my spare time I now _____
18. In my spare time I would_____
19. My closest friends now are _____
20. My closest friends would be _____

Look over your responses. How does your career actualization goal fit with the lifestyle reflected in the even-numbered sentences? How would attaining your goal improve your life?

Part 3: Skills Fit

Following is a set of skills or abilities needed for success in many types of careers. In the left-hand columns, check the importance of each to your career goals. Then rate each ability as (1) a major asset, (2) a minor asset, (3) an area needing improvement or (4) a liability.

Socializing With Others

Importance
High   Low

_____ _____ *Congeniality:* relate easily in situations that are primarily social in nature (parties, receptions)

        _____ 1   _____ 2   _____ 3   _____ 4

_____ _____ *Public relations:* relate on a continual basis with people who come to an establishment for information, service, or help, including a broad cross-section of people

        _____ 1   _____ 2   _____ 3   _____ 4

_____ _____ *Tastefulness:* dress presentably and appropriately for a variety of interpersonal situations or group occasions

        _____ 1   _____ 2   _____ 3   _____ 4

_____ _____ *Handling criticism or disagreement:* able to cope with negative reactions

        _____ 1   _____ 2   _____ 3   _____ 4

Communicating With Others

_____ _____ *Talking:* relate easily with people in ordinary conversational settings

        _____ 1   _____ 2   _____ 3   _____ 4

_____ _____ *Writing:* express myself well in written forms of communication

        _____ 1   _____ 2   _____ 3   _____ 4

_____ _____ *Compromising:* able to bargain or discuss with a view toward reaching agreement through negotiation

        _____ 1   _____ 2   _____ 3   _____ 4

_____ _____ *Persuading:* able to convince others to believe something that I hold to be true

        _____ 1   _____ 2   _____ 3   _____ 4

_____ _____ *Selling:* able to convince others to buy a product that I am selling

        _____ 1   _____ 2   _____ 3   _____ 4

_____ _____ *Public speaking:* able to deliver a talk or address to an audience

        _____ 1   _____ 2   _____ 3   _____ 4

Directing and Helping Others

_____ _____ *Supervising:* able to oversee, manage, or direct work of others

_____ 1 _____ 2 _____ 3 _____ 4

_____ _____ *Teaching:* able to help others learn how to do or understand something; able to provide knowledge or insight

_____ 1 _____ 2 _____ 3 _____ 4

_____ _____ *Coaching:* able to instruct or train an individual to improve his or her performance in a specific subject area

_____ 1 _____ 2 _____ 3 _____ 4

_____ _____ *Counseling:* able to engage in a direct helping relationship with another individual when the person's concern is not solvable through direct information-giving or advice

_____ 1 _____ 2 _____ 3 _____ 4

Organizing Others

_____ _____ *Organizing and planning:* able to develop a program project or set of ideas through systematic preparation and arrangement of tasks, coordinating the people and resources necessary to put a plan into effect

_____ 1 _____ 2 _____ 3 _____ 4

_____ _____ *Orderliness:* able to arrange items in a systematic, regular fashion so that such items or information can be readily used or retrieved with a minimum of difficulty

_____ 1 _____ 2 _____ 3 _____ 4

_____ _____ *Following through on details:* able to work with a great variety and/or volume of information without losing track of any items in the total situation; comfortable with small informational tasks that are part of the larger project responsibility

_____ 1 _____ 2 _____ 3 _____ 4

_____ _____ *Making decisions:* comfortable in making judgments or reaching conclusions about matters that require specific action; able to accept responsibility for the consequences of such actions

_____ 1 _____ 2 _____ 3 _____ 4

Working With Tools

_____ _____ *Mechanical reasoning:* able to understand the ways that machinery or tools operate and the relationship between mechanical operations

_____ 1   _____ 2   _____ 3   _____ 4

_____ _____ *Dexterity:* skill in using hands or body

_____ 1   _____ 2   _____ 3   _____ 4

_____ _____ *Visualizing size and shape:* able to judge the relationships of objects in space, to judge sizes and shapes, to manipulate them mentally, and to visualize the effects of putting them together or of turning them over or around

_____ 1   _____ 2   _____ 3   _____ 4

_____ _____ *Physical strength and stamina:* physical resistance to fatigue, hardship, and illness

_____ 1   _____ 2   _____ 3   _____ 4

_____ _____ *Working outdoors:* familiar with the outdoors, ability to work outdoors without encountering obstacles or knowledge deficiencies

_____ 1   _____ 2   _____ 3   _____ 4

Being Original and Creative

_____ _____ *Creating art and beauty:* keenly sensitive to aesthetic values, able to create work of art

_____ 1   _____ 2   _____ 3   _____ 4

_____ _____ *Imagination with things:* able to create new ideas and forms with various physical objects

_____ 1   _____ 2   _____ 3   _____ 4

_____ _____ *Imagination with ideas:* able to create new ideas and programs through conceiving existing elements of behavior in new ways; able to merge abstract ideas in new ways

_____ 1   _____ 2   _____ 3   _____ 4

Researching Problems

_____ _____ *Intellectual curiosity:* able to learn about scientific phenomena and investigate events that may lead to such learning

_____ 1   _____ 2   _____ 3   _____ 4

_____ _____ *Investigating:* able to gather information in a systematic way in an area of inquiry in order to establish certain facts or principles

_____ 1   _____ 2   _____ 3   _____ 4

_____ _____ *Technical skills:* able to work easily with practical, mechanical, or industrial aspects of a particular science, profession, or craft

_____ 1   _____ 2   _____ 3   _____ 4

Solving Numerical Problems

_____ _____ *Computational speed:* able to manipulate numerical data rapidly without the aid of a mechanical device, demonstrating considerable accuracy in the process

_____ 1 _____ 2 _____ 3 _____ 4

_____ _____ *Working with numerical data:* comfortable with large amounts of quantitative data, compiling, interpreting, presenting such data

_____ 1 _____ 2 _____ 3 _____ 4

_____ _____ *Solving quantitative problems:* able to reason quantitatively so that problems having numerical solutions can be solved without the aid of a computer or other mechanical equipment

_____ 1 _____ 2 _____ 3 _____ 4

_____ _____ *Computer use:* able to use electronic computers to solve quantitative problems; knowledge of programming, computer capabilities, software

_____ 1 _____ 2 _____ 3 _____ 4

Review your responses. Remember that you are not always the best judge of your abilities. Where you had doubt or difficulty, check with someone who has worked with you or supervised you in a related activity.

How do you assess the fit between your career actualization goals and your own abilities? Discuss this issue with others in as open and nondefensive a way as possible.

Part 4: Experience Fit

If you are to move toward your goals effectively, you must utilize as much of your prior experience as possible. Even when your goals take you in new directions, you can "transfer" many of the skills and understandings learned in one kind of experience and put them to use in a new setting or in the service of a new goal.

Look back at the strength audit that you completed earlier. Remember that worthwhile experiences may come from hobbies, clubs, athletics, and volunteer activities as well as from full-time work.

Now in each of the following categories record the relevant experiences that you have had in terms of your career actualization goals. Record the time, place, and extent of experience. Also try to think of the people who could document this experience for you by writing recommendations.

1. Mechanical experiences

    When?

    Where?

    Extent?

2. Physical or outdoor experiences

    When?

    Where?

    Extent?

3. Investigative and analytic experiences

    When?

    Where?

    Extent?

4. Mathematical experiences

    When?

    Where?

    Extent?

5. Artistic experiences

    When?

    Where?

    Extent?

6. Writing or editing experiences

    When?

    Where?

    Extent?

7. Selling or persuading experiences
   - When?
   - Where?
   - Extent?

8. Teaching or training experiences
   - When?
   - Where?
   - Extent?

9. Managerial or administrative experiences
   - When?
   - Where?
   - Extent?

10. Verbal communications or experiences
    - When?
    - Where?
    - Extent?

11. Directing or organizing experiences
    - When?
    - Where?
    - Extent?

12. Accounting or clerical experiences
    - When?
    - Where?
    - Extent?

Part 5: Revising Your Goals

You have now examined your tentative career goals in terms of their fit with (1) your personal strengths; (2) your desires; (3) your self-evaluated skills and abilities, and (4) your relevant practical experience.

Review carefully this reality-testing information. Also review Exercise 1.1 (Where Am I, etc.), your Career Actualization Lifeline (Exercise 4.3), and your Strength Audit (Appendix B).

Now review or revise your career goals based on this information. Add any exploratory, planning, or enabling goals that your review suggests. Remember that these types of goals may be just as important a part of your plans as are your ultimate or end goals.

Now write out a set of revised goals, those goals to which you are fully committed and willing to act upon *now*. Remember that these goals should be:

- *personally* chosen
- *publicly* affirmed
- *practically* attainable
- worth an *immediate* investment
- translatable into action *now*

Revised Goals

Index

A

ABC method (Ellis), 118
Abilities. *See* skills
Accomplishment, individual, 18, 19, 42, 96, 102
Achievement, 45, 82, 102
　motivation, 101, 102
　tests, 35
Action plans, 90, 101, 104–105
　steps in implementing, 129
Actualization, 4, 7
　career, 1, 6, 130, 131, 168
Adolescence
　changes during, 42
　socialization during, 58
　values acquired during, 47
Affirmation(s), 58, 113, 119, 169
　of goals, 102
African-American. *See* Black
Ageism, 67
Aggression, in response to stress, 127
Ainsworth, Mary, 7
Alienation, 47
Ambiguity, as factor in stress, 134–135
Anxiety, 128. *See also* Stress
Aristotle, 2
Aspirations, 5, 7, 28, 56, 61, 79, 80, 94, 107, 136
　during midlife, 44, 45, 46, 48, 49
Assessment
　on horizontal dimension, 95–96
　of interests, 31
　self-, 95
　on vertical dimension, 95, 96
Atkinson, Donald, 69, 70
Attitudes, 44, 47, 48, 101, 102, 121, 131
　toward male/female roles, 56
　racial identity, 69
Autonomy, 83
　state of white racial development, 71
Avoidance, 118
Awareness, 119
　of problems, 126

B

Balance, 113, 120–121, 168
Barriers, societal/institutional, 56, 61
BDA method, 106
Behavior(s)
　problem-solving, 126
　self-defeating, 118–119
　self-managing, 106
　target, 106–107
Beliefs, irrational, 118, 119
Betz, Nancy, 60
Bigotry, 67, 69
Biological clock, 44
Black racial identity, 69–70
Blaming, 127
Boys, socialization of, 56, 58, 60–61
Bulletin Boards (BBSs), computerized, in job search, 152–153
Business cards, 142

C

Card Sort, Missouri Occupational, 29–31; Appendix A
Career, 5, 168
　actualization, 1, 6, 130, 131, 168
　definition of, 17
　exploration, 31–32, 33, 34, 90
　development, 5, 16, 58
　information sources, 34
　nontraditional, 60
　pattern, 5
　planning, 6, 28, 32, 96, 114, 115, 168, 169

　transition, 118
Catastrophizing, 132, 134
Centering, 121–122
Challenge(s), 41, 42, 82, 94, 102, 104, 121, 129, 131
　during early adulthood, 43
Change(s)
　life, 41, 42
　managing, 20–21
　in midlife, 46
　in workplace, 16, 18
Choices, making, 80. *See also* Decision making
Chronicle of Higher Education, 152
Chunking, 135
Civil rights movement, 56
Coatsworth, 7
Commitment, 81, 82, 84, 95–96, 101, 103
　generating, 102-103, 105
　to goals, 103–104
　public, 107
Communication skills, 18, 155
Competence, 102. *See also* Control
Competition, 56, 81
Conflict
　racial, 67
　resolution, 18, 42
　role, 60
Complexity as factor in stress, 135
Consequences, 107
　in ABC method, 118
Consistency, 102
Contracting, self-, 107
Control, 1, 2, 3, 5, 6, 7, 48, 80, 82, 83, 85
　locus of, 102-103
　positive, 103
　in problem solving, 128
　self/personal, 44, 95, 101, 102, 105, 106, 107, 130, 134, 168
　in workplace, 22
Coping, and coping skills, 61, 103
　with stress, 130, 131, 132, 133, 134
Courage, 47
Cover letter, 145, 148–150, 156
Covey, Steven, 90
Creativity, 42, 46, 83, 168
　in problem solving, 125, 128, 129
Critical thinking, 21–22
Croce, Jim, 108
Crossover phenomenon, 6
Culture(s)(al), 66. *See also* Diversity
　American, 103
　clocks, 43-44
　diverse, 22, 68, 168
　entrepreneurial, 19–20
　heritage, 72
　of organization, 16, 19, 23

D

Daydreams, 102. *See also* Dreams
Decision making, 50, 129
　career, 32, 169
　in workplace, 17
Depression, 103, 116, 117, 118
Development, identity
　black, 69–70
　minority, 70
　white, 70–71
Developmental
　change, 7
　crises, 4, 5
　drives, 7, 80
　stages, 3
　transitions, 1, 2, 6
Diet
　and health, 116
　and stress, 133
Direction shock, 5

Discrimination, racial, 71
Diversity
　cultural, 68, 168
　in workplace, 16, 22, 61, 65, 66
Donne, John, 66
Dreams, 56–57, 61, 104, 168, 169

E

Eating habits. *See* Diet
Education, need for, 18
Effort, optimism, 101, 102, 103
Ellis, Albert, 118
E-mail, networking via, 153
Empathy, 67, 136
Empowerment, 3, 7, 28, 93
Environment. *See also* Workplace
　null, 58
　work, 31
Erikson, Erik, 46
Ethnicity. *See* Diversity
Evaluation, self-. *See* Assessment
Exercise
　and stress, 133, 136
　and well-being, 117
Expectations, 83, 118
　in entrepreneurial organizations, 20
　in midlife, 48
　others', of us, 94, 95
Experience(s), 32, 96, 103, 120

F

Fantasy goals, 79, 102
Feasibility study, 129
Flexibility, 49, 50
Freedom, 80, 83
Freud, Sigmund, 93
Friedan, Betty, 59
Friends. *See* Social support; Support system
Frustration, 126–127

G

Gender. *See* Sex-role
Genogram, 67; Exercise 6.1, p. 75
Girls, socialization of, 56, 58, 60, 61
Glass ceiling, 59
Goals, 44, 45, 81, 93, 94, 102
　accomplishing/attaining, 19, 96, 129
　affirming, 102
　balance, 121
　career, 27
　commitment to, 44, 103–104
　fantasy, 79, 102
　growth, need for, 81, 82–83
　life, 85, 90
　long-term, 105
　at midlife, 47, 48, 49
　organizational, 72
　planning and enabling, 90
　prioritizing, 93, 102, 104
　progress toward, 104, 105
　setting, 28, 50, 89, 90, 91, 104, 105, 168
　short-term/mini-, 90, 105
　style of setting, 92–93
　visualizing, 90–91, 92, 104
Growth, need for, 81, 82–83

H

Habits, 106, 107, 108
　work, poor, 107
Happiness, 6, 82, 84–85, 168
　definition of, 83
　in early adulthood, 42, 84–85
　nature of, 1, 2–3
Health, 114. *See also* Well-being
　diet and, 116
　emotional/mental, 115, 117–119

exercise and, 116
　spiritual, 115
　stress and, 131, 132, 133
Helms, Janet, 69, 71
Heritage. *See* Culture
Holland, John, 31, 33
Home-based businesses, 22
Honesty, 83
Hopes. *See* Aspirations
Horizontal dimension of assessing strengths, 95–96
Human development. *See* Development; Needs

I

Identity, 81, 119
　development
　　black, 69–70
　　minority, 70
　　white, 70–71
　at midlife, 48
　racial, 65, 68–69
Immersion, 82. *See also* Involvement
Impulsivity, 118–119
Inner self, 28, 45
Intensity as a factor in stress, 134
Interests
　assessing, 31
　girls', 60
　personal, 29–30, 44, 48
Internet, 22, 142, 169
　career sites, 150–151
　job search strategies, 153–154
　organizing job search on, 152–153
Interpersonal
　conflicts, 131
　relationships, 42, 49, 82, 83–84
　skills, 18, 19, 68, 155
Interview(ing), 142, 154–156, 168
Intimacy, importance of, 48
Intolerance. *See* Diversity
Involvement, 1, 2, 3, 6, 83, 84, 168
　as factor in stress, 135

J

James, William, 106
Job search
　cover letter in, 145–148, 149, 159
　information and service, 18
　by networking, 145
　by resume, 142–145, 146–147
Jung, Carl, 44, 46

K

Kanter, R.M., 58

L

Learning
　lifelong, 16, 17–18
　stress and, 132
Levant, Ron, 61
Life
　contexts, 17
　expectancy, 43
　planning, 1, 3, 5, 7, 41, 42, 49–50, 85, 90, 94, 114, 168
　roles, 17
Lifestyle, 5, 93, 168
　healthy, 114
　sedentary, 117
Listening, 67
Listservs in job search, 152–153
Locus of control, 102–103
Loneliness, 47

M

Magnusson, David, 7
Maslow, Abraham, 82

Masten, Rick, 7, 47
Mastery, 56, 85, 96, 102
   progressive, 81–82
Math avoidance, 60
Maturation. *See* Development
McGwire, Mark, 91, 92
Meaning, in life and work, 3, 7, 23–24, 80, 81, 84, 115, 119
Meditation, 131
Mental health, 117
Mentoring, 59
Midlife
   changes in men, 47
   changes in women, 46, 47
   planning, 47
   transitions/crisis, 43–46
Mini-goal, 105
Minority group(s). *See also* Diversity
   identity development, 70
Missouri Occupational card Sort, Appendix A, p. 171
Mobility, job, 23
Motivator(s), 5, 33, 79, 81, 82
   achievement, 101, 102
   and action planning, 105
   during midlife, 44
   goals as, 91
Multiculturalism. *See* Diversity

N

Need(s)
   achievement, 44
   deficit, 82
   for growth, 81, 82–83
   inner and outer, 80
   personal, 5, 6, 7, 17, 79, 80, 84
   psychological, 80–81
   satisfaction, 127, 130
   social, 82
   workers', 22
Negotiation
   roles at midlife, 48
   skills, 42
Networking, 145, 153, 168
Newsgroup, in job search, 152
Novelty, and stress, 133–134
Null environment, 58
Nutrition. *See* Diet

O

Objectives. *See* Goals
Obstacles, 129–130
   confronting, 125–126, 130, 132, 136
Opportunities, 3, 5, 6, 42, 45, 50, 81, 82, 95, 96, 102, 103, 104, 131, 142
   employment, 145
   through Internet, 152
   stress and, 133
   for successful people, 91
   in workplace, 16, 17, 32, 34, 67, 68
Optimism, 80, 85, 101, 102, 103
Order, need for, 80, 103
Organizations
   culture of, 19–20
   diamond-shaped, 17
   pyramidal, 17
   traditional, 20
Orwell, George, 2

P

Panic, 132, 136
Parents
   death of, 49
   relationship with, as we age, 48–49
Peer pressure, 58
Perceptions, 66, 67
   of self, 94, 96
Performance
   commitment and, 102
   stress and, 136
Personal best, 95
Personality, 6, 69
   changes in midlife, 46

development, 1, 61, 68
   types (Holland), 31, 33
   in workplace, 18, 21
Piaget, Jean, 7
Plan(ning). *See also* Career planning
   action, 90, 101, 104–105, 129
   definition of, 105
   life, 3, 5, 7, 41, 49–50, 85, 94, 114, 168
   long-range, 104
   during midlife, 47
   vocational/career, 5, 28, 32–33
Plato, 83
Power, 67
Predictability, need for, 80
Prejudice, 67, 69
Prevention, as necessary to well-being, 114
Prioritizing, goals, 93, 102, 104
Problem solving, 136, 168
   alternative solutions in, 128, 129
   creativity in, 42, 83, 125, 128, 129
   defining step in, 128
   identification step in, 127
   sensing step in, 127
   skills, 130
   and choosing solutions, 129–130
   stress and, 136
Procrastination, 104, 107, 108
Progressive mastery, 81–82, 96
Psychological
   aspects of middle age, 43, 44, 46
   needs, 80–81
   clocks, 43–44
   costs of racism, 73

Q

Quality of life, 83, 84–85

R

Racial identity, 68–69
Racism, 67, 70–71, 73
Readiness, 49, 50
Reality testing, 103, 104, 136; Appendix C, p. 217
Reflection, 56–58, 119, 142, 169
Relationship(s), 7
   during early adulthood, 42
   cultural/racial, 66, 69
   females and, 56, 61
   interpersonal, 49, 80, 84
   during midlife, 44, 48
   with parents in midlife, 48–49
   skills, 18
   stressful, 131
Relaxation, 83, 131, 136
Renegotiating. *See* Negotiation
Resilience, 126, 168
Respect, 90
Responsibility
   personal, 83, 107, 114, 115
   social, 82
   and strength, 94
   taking, 49, 102, 107, 114
Resume, 142, 153, 168
   electronic, 153
   guidelines for writing, 143–145
   sample, Figure 12.1, pp. 146–147; 156
   types of, 143
Reward and punishment, 106, 107
Risk
   as factor in stress, 135
   taking, 48, 94
Rogers, Carl, 85
Rogers, Will, 20
Role(s)
   conflict, 60
   life, 17
   male/female, 5, 56, 58, 60–61
   during midlife, 48
   stereotypic, 56, 58
Role models, 56, 60, 115

S

SAT (Scholastic Aptitude Test), 60

Security
   general factor, 133
   need for, 80, 116
   and stress, 135
Sedentary life, 117
Self
   authentic, 57, 58
   -reflection, 120
Self-assessment, 95
Self-awareness/self-identity/
   self-actualization, 1, 3, 44, 45, 50, 67, 82, 83, 106, 168
Self-care, 113
   diet and, 116
   emotional/mental, 117
   importance of, 114–115
   physical, 116–117
   spiritual, 119–120
Self-concept, 89, 93–94, 95
Self-contracting, in BDA, 107
Self-control, 95, 101, 102, 105, 106
Self-Directed Search (SDS), 28, 31, 33
Self-efficacy, 96
Self-employment, 22
Self-esteem/self-confidence, 85, 90, 93, 94, 117, 130
   as factor in coping with stress, 133
   male, 56, 59
Self-fulfilling prophecies, 103
Self-fulfillment, 28, 82–83
Self-management, BDA method of, 106–107
Self-talk, 119
Serenity Prayer, 128
Sexism, 67
Sex-role, 168
   boys', 56
   girls', 56, 60, 61
   socialization, 50, 56, 61
   in workplace, 58, 61
Sexual harassment, 59
Skills, 168
   communication, 18
   and happiness, 42
   identifying, 33
   interpersonal, 19
   negotiation, 42
   thinking, 21–22
   transportable, 19, 23
Skovolt, Tom, 59
Social
   comparison, 95
   support, 113, 120, 136
Socialization, sex-role, 50, 56, 58, 61
Socrates, 120
Solitude, 83
Solutions. *See also* Problem; Problem solving
   implementing, 129
Spirituality/spiritual
   health, 115, 116
   self-care, 119–120
Stagnation (Erikson), 46
Stereotyping, 66–67
   gender, 56, 58, 59, 61
Stimulation, need for, 81
Strength(s), 90, 96, 136
   Audit, Appendix B, p. 197
   assessing, 93, 94–96
   awareness of, 93–94
   potential, 94
Stress, 49, 84, 113, 114, 115, 118
   ambiguity and, 134–135
   causes of, 133–135
   chronic, 130, 131, 133
   complexity and, 135
   definition of, 130
   diet and, 116
   drugs and, 131
   duration of, 132–133
   exercise and, 117
   gender and, 61
   intensity of, 132, 134

   interpersonal conflict and, 131
   in interviewing, 156
   management/coping with, 43, 130–132, 135–136, 168
   sources of, 131
   using structure to manage, 136
   tolerance limits to, 135
   work, 29
Structure, to manage stress, 136
Success
   behaviors leading to, 21
   characteristics of, 102, 121
   in early adulthood, 42
   gender issues related to, 60
   in life goals, 85, 91
   obstacles to, 126
   stress and, 133
   in workplace, 68
Support system, 136. *See also* Social support
   in job search, 145, 156

T

Task analysis, 135
Teams and teamwork, 18–19, 61, 68, 72
Technology in workplace, 18, 22, 23
Tension. *See* Stress
Thinking skills, 21–22
Time management, 42, 106, 107–108
Timing, 34
Tolerance limits to stress, 134
Transitions, 2, 6, 41, 119, 120
   adult, 42, 45, 48, 96
   career, 118
   developmental, 1, 3, 4
   early adult, 42, 43
   midlife, 43–44, 48
Traumas, 133

U

Useem, Jerry, 150

V

Values, 168
   of adolescents, 47
   and goals, 104
   during midlife, 44, 45, 48
   personal, 17, 44–45, 50, 79, 81, 83, 90, 93, 118, 120
   work-related, 33–34; Exercise 3.6
Vertical dimension of assessing strengths, 95, 96
Visualizing goals, 90–91, 92, 104
Vocational. *See also* Career; Workplace
   environments, 31
   mission, 115
   planning, 5

W

Well-being, 84, 114, 116, 131. *See also* Happiness
Wellness, 115
White racial identity development, 70–71
Wide Area Information Servers (WAIS), 154
Willpower, 106
Withers, Bill, 120
Women's movement, 56
Work
   definition of, 6
   meaningful, 23–24
Workplace, 16
   changing, 20–21, 58, 72
   diverse/global, 22, 23, 61, 65
   gender issues in, 58–59, 61
   isolation in, 23
   success in, 68
   technology in, 18, 22, 23
Worldview, 65, 72–73
World Wide Web, using, in job search, 154